SEP

W9-BCS-551

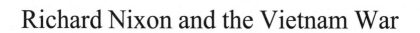

Richard Nixon and the Vietnam War

Vietnam: American in the War Years
Series Editor: David L. Anderson
California State University, Monterey Bay

The Vietnam War and the tumultuous internal upheavals in America that coincided with it marked a watershed era in U.S. history. These events profoundly challenged America's heroic self-image. During the 1950s the United States defined Southeast Asia as an area of vital strategic importance. In the 1960s this view produced a costly American military campaign that continued into the early 1970s. The Vietnam War was the nation's longest war and ended with an unprecedented U.S. failure to achieve its stated objectives. Simultaneous with this frustrating military intervention and the domestic debate that it produced were other tensions created by student activism on campuses, the black struggle for civil rights, and the women's liberation movement. The books in this series explore the complex and controversial issues of the period from the mid-1950s to the mid-1970s in brief and engaging volumes. To facilitate continued and informed debate on these contested subjects, each book examines a military, political, or diplomatic issue; the role of a key individual; or one of the domestic changes in America during the war.

Volumes Published

Allies at Odds: America, Europe, and Vietnam, 1961-1968, by Eugene M. Blang
Antiwarriors: The Vietnam War and the Battle for America's Hearts and Minds, by Melvin Small
Democracy's Children: The Young Rebels of the 1960s and the Power of Ideals, by Edward K. Spann
Like Rolling Thunder: The Air War in Vietnam, 1964-1975, by Ronald B. Frankum, Jr.
The Deadly Bet: LBJ, Vietnam, and the 1968 Election, by Walter LaFeber
Crossroads: American Popular Culture and the Vietnam Generation, by Mitchell K. Hall
The Tet Offensive: Politics, War, and Public Opinion, by David F. Schmitz
Cold War Mandarin: Ngo Dinh Diem and the Origins of America's War in Vietnam, by Seth Jacobs
Debating Vietnam: Fulbright, Stennis, and Their Senate Hearings, by Joseph A. Fry

Richard Nixon and the Vietnam War

The End of the American Century

David F. Schmitz

ROWMAN & LITTLEFIELD
Lanham • Boulder • New York • Toronto • Plymouth, UK

Published by Rowman & Littlefield
4501 Forbes Boulevard, Suite 200, Lanham, Maryland 20706
www.rowman.com

10 Thornbury Road, Plymouth PL6 7PP, United Kingdom

British Library Cataloguing in Publication Information Available

Library of Congress Cataloging-in-Publication Data

Schmitz, David F.
Richard Nixon and the Vietnam War : The end of the American century / by David F. Schmitz
p. cm.
Includes bibliographical references and index.
ISBN 978-1-4422-2709-5 (cloth : alk. paper) -- ISBN 978-1-4422-2710-1 (electronic)
1. Vietnam War, 1961-1975--United States. 2. Nixon, Richard M. (Richard Milhous), 1913-1994. 3.
United States--Politics and government--1969-1974. Title.
DS558.S346 2014
959.704'31--dc23
2013949313

™ The paper used in this publication meets the minimum requirements of American
National Standard for Information Sciences Permanence of Paper for Printed Library
Materials, ANSI/NISO Z39.48-1992.

Printed in the United States of America

Contents

Abbreviations

ARVN Army of the Republic of Vietnam
AWF Papers as President of the United States, 1953–1961 (Ann Whitman Files), Dwight D. Eisenhower Papers, Dwight D. Eisenhower Presidential Library
    CIA Central Intelligence Agency
    COSVN Central Office for South Vietnam
    DDEL Dwight D. Eisenhower Presidential Library
    DH Series Dulles-Herter Series, Dwight D. Eisenhower Presidential
Library
    DMZ demilitarized zone
    FRUS Foreign Relations of the United States
    GVN government of South Vietnam
    HAK Henry A. Kissinger
    JCS Joint Chiefs of Staff
    LBJL Lyndon B. Johnson Presidential Library
    MACV Military Assistance Command, Vietnam
    NATO North Atlantic Treaty Organization
    NIE National Intelligence Estimate
    NLF National Liberation Front
    NSC National Security Council
    NSCH National Security Council Institutional (H) Files
    NSDM National Security Decision Memorandums
    NSSM National Security Study Memorandum
    NVA North Vietnamese Army
    NVN North Vietnam(ese)
    POW prisoner of war
    RNPL Richard Nixon Presidential Library
    SALT Strategic Arms Limitation Treaty
    SEATO Southeast Asian Treaty Organization
    SVN South Vietnam(ese)
    VC Viet Cong (Vietnamese communists)
    VSSG Vietnam Special Studies Group
    VVAW Vietnam Veterans against the War

Acknowledgments

I thank David Anderson for encouraging me to write a second volume for the "Vietnam: America in the War Years" series. He responded enthusiastically to my topic and was a source of wise counsel throughout. Jon Sisk, my editor at Rowman & Littlefield, asked good questions and provided wise suggestions and advice. I was fortunate to be able to work with them on this project. Elaine McGarraugh expertly guided the book through production.

Provost and dean of the faculty at Whitman College, Timothy Kaufman-Osborn, has supported me in all of my work, and I thank him and the College for the financial support provided that allowed travel to archives, especially the National Archives in College Park, Maryland, and the Richard M. Nixon Presidential Library in Yorba Linda, California. Through the College's Lewis B. Perry Summer Research Scholarship Program, I was able to have Carolyn Hart work with me one summer on Nixon's views toward protest and Vietnam and his initial policies toward Vietnam, and to accompany me on a research trip to the Nixon Library where she assisted me in examining the most recently declassified records, especially those related to Cambodia. The same fund also allowed me to employ Kathryn Witmer the next summer. While working mainly on a different project, she nonetheless provided invaluable assistance in locating documents on Nixon, particularly prior to his becoming president, and with my thinking through many of the questions relating to Nixon's policy toward Vietnam. She also read parts of the manuscript and provided excellent advice concerning its organization. Jacob Harwood assisted me with finding information as I was finishing the book

My former student Gabrielle Westcott graciously read the entire manuscript. She proved to be a trenchant critic with a sharp editorial pen and in the process made invaluable suggestions that improved all parts of this study and made this a better work. The faults that remain are mine alone.

I am pleased to thank Lee Keene of Whitman's Penrose Library for all of his assistance with finding documents and sources. He is an exemplary librarian whose sage advice, willingness to assist, and professionalism helped in so many ways. The archivist at the National Archives and the Nixon Library were, as always, excellent and professional. I want to particularly thank Jonathan M. Roscoe at the Nixon Library for his assistance with understanding the collection and using the most recently declassified records. Jon Fletcher, the AV Archivist at the Nixon Library, graciously assisted me in locating the photographs for the book. Kathryn Farrell Guizar of Image Management in Walla Walla helped me prepare the photographs for the press, and Benjamin Verdi of Rowman & Littlefield made all parts of the production process clear and easy.

I especially thank Professor Steven Brady of the University of Notre Dame for inviting me to speak to his class on the Vietnam War. It provided me an opportunity to work through my ideas on Nixon and Vietnam with an enthusiastic and engaged group of students.

My family, immediate and far-flung, continues to provide the necessary support one needs to sustain them while writing. From her perspective form working in Washington D.C., to his from his classes in college, my children Nicole and Kincaid asked difficult questions, discussed many of the themes addressed in this book, and challenged me all along the way. My wife Polly enhances it all in ways too numerous to list. Together, they made it worthwhile.

Since I arrived at Whitman College, I have taught my course on the Vietnam War every fall semester. For all of their tough questions, thoughtful papers, insightful comments, and desire to learn about America's most divisive war of the twentieth century, and for once again, as they did with my work on the Tet Offensive, inspiring me to look closer at a key moment in the war and write about it, I dedicate this book to all my students in the class over the past thirty years.

Introduction

The first two years of President Richard Nixon's first term marked a crucial turning point in the Vietnam War. Nixon assumed office at the height of the conflict. In the wake of the Tet Offensive, the Clifford Task Force's strategic review of American policy, and the March 1968 meeting of the Wise Men, President Lyndon Johnson had capped escalation and placed restrictions on the bombing of North Vietnam in an effort to begin negotiations on the war. Yet the fighting raged on in the South as the talks in Paris made no progress in addressing the issues of the war. American forces in Vietnam had reached their peak of 545,000 men. Casualties continued to mount, with 1968 and 1969 being the bloodiest years of the war, and the fighting was costing the United States over $30 billion a year. The result was a stalemate. As the war brought increasing casualties with no end in sight, deep divisions developed in society between those who wanted to see the war through to a military victory and others who sought the removal of American forces and peace. By 1968, a plurality of Americans saw the decision to send American troops to Vietnam as a mistake. Opposition to the war caused Johnson to withdraw from the presidential race that year and led to massive protests and disruptions that reflected a desire among a majority of Americans for an end to the conflict. The election of 1968 was one of the closest in American history. Both Nixon and Democratic candidate Hubert H. Humphrey campaigned on promises to end the war, although neither offered a clear plan as to how to achieve that goal.

Nixon saw the war in Vietnam in Cold War terms and supported the escalation of American involvement as necessary to contain the expansion of communism in Asia, deter future wars of national liberation, and demonstrate American credibility as a great power. For these reasons, when he became president, Nixon was determined to use American force to achieve victory in Vietnam, defined as maintaining an anticommunist government in Saigon and upholding American credibility, which had eluded President Johnson. In 1969 and 1970, Nixon sought a military victory in Vietnam. As H. R. "Bob" Haldeman noted in April 1970, the president and his national security advisor, Henry Kissinger, still believed they could get the war "wound up this year, if we keep enough pressure on, and don't crumble at home."[1] Nixon decided to escalate and expand the conflict to try to break the stalemate and settle the war on the battlefield. The president believed this policy—which he called the "madman theory"—would demonstrate his willingness to take military action in order to win that Johnson had not and, in the process, deliver a military victory that would force Hanoi to quit fighting and capitulate to American terms for ending the war. Much of this was done covertly to avoid stirring up domestic opposition. At the same time, Nixon knew he had to buy political time to fully implement his strategy. To that end, the president created the impression that he was winding the war down. Nixon announced his willingness to negotiate an end to the fighting, enacted the policy of Vietnamization, and implemented the first de-escalation of American forces. He also engaged in a policy of positive polarization designed to place the antiwar movement on the defensive by rallying support for the war.

It was all for naught. Nixon's quest for a military victory lasted eighteen months and ended in defeat. The secret bombing of Cambodia, threatened escalation of the war against the North through Operation Duck Hook, and the invasion of Cambodia in April 1970 all failed to break the stalemate or force concessions from North Vietnam at the negotiating table. In addition, rather than keeping the antiwar movement at bay, Nixon's policy of Vietnamization and withdrawal of American forces created an expectation that the war was coming to an end, increased demands for an expedited withdrawal, and contributed to mainstreaming the antiwar movement. By 1971, the president was forced to significantly de-escalate the American presence and seek a negotiated end to American involvement in the fighting of the war. The period Henry Luce had dubbed the "American Century" in 1941 was over after only thirty years.

Nixon's decision to pursue a military victory became a missed opportunity to bring the war to an earlier end—with devastating consequences. In Vietnam, the policy resulted in seven more years of fighting that included the most intensive bombing campaigns of the war, an expansion of the war to Cambodia and Laos, and ever-increasing numbers of Vietnamese soldiers killed on both sides. For the United States, prolonging the war led to the deaths of over twenty-five thousand more soldiers, a deepening of the political and economic problems in the nation, and the Watergate crisis.

Starting in the summer of 1970, in an effort to salvage his policy in Vietnam, Nixon redefined notions of both victory and peace. The president would not abandon the Saigon regime; yet he knew he had to change the American military role in the war in order to maintain some influence over events. Toward that end, Nixon shifted the definition of success away from victory to creation of an illusory peace through the de-escalation of American forces and maintenance of the Saigon government intact until after his reelection. This would allow him to claim that he had successfully brought peace despite a failure to resolve the fundamental issue of the war: the political future of Vietnam. The emphasis of

American foreign policy shifted from seeking a military victory in the Vietnam War to implementing Vietnamization and reducing Cold War tensions through détente with the Soviet Union and the opening up of talks with China. Although this allowed Nixon to remove American troops without the collapse of Saigon, it also meant that he expected the war between North and South Vietnam to continue as long as he was president.

Remarkably, given Nixon's efforts to win the war, no study examines only the crucial first years of his policy toward Vietnam and quest for a conventional military victory. Using the most recently declassified documents, new *Foreign Relations of the United States* publications, and the latest scholarship on the war, this work examines the first three years of the Nixon presidency to demonstrate that the turning point in the Vietnam War that began with the Tet Offensive in 1968 was not complete until the summer of 1970 when Nixon abandoned his madman policy and quest for a military victory that would end the war with the defeat of enemy forces. In the process, it demonstrates that a new periodization of the war is called for—one that recognizes that, in his first two years in office, Nixon sought victory on the battlefield, and this period should be treated as distinct from that of the president's later shift toward de-escalation and a negotiated withdrawal of American forces.

In order to fully understand Nixon's policy, we must situate it in the context of American Cold War foreign policy, Nixon's views on the Vietnam War, and the state of the war when he took office. The first chapter provides an overview of Nixon's thinking on the Vietnam War and the necessity of American intervention from 1953 to 1967. Chapter 2 focuses on the 1968 election campaign, how Nixon responded to the impact of the Tet Offensive, and his need to moderate his positions in order to secure the presidency. Chapter 3 examines Nixon's strategy for victory, including the secret bombing of Cambodia, the madman theory, the Nixon Doctrine, and Operation Duck Hook, and culminates with the president's "Silent Majority" speech, paying critical attention to the interplay between the administration's efforts to win the war and the antiwar protests in the nation. Chapter 4 investigates the expansion of the war into Cambodia and the political crisis this produced for the Nixon administration, most notably the killings at Kent State, the demonstrations that followed, and the Cooper-Church Amendment, leading to the abandonment of the victory strategy. The last half of 1970 and the first six months of 1971 comprised the year of decision for Nixon. Chapter 5 examines how and why the president shifted the focus of policy to negotiations, détente, and pacification while he continued to deal with the problems of the economy and his reelection. The final chapter evaluates Nixon's policy, the ending of the American Century, and the impact of the years from 1969 to 1971 on Nixon's reelection, the Paris Peace Treaty, and Watergate;

it also looks at how these three tumultuous years foreshadowed many of
the problems that continue to beset the United States today.

NOTE

1. Jeffrey Kimball, *The Vietnam War Files: Uncovering the Secret History of Nixon-Era Strategy* (Lawrence: University Press of Kansas, 2004), 26.

ONE

The Necessity of the War in Vietnam

Richard Nixon was one of the most important figures in the history of the Vietnam War. From the time he was in Congress urging President Harry S. Truman to support France, through his 1953–1961 tenure as Dwight D. Eisenhower's vice president and then his years outside elected office as a critic of Presidents John F. Kennedy's and Lyndon B. Johnson's policies, until his candidacy for president in 1968, Nixon advocated an ever larger American commitment to Southeast Asia and role in the fighting in Vietnam. For Nixon, Vietnam's importance stemmed from its place in the global Cold War struggle to contain communism and maintain US power and credibility in Southeast Asia. In a bipolar world, the significance of the conflict derived from how Vietnam fit into the Cold War battle with the Soviet Union and the People's Republic of China. Nixon therefore emphasized Vietnam's importance, claiming that it was vital to the interests of the United States and the entire free world. From 1953 to 1965, Nixon's analysis of events in Vietnam and the rhetoric he employed remained remarkably consistent as he pushed for a greater American role. For Nixon, Vietnam was indistinguishable from the rest of Asia and was significant due to the potential consequences of its loss to communism. Once the United States committed forces in 1965, Nixon consistently called for a greater effort in the quest for a military victory. What disagreements he had with the Kennedy and Johnson administrations stemmed from the pace and extent of escalation, not from a questioning of the need for American involvement in Vietnam.

The initial American commitment to Vietnam stemmed from the postwar policy of containment. After World War II, American officials came to see the Soviet Union as a new threat to American interests and world peace. The Truman administration saw Russian policies as inherently aggressive, expansive, and hostile to the West and understood communism as a monolithic force directed by Moscow that threatened to spread to all parts of the world. As such, it constituted another totalitarian threat to freedom, similar to fascism, with which there could be no compromise. The United States again faced an enemy that represented the antithesis of its values and a threat to its security. At Munich, American officials had learned the key lesson of the 1930s: aggression cannot be appeased. From Washington's vantage point, it was a bipolar world, a struggle between freedom and totalitarianism, in which all international events were linked to the battle against communism.

France's post-World War II struggle to regain control of its colony in Vietnam was quickly fit into the Cold War paradigm. Ho Chi Minh's declaration of Vietnamese independence on September 2, 1945, and the Vietminh's attempt to block the return of French power came to be seen as part of a larger communist effort to gain control over all of East Asia. As understood by American policymakers, the struggle in Vietnam was not an anticolonial independence struggle but rather one front in the global effort to contain communism. The United States therefore provided military aid and political backing in support of the French attempt to crush the Vietminh. In 1950, the Truman administration formally recognized the government of Bao Dai as an independent state within the French Union and began to send aid directly to Vietnam.

The consensus on American containment policy was made clear when Eisenhower became president in January 1953. He agreed with the logic and assumptions of Truman's policy and continued his efforts to support the French in Vietnam. When in his January 20, 1953, inaugural address Eisenhower set out the bipolar worldview, which served as the basis for containment, that "freedom is pitted against slavery; lightness against the dark," Vietnam was one of the places he had in mind. The struggle there conferred "a common dignity upon the French soldier who dies in Indo-China . . . [and] the American life given in Korea."[1] American leaders saw the two wars as two different fronts in the same struggle against international communism. The president called on the nation to do more in East Asia and asked Congress "to make substantial additional resources available to assist the French and the Associated States in their military efforts to defeat Communist Viet Minh aggression."[2] According to Eisenhower's secretary of state, John Foster Dulles, the administration saw the situation in Vietnam as "even more dangerous in its global aspects than is the fighting in Korea, for a collapse in Indo-China would have immediate grave reactions in other areas of Asia."[3]

Eisenhower summarized the importance he placed on Indochina for the "free world" at his famous press conference on April 7, 1954, in which he outlined the "domino theory":

> First of all, you have the specific value of a locality in its production of materials that the world needs. Then you have the possibility that

many human beings pass under a dictatorship that is inimical to the free world. Finally, you have broader considerations that might follow what you would call the "falling domino" principle. You have a row of dominoes set up, you knock over the first one, and what will happen to the last one is the certainty that it will go over very quickly. So you could have the beginning of a disintegration that would have the most profound influences.

Eisenhower noted that for the first point, tin, tungsten, rubber, and other items would be lost. More importantly, the free world could not afford greater losses in Asia where "already some 450 million of its people" had fallen "to the Communist dictatorship." Finally, the loss of Indochina to communism would lead to the loss "of Burma, of Thailand, of the Peninsula, and Indonesia" and to threats against Japan, Taiwan, the Philippines, and eventually Australia and New Zealand. In addition, it would deny Japan that region where it must trade or "Japan, in turn, will have only one place in the world to go—that is, toward the Communist areas in order to live. So," Eisenhower concluded, "the possible consequences of the loss are just incalculable to the free world."[4]

As early as 1953, Nixon advocated US involvement in Vietnam and inserted himself into the debate about the French presence in Indochina. Nixon cast France's struggle to retain its colony as an effort to provide independence for Vietnam against communist imperialism. In the fall of 1953, Nixon traveled to Asia to meet with American allies, assess the threat of communism and the aid necessary from the United States, and provide assurances of American support. In Saigon, where he met with both French and Vietnamese officials to discuss France's war against the communist-led Vietminh, he declared, "What is at stake in this war is fundamentally the freedom and independence of Southeast Asia. If the Communists should win in Indo-China, independence would be lost to this whole part of the world." Nixon elevated the French to the status of liberators and claimed that France and the United States were allied in an effort to protect freedom in the region. "We believe that the objective of France, the United States, and Vietnam are the same, that is freedom and independence" in a struggle against a common enemy.[5] He held that "victory will be possible only if Frenchmen and Vietnamese fight together and remain united."[6]

On his return to the United States, the vice president gave his first major address on foreign policy. Speaking on television and radio, Nixon portrayed the events in Southeast Asia as critical to US national security and the fate of the free world. He asked rhetorically why Americans should care about what happened on the other side of the world in a place few people knew about. The answer, he stated, was that "the Communists are making an all-out effort to win this area." After their victory in China and the war in Korea, the communist were "waging war now in Indochina and in Malaya. They have stirred up revolutions in Burma and

Indonesia and the Philippines, and they have supported subversion everywhere in this area." Anticipating Eisenhower's April 7 comments, Nixon argued that the cost to the United States and the free world of losing
Southeast Asia were incalculable in terms of resources, markets, and defense. If communism triumphed in Indochina, all of Southeast Asia
would fall "under Communist domination or Communist influence,
[and] Japan, who trades and must trade with this area in order to exist,
must inevitably be oriented toward the Communist regime." Moreover,
"the balance of power in the world in people and resources will be on
their side, and the free world eventually will be forced to its knees. It is
vital therefore to keep this part of the world from falling into Communist
hands."[7]

Nixon presented Vietnam as a unique opportunity for the United
States to prove that its system of government and way of life were best
and that it was Washington's obligation to lead the world. According to
Nixon, the communists had made a "vicious smear of America and the
Americans." In the process "they have created in the minds of the people
that we are arrogant, that we are mean, that we are prejudiced, that we
are superior, that we are bent on war rather than on a program that will
lead to peace. And the only answer to such propaganda is not words. The
only answer is deeds." The vice president claimed that the people of
Vietnam wanted what America had to offer, as "we were very much
more alike than we were different," and that "they can and would like to
be friends of America and the free world." The Vietnamese "want independence. They want economic progress. They want peace" and freedom.[8]

Nixon was fond of quoting President Woodrow Wilson when explain-
ing the appeal of the United States to other nations. Wilson, Nixon declared, believed that "a patriotic American is never so proud of the great
flag under which he lives as when it comes to mean to other people as
well as to himself a symbol of hope and liberty." America's expenses on
military strength in the global battle against communism were designed
to bring that hope to others. "Why this huge expenditure of money and
manpower?" Nixon asked. "Not because we want territory. We have
never asked for any, and we have acquired none. Not because we want
the countries we aid to be dependent, but because we want them to be
independent."[9] In contrast, Nixon argued that communism "runs counter to human nature. Communism in practice goes against all the fundamental desires of the peoples of Asia. Instead of independence it has
brought colonial imperialism and slavery. Instead of economic progress it
has brought poverty. Instead of peace, it has brought war. It denies a
choice of culture, a choice of religion, or an economic system to those
who are under Communist domination."[10] American support of France
in Vietnam was therefore a critical component of containment in East
Asia. Nixon argued, "The day the French leave Indochina, the Commu-

nists will take over. We realize as they do that the only way they can assure their independence and the only way they can defend it is to continue the fight side by side with their partners in the French Union against the forces of Communist colonialism which would enslave them."[11]

While in Hanoi, Nixon had said that the United States rejected any negotiations for peace in Indochina that would lead to communist rule in Vietnam. "Under no circumstances could negotiations take place that would place people who want independence under a foreign bondage."[12] He expanded on this point in his speech. Setting out an early version of the domino theory, Nixon asserted, "If Indochina falls, Thailand is put in an almost impossible position. The same is true of Malaya with its rubber and tin. The same is true of Indonesia." Moreover, Nixon emphasized fears that Japan, the cornerstone of the great crescent of containment and America's most successful Asian partner in the Cold War, would fall and set off a chain of events, culminating in another world war. For all of these reasons, "it is vitally important that Indochina not go behind the Iron Curtain." Fortunately, Nixon assured the nation, "we are finally getting the kind of leadership which is bringing to the world the true picture of American policy" under President Dwight Eisenhower. "For the first time the Communists are on the defensive all over the world" in the global struggle for freedom.[13]

There had to be a period of transition, Nixon and the rest of the Eisenhower administration believed, between colonialism and independence for the Vietnamese to learn self-government, and it was crucial that the United States provide protection against communism during this critical time. If France granted full independence to Vietnam, Bao Dai could not prevent a communist victory. As Dulles stated in January 1954, the problem was "the lack of political maturity on the part of the people themselves, and their inability to make up their own minds as to what it is they want." The secretary of state continued by noting that he was "a great believer in the general idea of giving independence to people who want it, but I think that—I don't know really whether some of these people are qualified, well qualified yet for independence. I am not sure that these people are qualified to be fully independent." Although the communists tested the Filipinos' capacity for independence, Dulles opined, the latter had years of American tutelage and "quite a lot of experience and training and development." Granting "independence to a lot of these people in a world where the Communists are prowling around to grab you, it is not a thing which is easily accomplished." The question was "whether there is a political maturity among the people to organize their own institutions, establish a strong government needed to meet the disturbing conditions that prevail there."[14] This meant that Vietnam needed the protection of a Western nation, or it would fall to the international communist movement.

Despite his attempts to bolster the French war effort in Indochina, Nixon had little confidence in France's ability to win the war. The vice president stated that the United States might have to send its own troops if France quit fighting. The biggest difficulty facing the United States, in his view, was the faltering French will to continue.[15] Nixon's assertion that if France stopped fighting and the situation demanded it, Washington should send American boys to prevent the communists from taking over this gateway to Southeast Asia contradicted the official position of the Eisenhower administration. With the French defeat at Dienbienphu in May 1954, Nixon's projection alarmed many commentators and brought a mild public rebuke from Secretary of State Dulles, who dismissed Nixon's projection of the need to send American forces as "highly unlikely." Rather, the "essential thing in the discussions of Indo-China at Geneva" was that there was a "unity of purpose of the free nations . . . to assure that that area cannot be conquered by the Communists." Southeast Asia was an area "of vital concern to the free world," and the Europeans recognized along with the United States "that the armed Communist threat endangered vital free world interests and made it appropriate that the free nations most immediately concerned should explore the possibility of a collective defense."[16]

For his own part, Nixon stated that he meant that the United States would oppose any outright surrender of Vietnam to the communists at the upcoming Geneva talks. Such an action would unfavorably shift the balance of power in the world to a point where "the Kremlin would think it is time for a world war." "This is just not a civil war, it is a war of aggression by the Communist conspiracy against all free nations. The Chinese Communist Government supports, controls and directs it. It is not a war to perpetuate French colonialism but to resist extension of Chinese communism." The administration aimed to hold onto Indochina without a war involving the United States "if we can." Nixon praised Eisenhower's policy because it was designed to prevent war by "letting any aggressor know the consequences" of any attempt to expand. It was important that the communist world understand that the policy of the Eisenhower administration was "firm, consistent, and courageous." Compromise, "vacillation and weakness lead to war. Firmness is the only thing that has a chance to lead to peace." American will was being tested in Vietnam, currently the most crucial spot in the Cold War struggle. If the United States failed to demonstrate its determination, the whole region could be lost. "You don't keep Communists out of an area by telling them you won't do anything to save it." Thus, if Indochina fell, all of "Southeast Asia would be put in jeopardy."[17]

The Geneva Accords, which brought an end to the fighting between the French and the Vietminh, provided for an armistice and a temporary military partition of Vietnam at the seventeenth parallel, with the Vietminh pulling their forces to the north and the French to the south. The partitioned areas were to be administrative units designed to separate the two armies. Neither side was to act as a sovereign nation. The political question was to be resolved by elections, supervised by an international commission, to be held within two years to establish a unified Vietnam. Dulles immediately made it clear that the United States was not bound by the settlements reached at Geneva and that the Eisenhower administration intended to work against the enactment of the provisions. In particular, he noted that, unlike in Germany or Korea, the United States "was not anxious to see an early election" held in Vietnam "because as things stand today, it is probable that Ho Chi Minh would get a very large vote."[18] Eisenhower wrote in his memoirs, "I have never talked or corresponded with a person knowledgeable in Indochinese affairs who did not agree that had elections been held as of the time of the fighting, possibly 80 per cent of the population would have voted for the Communist Ho Chi Minh as their leader rather than Chief of State Bao Dai." He noted that the lack of leadership demonstrated by Bao Dai had led the Vietnamese to believe they had nothing to fight for.[19]

Ideally, Dulles would favor "genuinely free elections" in Vietnam, but currently it was not possible. "At the present time in a country which is politically immature, which has been the scene of civil war and disruption, we would doubt whether the immediate conditions would be conducive to a result which would really reflect the will of the people." Further, the United States would not "stand passively by and see the extension of communism by any means into Southeast Asia."[20] Dulles did not believe that the people of Southeast Asia could govern themselves. Without continued guidance from the West, these nations would fall to communism. American officials believed that until the Vietnamese gained the same level of political maturity that American guidance had provided the Filipinos, they would need support, and the United States was obligated, in the face of France's failure, to provide it. A strong anticommunist leader who could combat Ho's forces and develop South Vietnam with the backing of the United States was needed. That would allow time for the people to learn the benefits of a US-supported government as opposed to the current conditions. At that point, they could cast more informed votes.

Success in South Vietnam would take two years, Dulles believed, "and would require in large part taking over the training responsibility by the US."[21] Still, it could be done. As Dulles told a friend, with the French defeat "we have a clean base there now without a taint of colonialism. Dienbienphu was a blessing in disguise."[22] Over and over, administration officials pointed to the examples of Greece, Iran, and, most notably, the Philippines as proof that they could build a new nation in South Vietnam. American policymakers saw the progress of the Philippines from chaos to order and the defeat of communism as a remarkable success story for which they could take full credit, a shining example of

American leadership and nation building. In the Philippines, the United States had backed Ramon Magsaysay first for the position of secretary of defense and in 1953 for president at a time when the communist-led Huk rebellion threatened to overthrow the government in Manila. He was credited with suppressing the Huk uprising and averting economic collapse in the archipelago. This was mainly due, officials believed, to his willingness to listen to and follow American advice. Magsaysay had secured a strategic outpost of the United States, established order, and turned the newly independent former colony firmly toward the West.[23] If the United States could successfully create a stable, independent, pro-US Philippines, it could do the same in South Vietnam.

The man the United States entrusted to effect its political will in Vietnam was Ngo Dinh Diem. With Washington's backing, he was appointed premier of South Vietnam by Bao Dai on June 17, 1954. Diem, a Catholic, enjoyed important political support within the United States, particularly from leading Catholic politicians such as Senators Mike Mansfield and John Kennedy and the American Friends of Vietnam. In August, the United States informed France that it intended to deal directly with the new state of South Vietnam and would no longer funnel aid through Paris or have its military advisors work with French officers. The Eisenhower administration's decision was motivated by Cold War concerns. It was essential, Dulles argued, that "in South Vietnam a strong Nationalist Government . . . be developed and supported if the world is not to witness an early Communist take-over in Indochina and a still greater menace to South and Southeast Asia with repercussions in Africa." In order to help ensure its success and "preserve freedom in Vietnam," the United States would now treat Diem's government as an independent state, and American assistance would flow directly to it "rather than through the French government."[24]

As the United States maneuvered to secure Diem's rule in the new nation of South Vietnam, Nixon explained that the "guiding principle of our policy is peace without surrender." Success had to come from a demonstration of will and the credibility of America's power, and strength and firmness were the watchwords of the day. "Aggressive international communism presents the only threat to world peace," and it could only be deterred when "firmness in our will and determination to use our strength against aggression when it occurs is made clear to the world." The Munich analogy was central to Nixon's thinking. At the end of the 1930s, he opined, "we heard the cry 'Why die for Danzig?' No one died for Danzig then—millions died later. History shows that surrender of territory in itself never satisfies an aggressor; it only increases his appetite." The best means to contain communism, avoid world war, and create a chance for peace "will be created through following a policy of strength and firmness with the door always open to negotiation but never to appeasement."[25] With Diem firmly ensconced in Saigon, the vice president declared in October 1955 that the United States would always be open to negotiations as a means to settle disputes but would oppose any concessions to the communists. "We have learned from history that where potential aggressors are concerned, weakness invites attack— strength deters it."[26] The United States could not allow itself to become complacent based on success in South Vietnam.

As Nixon declared in June 1956, in the "titanic struggle between two opposing concepts of life in which we are engaged," the outcome would be decided in the Third World. "The next few years will determine whether we can live in peace and at the same time avoid surrender. And that question will be answered by how well we are able to meet and defeat the changing tactics of the dictatorial forces which threaten the free world." Moscow's shift from Stalin's policy of conflict and aggression in Europe to insurgency and revolution in Asia and Africa meant a threat to the "600 million people [that] live in the so-called uncommitted or neutral nations." Military strength was important, Nixon argued, but equally so was nation building and an "emphasis on developing the kind of ideological program which is designed to win the minds and hearts of men." This was the crucial task, as "it is not enough to denounce or expose communism. We must show that we have a better alternative. . . . There is no question but that we have the better case to sell. Because basically we are on the right side—the side of freedom and justice, of belief in God, against the forces of slavery, injustice, and atheistic materialism. Ours is the truly revolutionary, dynamic idea. It is the Communist idea which is repressive and reactionary."[27]

The battle to maintain the free world was still undetermined and would be decided by what happens to the millions of people now neutral who are trying to decide whether they will align themselves with the Communist nations or with the free nations," Nixon stated. "There is no place for complacency, no matter how well-founded it may appear. None of us can be blind to the fact that a cloud hangs over our heads. It is a cloud of anxiety and even of fear. We see it as a mushroom-shaped cloud that spells a solemn warning, a warning that this prosperity could be wiped out in the awful flash of thermo-nuclear warfare." Vietnam was the test case for the United States to develop a pro-Western nationalism between imperialism and the discredited colonial model, on the one hand, and communist revolution, on the other; it was a stage on which Americans could once again demonstrate their character and integrity to the world. Since American leadership was "moral as well as military and economic," Americans "must never acquiesce in oppression or slavery any place in the world. We must offer assistance and encouragement to the peaceful liberation of enslaved peoples."[28] As Nixon noted in July 1956, when he visited Saigon and President Diem, the creation of the state of South Vietnam meant that "the military march of communism had been halted" in Southeast Asia. "I do not exaggerate when I say that your friends everywhere have derived great inspiration from the successes which have marked the first two years of President Ngo Dinh Diem's administration."[29]

The theme of Vietnam as vital to America's global interests in a bipolar world remained at the center of all of Nixon's analysis and commentary on Vietnam after his defeat by John F. Kennedy in the 1960 presidential election, and he would consistently pressure first Kennedy and then Lyndon Johnson to escalate the American commitment. In his first post-election speech, in May 1961, Nixon stated that, in the wake of the failed Bay of Pigs operation in Cuba and communist gains in Laos, there was "an obvious need for us to develop more effective programs to meet the threat of Communist aggression." The Democrats had to realize that it was a "time of crisis" and that the "forces of Communism are determined to conquer the entire world." Yet the Kennedy administration was acting timidly and defensively and showing signs that it was afraid to use American force to stay the communist hand. Nixon assured Kennedy that he would "support him to the hilt in backing positive action he may decide is necessary to resist further Communist aggression." In a thinly veiled reference to the Bay of Pigs, he added that if the Kennedy administration committed the prestige of the United States "on a major scale, we must be willing to commit enough power to obtain our objective even if all of our intelligence estimates prove wrong."[30]

Nixon criticized Kennedy for failing to back up his words with strong action. Rhetoric about paying any price and asking what people could do for the nation was not enough to win the battle against communism. "Our deeds must match our words. We must never talk bigger than we are prepared to act." No areas of the world were peripheral or unimportant, and the danger was that "if the smaller nations get the idea that we don't consider them important enough to fight for and that the Communists do, they will go down the Communist line like a row of dominoes."[31] When Kennedy did begin to escalate the American commitment in Vietnam in the fall of 1961, taking steps that would increase the number of military advisors from six hundred to sixteen thousand by 1963, adopting new counterinsurgency efforts, and sending more sophisticated military equipment, Nixon praised his actions while expressing his hope that Kennedy would "step up the build-up and under no circumstances curtail it because of possible criticism." It was "essential that the United States commit all the resources of which it is capable to avoid a Communist take-over in Vietnam and the rest of Southeast Asia."[32]

For Nixon, monolithic communism remained an accurate portrayal of the enemy America faced. Although "Red China and Russia [were] having their differences," Nixon believed these concerned tactics for destroying the West, not substantive matters: "they are simply arguing about what kind of a shovel they should use to dig the grave of the United States." Communism continued to expand while suffering no loss of territory. "Communism is on the move," Nixon argued. "It is out to win. It is playing an offensive game. Where in the world today do we expect trouble? In the Communist satellites of Eastern Europe? No, in the free nations of Latin America, Africa, and Asia." [33]

Speaking before the American Society of Newspaper Editors in April 1963, Nixon declared that the United States needed a victory strategy to meet the communist challenge. Such a strategy entailed a strengthening of American alliances, more effective assistance to Third World nations threatened by communism, and a renewed effort "to extend freedom to match the Communist efforts to extend slavery." The third prong was vital, Nixon believed, and he focused most of his attention on it during his talk. The setback in Cuba at the Bay of Pigs made it clear that the United States had to be more proactive in using its strengths, economically, politically, and militarily, in the defense of freedom. "I say it is time for us proudly to declare that our ideas are for export. We need not apologize for taking this position." The United States had sacrificed over 1 million men in two world wars, fought in Korea, and given out over $100 billion in foreign aid. "For what purpose? Not for an acre of territory or to gain domination over any other people but because we believe in freedom, not just for ourselves but for others as well." The communist goal was to overthrow the American government and make the United States a communist nation. The American answer must be that "our goal is nothing less than a free Russia, a free China, a free Eastern Europe, and a free Cuba. Only such a great goal, deeply believed in . . . is worthy of the efforts of a great people in the gigantic struggle. Only such a goal will blunt the Communist ideological offensive and regain the initiative for the cause of freedom." [34] Nixon believed the United States had to begin in Vietnam, where the Cold War was hottest.

The multiple crises in South Vietnam throughout 1963—the military defeats, urban protests by students and Buddhists, self-immolations by Buddhist monks, violent crackdowns on protestors, and imposition of martial law—did not deter Nixon from supporting Diem. Speaking in Paris in October 1963, he recognized the validity of the widespread criticisms of the Diem government due to its repression of protests in South Vietnam but argued that it was still necessary for the United States to work with him in order to defeat communism. Diem's regime might by unsatisfactory, but "the choice is not between President Diem and somebody better, it is between Diem and somebody infinitely worse." Any change would just benefit the communist insurgents. This was "the most dangerous period of the cold war," and the United States could not flinch in the face of the challenge presented in Vietnam. [35]

A week later, Diem was ousted in a coup supported by the Kennedy administration. For Nixon, this perfectly demonstrated his belief that the United States had committed its prestige but the Democrats had not taken the necessary measures to win in Vietnam. His fixation on total victory

over the communist enemy led him to amplify his call for military escalation during the 1964 presidential campaign. Nixon campaigned exten-
sively for Barry Goldwater, making foreign policy and the war in Vietnam central to his argument in support of the Republican nominee
against Johnson. Throughout the campaign, he held on to Cold War assumptions about monolithic communism and the logic of the domino
theory, arguing that the war in Vietnam was an extension of China's
efforts to expand its influence throughout Southeast Asia. Not just Vietnam but all of Southeast Asia, Australia, and New Zealand were threatened. Even more importantly, American credibility was on the line.

During another visit to Vietnam in April 1964, Nixon insisted that any
withdrawal of American support from Saigon would lead to a communist victory, and he called for an increase in the American commitment to
South Vietnam instead. He stated that the Johnson administration's strategy for winning the war was "inadequate" and that the goal had to be
"nothing less than victory." He questioned whether the current administration had "a plan which is adequate to reach that goal." Speaking in
Tokyo a few days later, Nixon was more direct, saying he favored an
expansion of the war by taking the fighting directly to North Vietnam.
There would be no success in a policy that "restricted the South Vietnamese to simply dealing with the Communist guerrillas in South Vietnam," and it was necessary to consider attacking the "privileged sanctuary" of North Vietnam.[36] He went so far as to suggest in 1964 that the
United States should increase the South Vietnamese air force to allow it to
extend its bombing of the communist supply routes to the South and that
Saigon "should extend guerrilla warfare over the border and harass the
enemy in the north."[37]

Nixon's most complete statement of his views on the war in Vietnam
came in his August 1964 article in *Reader's Digest* titled "Needed in Vietnam: The Will to Win." He asserted that far more than the fate of Vietnam
was at stake in the war. Due to the weakness of the Democrats, the
United States faced "the prospect of a grave, and irreparable, defeat." The
situation was getting worse by the year as the Johnson administration, in
Nixon's estimation, sought to do the minimum to prevent defeat instead
of devising a strategy for victory. This approach, he contended, was leading to fear among American allies in Asia that the United States could not
protect them and that communism was "the wave of the future." In the
"worldwide struggle against communism," the war in Vietnam was part
of a larger campaign for Asia; any weakening of American support for
Saigon or failure to contain communism would deal a fatal blow to US
credibility, with dire consequences.[38]

If the United States did not act, the former vice president asserted, the
Johnson administration's policy would be tantamount to appeasement,
akin to when "Chamberlain reached an agreement with Hitler at Munich
in 1938." It was clear that "on the fate of South Vietnam depends the fate

of all of Asia. For South Vietnam is the dam in the river. A communist victory there would mean, inevitably and soon, that the flood would begin" and the surrounding dominoes of Laos, Cambodia, Thailand, Malaysia, and Indonesia would fall. "Can anyone seriously suggest," Nixon asked rhetorically, "that in such a circumstance the United States would not have to engage in a major war to save the Philippines from the same fate as Vietnam? And what of Japan?" Asia's only industrial nation, denied access to the markets and resources of Southeast Asia, would be forced to make an accommodation with communist China. Nor did the repercussions stop with East Asia. "Can anyone doubt the effect of this defeat in Africa, Latin America, and even on our allies in Europe"—or that it would lead to World War III?[39]

Nixon dismissed calls for a neutral South Vietnam as a failure to learn the lessons of history. "Neutralization is but another name for appeasement. It is surrender on the installment plan." In Laos, the United States pursued neutrality under Kennedy but did nothing to hold the line. "We talked big and acted little." The Kennedy administration trusted the communists to honor their word. Yet "when the chips were down, the United States backed away from its brave words and agreed to a compromise. As a result, Laos is going down the drain." Now North Vietnam was continuing to aid the communists in Laos, using that country as "a corridor for supplying the Viet Cong guerrillas in South Vietnam." Thus, the "present administration's policies, which cannot lead to victory in Vietnam, do not reduce the danger of major war. It increases it."[40]

With the proper leadership and political will, Nixon argued, there was still time to save South Vietnam and turn the tide against the communists in Asia. The right policy and a full effort could protect Saigon, reassure American allies, and lessen the chances of a larger war. "The only way to avoid a major war later is to win the smaller war in Vietnam—and to take the risks involved in accomplishing that objective." This was a military issue, not a political one. "The problem is not one of tactics and strategy. It is a problem of will—and morale." The tough decisions had to be faced. "What we *must* do is instill in ourselves and our allies a determination to win this crucial war—and win it decisively." It was essential that Americans "recognize that we are in a life-and-death struggle that has repercussions far beyond Vietnam, and that victory is essential to the survival of freedom." Immediate action was necessary. "If we are ever to stop the communist advance in Asia the time is now. The place is Vietnam."[41]

Nixon proposed a strategy for how the communist challenge could be met. Communist appeal and power in Asia, he claimed, were at the lowest point since World War II, and victory could be obtained in a limited war that did not call for the use of nuclear weapons. "The Red guerillas in South Vietnam are winning because they are supplied from positions in Laos and North Vietnam which we refuse to seal off." The United States

could use its airpower to deny the communist these sanctuaries and destroy the supply routes to the South. With the South isolated and "the
northern border sealed, the same tactics that were used successfully to
clean out the guerillas in the Philippines and in Malaya can be used
effectively in South Vietnam." Nixon was confident that "assum[ing] a
determined, offensive policy" would bring the United States victory, restore American credibility, and rally the anticommunist forces in Asia.
Further emphasizing that now was the time to act in Vietnam, he argued,
"History shows that the appeasers, the compromisers who refuse to
stand up against aggression, *have* to take a stand sooner or later—and
always at a less favorable time and place."[42]

It was imperative, Nixon exhorted, that the United States make the
right decision to stand and fight in Vietnam. "The decision is upon us. If
we fail to win in South Vietnam—whether through following our present
equivocal policy, through neutralization or through outright surrender—
communism in Asia will achieve a new and vastly increased momentum." Moreover, "our defeat will confirm the Chinese communist conten-
tion that the United States is a paper tiger, careless of commitments to its
allies and readily susceptible to defeat by terrorism, subversion and guerilla warfare." This would lead to further global aggression by the communists and a major war most likely involving nuclear weapons. "Con-
versely, a victory for us in South Vietnam will shatter the myths of communist invincibility and of the inevitability of a Chinese take-over in
Southeast Asia. It will restore all the prestige we have lost and give us
more besides." In the end, the fight in Vietnam was winnable; the crisis
was not "one of competence but of *confidence*." What was being tested
was not the United States' power but its "capacity to use [that] power
correctly and with courage. All that is needed, in short, is the will to
win—and the courage to use our power—*now*."[43]

The Republican defeat in 1964 did not deter Nixon when it came to
Vietnam. He increased his calls for escalation and military victory. In
December, he recommended the bombing of communist bases in North
Vietnam and Laos and claimed that if South Vietnam fell to communism,
the United States would find itself soon in a major war with communist
China or even the Soviet Union. With control of Southeast Asia, he declared, China would exert "tremendous pressure on Japan—the big prize
in Asia." Escalation could bring war with the Chinese, but the risk was
worth taking "so we won't have to fight a major war three or four years
later."[44]

In January 1965, Nixon delivered a well-covered speech to the Executive Club in New York titled "Facing the Facts in Vietnam: Get Out,
Neutralize or Win." He began by invoking the now familiar fear of appeasement by quoting Winston Churchill from 1938 after Munich: "The
belief that security can be obtained by throwing a small state to the
wolves is a fatal delusion." Given this lesson, Nixon insisted, "the battle

for Vietnam is the battle for Asia." The fighting in Vietnam, "in the final analysis," was "not between the Vietnamese and the Viet Cong nor between the United States and the Viet Cong, but between the United States and communist China. If communist China was not instigating and supporting the Viet Cong, there would be no war in Vietnam today." Yet the United States was currently "losing the war in Vietnam, and if there is not a change in strategy," it would be defeated within the year. In order to win in Vietnam and prevent a Chinese conquest of all of Asia, the struggle to save Saigon had to be expanded. "We must realize that there is no easy way out. We either get out, surrender on the installment plan through neutralization, or we find a way to win!" It was time for the United States to "quarantine" South Vietnam by cutting off the ability of North Vietnam to interfere in the South through the use of "American air and sea power to cut supply lines and destroy staging areas in North Vietnam and Laos which now make it possible for the guerillas to continue their actions." He ended his dire warning by again quoting Churchill and calling upon the United States to honor the former British prime minister's memory by heeding his words and taking the necessary action to stop communism and to preserve American strength, credibility, and interests.[45]

The next month, commenting on the attack on the American military base at Pleiku, Nixon called for around-the-clock — "day by day, and for that matter, night by night" — air strikes against North Vietnam. A failure to take action by the United States would "mean loss of the war . . . to imperial communism." America had to act. "The choice today is not between this war and no war, but this war and another much bigger war" in the near future if Washington did not respond.[46] That summer, he would go a step further, arguing that the United States should not restrict its bombing targets to North Vietnam out of fear of Soviet retaliation. American policy had to be firm and militarily effective to demonstrate the nation's willingness to stop communist aggression.[47]

The Johnson administration did take action, announcing Operation Rolling Thunder, a sustained bombing campaign against North Vietnam and the Ho Chi Minh Trail, later that month. In March, the first US marines landed in Danang to protect the American air base there, and in April the president spoke to the nation at Johns Hopkins University to explain why he had to escalate the American commitment to South Vietnam and fight. He cast the confrontation in Cold War terms similar to the arguments Nixon employed. "The first reality," the president explained, "is that North Viet-Nam has attacked the independent nation of South Viet-nam." In this effort, it was acting as part of a larger communist plan to conquer Asia. "Over this war — over all Asia — is another reality: the deepening shadow of Communist China. The rulers of Hanoi are urged on by Peking." The Munich analogy was clear to Johnson. "Let no one think for a moment that retreat from Viet-nam would bring an end to conflict. The battle would be renewed in one country and then another. The central lesson of our time is that the appetite of aggression is never satisfied. To withdraw from one battlefield means only to prepare for the next." America's containment policy and credibility were being tested, and the world was watching to see how Washington would react. Johnson was adamant. "We will not be defeated. We will not grow tired. We will not withdraw, either openly or under the cloak of a meaningless agreement."[48]

After Johnson made the decision to send troops in July 1965, Nixon praised the president's course of action but continued to suggest that he was not doing enough and to warn that the goal had to be a military victory. Using the Vietnam War to stay in the public eye, Nixon again traveled to Saigon in September. He argued that it was of the utmost importance for US prestige that the victory be complete: the United States could not "afford to leave without a victory over aggression." Nixon therefore criticized those who called for "peace-feelers," such as those suggested by Senator William Fulbright, as "advocating a 'soft line' toward North Vietnam" and making concessions "to the Communists in order to get peace.'" For Nixon, "whenever any individual talks about negotiations that would reward aggression, all that he does is rather than hastening peace, he prolongs the war. He encourages our enemies, he discourages our friends and he confuses even the neutrals." There was only one basis for negotiations: "a Communist withdrawal of their forces and for the Communists to agree to quit infringing on the independence and territorial integrity of South Vietnam." Anything else, he asserted, would mean a loss of American credibility, and that "would be a defeat for the United States and for the forces of freedom in Asia." With the stakes so high in Vietnam, Nixon opined, Johnson had yet to send enough troops to win the war, and the level of forces would "have to be more substantial and larger than we have at present."[49]

Now that the United States had committed its own forces, Nixon perpetuated the idea that the fight in Vietnam was noble and that negotiations were not only misguided but immoral and dangerous. Turning again to the pages of *Reader's Digest* in December 1965, Nixon stated, "I am convinced that the major danger today is not a military defeat on the battlefield, but a diplomatic defeat at the conference table." It was understandable that pacifist and so-called peace groups sought negotiations, Nixon said. "More disturbing," however, "than these scattered and irresponsible outcries are the powerful and respected voices calling for a negotiated truce in Vietnam." He charged that they failed to understand history or the communist threat and equated their calls for negotiations with "appeasement and retreat." The source of the war was the "naked aggression on the part of North Vietnam" backed by China. Those who called for talks with Hanoi did not "understand that the course they advocate is filled with far more danger of war than any other that could be presented." For Nixon, negotiations were the road to a larger war, not peace. "Those who advise us to stop fighting now because they believe we can't win would negotiate out of fear—and this way lie appeasement and the seeds of disaster." It should be clear to a generation that had fought World War II that "the lesson of all history warns us that we should negotiate only when our military superiority is so convincing that we can achieve our objective at the conference table—and deny the aggressors theirs." Therefore, negotiations at that point of the war "would be like negotiating with Hitler before the German armies had been driven from France."[50]

The road would not be easy. It would take, Nixon believed, "two years or more of the hardest kind of fighting" to prevail, but he was "convinced that the communists are losing ground and that the South Vietnamese with our help have a good chance of victory. What has made the difference is the impact of American air strikes in North Vietnam and our commitment of grounds troops in South Vietnam." The United States had to guarantee "South Vietnam's independence and freedom from communist control." With this goal, "there can be no substitute for victory when the objective is the defeat of communist aggression." After all, Nixon concluded, the United States was fighting for more than just South Vietnam. It was engaged in a battle to maintain American credibility and, in the process, was fighting "for peace, freedom and progress for all peoples."[51] Nixon held to this position throughout the war, and it served to guide his criticisms of Johnson's conduct of the war and his own policies when he assumed the presidency.

Throughout 1966, Nixon continued to support the war in Vietnam and to criticize President Johnson for not escalating fast enough or using the full extent of American power to succeed. This caused, he claimed, the slow pace of progress in Vietnam and disunity at home, and the communists were counting on this disunity to win the war. Nixon consistently attacked critics of the war and called for a greater American military effort. He claimed that the opponents of the war were taking the "soft line, the appeasement line" and thereby irresponsibly lending support to the enemy. There should be no reward for aggression. If the United States, Nixon stated in April, "cuts and runs in Vietnam we will have a temporary peace and then a certain world war." This made it necessary for the United States to use even more force than the Johnson administration had currently deployed in order to achieve victory.[52]

In August, on yet another trip to Vietnam, Nixon called for a "substantial increase" in American ground forces, by about 25 percent to five hundred thousand, and an expansion of the air war. Those who argued for a lesser number, Nixon asserted, were actually calling for a longer, costlier war. He thought those who objected to his view "should realize that in the long run [a greater buildup] means a lesser American commitment." "Maximum force" would bring the war to a swift conclusion.

Pulling his two themes together, Nixon insisted at the end of the month that the Johnson administration was resigned to a long, drawn-out war in Vietnam that would lead to increased calls for negotiation. The United Stated needed "new tactics, new leadership, new methods to shorten this war and bring it to a conclusion without appeasement of the enemy." Nixon warned, "If Vietnam falls, the Pacific will be transformed into a Red ocean and the road will be open to a third world war."[53]

Just prior to the midterm elections, President Johnson traveled to Manila to meet with South Vietnamese and American officials from Saigon to assess the war. In what became known as the "Manila formula" for peace, the United States, it was announced, would withdraw its forces from South Vietnam six months "after the military and subversive forces of North Vietnam are withdrawn, infiltration ceases and the level of violence thus subsides." Nixon quickly criticized the plan as revealing the weaknesses of the administration's policy in dealing with "one of the central issues of our time." Mutual withdrawal, as Nixon termed it, appeared on the surface to be a reasonable approach, when in fact it surrendered all that the United States had accomplished in two years of fighting, demonstrated the inability of the Democrats to make the hard choices necessary to win the war, and "jeopardize[d] every strategic American objective in Vietnam." It returned the war to a battle between Saigon and the Viet Cong, a situation in which "the South Vietnamese government could not prevail for any length of time over the Communist guerrillas without American advisers, air support and logistical backing. Communist victory would most certainly be the result of 'mutual withdrawal.'"[54]

Such an agreement, therefore, threatened "a worldwide crisis of credibility." Honoring the American "commitments to defend freedom" in Vietnam was costly but working. Why, Nixon asked, "endanger our hard-won credibility for this temporary propaganda advantage?" The administration had "offered to surrender a decisive military advantage" and to "leave it to Communist generals to determine the timing and intensity of the war," a return to a policy of "gradualism" in fighting that had failed earlier in the decade. Nixon stated that he agreed with Dwight Eisenhower, who believed "in putting in the kind of military strength we need to win and getting it over with as soon as possible."[55] As he stated in early 1967, Nixon believed that any consideration of negotiations or bombing halts by the United States had "the effect of prolonging the war by encouraging the enemy. They are led to believe there is division in the United States and they can win." Republicans, Nixon declared, wanted a "constructive attitude" that would bring "peace without surrender."[56]

In April 1967, during his fifth visit to Vietnam in four years, Nixon insisted on the necessity of the war in Vietnam and military victory to uphold American credibility as the leader of the free world. Nixon warned that "if the credibility of the United States is destroyed in Vietnam, it will be destroyed in Europe as well." He was encouraged by the unity among the nations of Asia in support of the war, stating that all of America's Asian allies were "committed alike to freedom . . . and resistance to aggression," but Nixon was concerned about criticism in Western Europe and in the United States. The war would be shortened and victory achieved quicker "by mobilizing free world opinion and by uniting the United States."[57]

Division only served to prolong the war and provide "aid and comfort to the enemy." It was essential that the United States convince the North Vietnamese that they could not win the war militarily or by holding out for a diplomatic deal, and he supported a dramatic increase in American efforts to win the war. "It can be said now," Nixon declared in Saigon, "that the defeat of the Communist forces in South Vietnam is inevitable. The only question is, how soon?" Here, Nixon criticized Johnson for not making a strong enough effort and stated his belief that victory could be "speeded up" by using more airpower, by mining North Vietnamese harbors to cut the flow of supplies, and by taking stronger steps to pacify South Vietnam. He was certain that the Republicans would not make negotiations a part of their platform in 1968. Rather, they would stress "how to bring more pressure to bear for victory."[58]

Starting in mid-1967, Nixon's comments on the war were calculated with the 1968 presidential election in mind as he worked to position himself as an experienced voice with the right approach to winning the war. Nixon did not officially announce his candidacy until January 1968, but he spent most of the fall of 1967 campaigning in key states. While in Oregon in late November, he was forced to respond to a call for an expansion of the war by Eisenhower. The former president's endorsement of a policy of "hot pursuit" that allowed US troops to operate in the demilitarized zone and chase enemy forces into Cambodia and Laos placed Nixon in a difficult position. He had decided to limit his comments on Vietnam during the campaign to middle-of-the-road pronouncements and vague statements that would appeal to the broadest constituency possible. Using all of his skill as a politician in walking a tightrope, Eisenhower's vice president stated that from a military point of view, General Eisenhower was "absolutely right," but the actions he recommended ran the risk of "widening the ground conflict in Vietnam—a risk that should be carefully weighed." From a political perspective, Nixon said he "would be very reluctant to take action that would be regarded as an invasion of North Vietnam, Cambodia or Laos" and that the diplomatic and political risks "outweighed" the military gain.[59] This was an example of what would come to be called the "new" Nixon—less belligerent, willing to concede certain realities about the limits of American power, and indicating that he sought to end the war. Thus began Nixon's effort to position himself as a centrist voice on the Vietnam War.

NOTES

1. *Public Papers of the Presidents: Dwight D. Eisenhower, 1953* (Washington, DC: Government Printing Office, 1960), 4.

2. *Public Papers of the Presidents: Eisenhower, 1953*, 258.

3. US Congress, Senate, *Executive Sessions of the Senate Foreign Relations Committee, 1953* (Washington, DC: Government Printing Office), 5:139–40 (hereafter *Executive Sessions* followed by year, volume, and page number).

4. *Public Papers of the Presidents: Dwight D. Eisenhower, 1954* (Washington, DC: Government Printing Office, 1960), 382–83.

5. "Nixon Bids Vietnam Spur War Effort," *New York Times*, November 1, 1953, 13.

6. *New York Times*, November 5, 1953, 8.

7. US Department of State, "Meeting the People of Asia," *Department of State Bulletin* (Washington, DC: Government Printing Office, 1954), 10.

8. US Department of State, "Meeting the People of Asia," 11.

9. Richard M. Nixon, "The Chances for Peace Today: Dynamic Forces at Work on World Problems," *Vital Speeches of the Day*, October 17, 1955, 72.

10. US Department of State, "Meeting the People of Asia," 11, 13.

11. US Department of State, "Meeting the People of Asia," 12.

12. *New York Times*, November 5, 1953, 8.

13. US Department of State, "Meeting the People of Asia," 12.

14. *Executive Sessions*, 1954, 6:23–24.

15. *New York Times*, April 18, 1954; April 20, 1954.

16. *New York Times*, April 20, 1954.

17. *New York Times*, April 21, 1954, 4.

18. *Executive Sessions*, 1954, 6:642–43.

19. Dwight D. Eisenhower, *Mandate for Change, 1954–1956* (Garden City, NY: Doubleday, 1963), 372.

20. Dulles, quoted in Lloyd Gardner, *Approaching Vietnam: From World War II through Dienbienphu, 1944–1954* (New York: Norton, 1988), 270.

21. Dulles, quoted in Gardner, *Approaching Vietnam*, 258.

22. Dulles, quoted in Marilyn B. Young, *The Vietnam Wars, 1945–1990* (New York: HarperCollins, 1991), 46.

23. Stanley Karnow, *In Our Image: America's Empire in the Philippines* (New York: Random House, 1989), 346–55.

24. Dulles to Eisenhower, August 18, 1954; Dulles to Mendes-France, August 16, 1954, AWF, DH Series, Box 4, DDEL.

25. Richard M. Nixon, "Peace without Surrender," *US News & World Report*, April 15, 1955, 66.

26. Nixon, "The Chances for Peace Today," 70.

27. Richard M. Nixon, "A Peaceful Crusade for Freedom," *Department of State Bulletin*, June 25, 1956 (Washington, DC: Government Printing Office, 1956), 1043–45.

28. Richard M. Nixon, "In the Cause of Peace and Freedom: Rule of Law Upheld," *Vital Speeches of the Day*, December 6, 1956, 165.

29. *New York Times*, July 7, 1956, 4.

30. Richard M. Nixon, "Now Is the Time," *Time*, May 12, 1961, 14.

31. Nixon, "Now Is the Time," 14.

32. *New York Times*, February 16, 1962, 3.

33. Richard M. Nixon, "American Policy Abroad," *Vital Speeches of the Day*, April 20, 1963, 487.

34. Nixon, "American Policy Abroad," 488–89.

35. *New York Times*, October 25, 1963.

36. *New York Times*, April 2, 1964; April 3, 1964; April 10, 1964.

37. Richard M. Nixon, "Needed in Vietnam: The Will to Win," *Reader's Digest* 85 (August 1964): 42.

38. Nixon, "Needed in Vietnam," 37–43.

39. Nixon, "Needed in Vietnam," 37–43.

40. Nixon, "Needed in Vietnam," 37–43.

41. Nixon, "Needed in Vietnam," 37–43 (emphasis in the original).

42. Nixon, "Needed in Vietnam," 37–43 (emphasis in the original).

43. Nixon, "Needed in Vietnam," 37–43 (emphasis in the original).

44. *New York Times*, December 3, 1964.

45. Richard M. Nixon, "Facing the Facts in Vietnam: Get Out, Neutralize, or Win," *Vital Speeches of the Day*, January 26, 1965, 339. The speech received front-page coverage in the *New York Times* the next day. The day after Nixon's speech, National Security Advisor McGeorge Bundy sent a memorandum to President Johnson saying many of the same things as Nixon. Writing on behalf of himself and Secretary of Defense Robert McNamara, Bundy stated that the administration's "current policy can lead only to disastrous defeat," that America's credibility was being questioned, and that the only way to achieve victory was through the employment of American "military power . . . to force a change of Communist policy." Bundy to Johnson, "Basic Policy in Vietnam," January 27, 1965, NSF: Memos to the President, Bundy, Box 2, LBJL.

46. "Nixon says U.S. should Attack Red Supply Lines Day and Night," *New York Times*, February 11, 1965, 12; Andrew Johns, *Vietnam's Second Front: Domestic Politics, the Republican Party, and the War* (Lexington: University Press of Kentucky, 2010), 83.

47. *New York Times*, July 11, 1965.

48. *Public Papers of the Presidents: Lyndon B. Johnson, 1965* (Washington, DC: Government Printing Office, 1966), 1:394–98.

49. *New York Times*, September 6, 1965.

50. Richard M. Nixon, "Why Not Negotiate in Vietnam?" *Reader's Digest* (December 1965): 49–54.

51. Nixon, "Why Not Negotiate in Vietnam?" 49–54.

52. *New York Times*, May 1, 1966; for examples of Nixon's views, see also *New York Times*, January 31, 1966; February 6, 1966; April 17, 1966; May 27, 1966.

53. *New York Times*, August 8, 1966; August 12, 1966; August 27, 1966; September 1, 1966.

54. *New York Times*, November 4, 1966.

55. *New York Times*, November 4, 1966.

56. *New York Times*, March 6, 1967.

57. *New York Times*, April 8, 1967.

58. *New York Times*, April 15, 1967; April 18, 1967.

59. *New York Times*, November 30, 1967.

TWO

The Middle Road to the White House

As the 1968 campaign began in earnest, Richard Nixon's strategy was to allow himself the greatest flexibility in his positions on the Vietnam War by keeping his comments as general as possible. He aimed to appeal to both supporters and opponents of the war. If in favor of the war and a military victory, one could interpret many of Nixon's statements as in line with that policy. On the other hand, if one hoped for negotiations and a de-escalation of the American role in the world, Nixon indicated that he was willing to pursue this course of action if elected president. As noted by many critics at the time and since, Nixon's positions were often contradictory and hypocritical. This Janus-faced approach, however, was intentional. Moreover, for much of the campaign, particularly after Lyndon Johnson's March 31 speech and withdrawal from the race, Nixon conveniently avoided taking a definite position on the war by claiming that he did not want to state any specific positions or take any actions that might jeopardize the Johnson administration's efforts toward achieving peace.

After holding a commanding lead over the Democratic candidate, Vice President Hubert Humphrey, for most of the race, Nixon's advantage began to slip away in October. As Humphrey distanced himself from Johnson and became a clear advocate of a negotiated peace, Nixon continued to talk in public of attaining peace and achieving victory in Vietnam while simultaneously working covertly to prevent any breakthrough in the negotiations that would aid Humphrey's campaign. It was a dangerous but ultimately successful strategy. On November 5, Nixon barely defeated the vice president by less than five hundred thousand votes.

Nixon entered the race with a well-deserved reputation as a hawk who advocated escalation and a military solution, who saw the war as

23

part of a larger effort by China to export revolution and wars of national liberation to other nations in Asia, and who believed that the United States had to meet this challenge to peace and stability in order to preserve its interests, credibility, and policy of containment. Vietnam was a necessary war that the United States had to win. With his position in 1954 that the United States might have to send forces to save Vietnam, his consistent calls for greater escalation once the United States went to war, and his claims that the American presence in Vietnam was preventing further Chinese expansion in Asia and World War III,[1] Nixon was the leading proponent of the use of force to uphold containment in Southeast Asia. His views stemmed from his conviction that toughness and resistance were necessary against the communist world to frustrate Moscow's and Beijing's efforts at expansion. Any weakness would lead to defeat and a later, larger war. As Nixon stated in January 1968, he believed it mattered greatly how the war ended. "There are some people running around saying we could end it in a couple of days. I can show you how to do that—and it's unthinkable. . . . The only course is to increase pressure on all sides—militarily, diplomatically, economically." Yet this would all be for naught if the home front was lost. "Every time somebody says we should pull out, Ho is encouraged to think he can win militarily in Vietnam."[2]

Going into the 1968 campaign, Nixon set out the main outlines of his thinking on the Vietnam War—which would become his policy once president—in an October 1967 *Foreign Affairs* article titled "Asia after Viet Nam." He began by reaffirming the American commitment to Asia and the need for containment. The US commitment of force in Vietnam had played a "vital role" in protecting all of East Asia from communism. "Whatever one may think of the 'domino' theory," US presence and credibility "provided tangible and highly visible proof that communism is not necessarily the wave of Asia's future." The threat from China, he wrote, "is clear, present, and repeatedly and insistently expressed," as demonstrated by its aggression by "proxy" in Vietnam. Beijing could repeat this strategy in any of a half dozen other countries in Asia. Nixon believed that the American presence in Vietnam, however, was allowing for an "extraordinarily promising transformation" in Asia. He specifically noted the coming to power of Suharto in Indonesia as evidence of the positive impact of the war. The "U.S. presence," he claimed, had been "a vital factor" in blocking an attempted communist takeover in Jakarta and saved the "greatest prize" in Southeast Asia. "It provided a shield behind which the anti-communist forces found the courage and the capacity to stage their counter-coup and . . . rescue their country from the Chinese orbit." There was no question, Nixon asserted, "that without the American commitment in Viet Nam, Asia would be a far different place today," with the communist world holding control over most of the mainland.[3]

Nonetheless, Nixon realized that the rising costs of the Vietnam War and growing domestic opposition threatened to force the United States to unilaterally withdraw if no alternative strategy was developed. "One of the legacies of Viet Nam," he wrote, "will be a deep reluctance on the part of the United States to become involved once again in a similar intervention on a similar basis." The war had generated political, social, and economic strains in the United States. The bitter opposition at home "has torn the fabric of American intellectual life, and whatever the outcome of the war the tear may be a long time mending." Recognizing the end of the consensus on containment, he doubted whether "the American public or the American Congress would now support a unilateral American intervention" if another friendly nation were threatened by "an externally supported communist insurrection." This did not mean that the United States would not "respond militarily to communist threats in the less stable parts of the world," but other nations had to "recognize that the role of the United States as world policeman is likely to be limited in the future."[4]

The upshot was that local governments had to take on a greater share of the costs and burdens of their own defense and containment, foreshadowing what would become the Nixon Doctrine. The United States would continue to provide military support and economic assistance, but more countries had to take responsibility for regional security. For Nixon, this was not a way out of Asia for the United States. Rather, it would allow Washington to continue to meet its commitments, stay in the area, and reject the calls of the "new isolationists" for an American withdrawal from the world. "The United States is a Pacific power," he declared, and Asia was the region where communism posed the greatest threat to its interests. Nor was it a call to revive the Southeast Asia Treaty Organization, whose usefulness had passed because it was too dependent on the United States. It did mean, however, that other nations had to be willing to fight for their own defense without American troops. Turning to the question of what type of nations the United States should support, Nixon stated that these countries would not fit the Western ideal of democracy. Americans "must recognize that a highly sophisticated, highly advanced political system, which required many centuries to develop in the West, may not be best for other nations which . . . are still in an earlier stage of development." What mattered was maintaining stability and preventing the spread of communism. America, therefore, had to reject the calls "of the new isolationism" while simultaneously finding better, less costly ways to contain communism.[5]

Merging the hard-line themes that represented his views up to 1968 with the message of his *Foreign Affairs* article, Nixon gave an interview to the *Nation's Business* in January 1968 in which he stated that it was essential that the United States engage in what he termed "preventive diplomacy" both to win the war in Vietnam and to prevent future wars. This meant creating "regional, buffer, collective security arrangements which would take the responsibility for handling guerrilla outbreaks in those areas." In order to "bring the war in Viet Nam to an end, it is necessary to convince the North Vietnamese that they cannot win the war militarily, that they cannot win politically." In addition to military pressure, another way forward was to "use our economic and diplomatic leverage with the Soviet Union to get them to use their influence with North Viet Nam to bring the war to a conclusion." Most importantly, "it is necessary to mobilize public opinion in the United States behind the war effort" and to build unity at home. "I think," Nixon opined, that "the Administration's failure has been most marked in this area."[6]

On January 30, 1968, approximately eighty-four thousand National Liberation Front (NLF) and North Vietnamese Army (NVA) forces attacked over one hundred cities and military bases across South Vietnam. The large, coordinated Tet Offensive caught American officials by surprise as it contradicted the optimistic claims of the administration the previous fall that the war of attrition had succeeded in wearing down the enemy to the point that it could no longer replace losses or engage in sustained military action. Tet had a dramatic impact on the presidential race. While General William Westmoreland and President Johnson portrayed it as a dramatic defeat for the NLF and NVA, the Tet Offensive quickly damaged the president's political fortunes and raised significant questions about the war and the chances for victory.[7] The response of respected CBS news anchor Walter Cronkite captured the sentiment of many Americans. Reacting to the news of the initial attacks, Cronkite asked, "What the hell is going on? I thought we were winning the war!" At the end of February, in a special report on Vietnam, he presented the fighting as a stalemate, questioned any optimistic reports, and called for negotiations.[8]

The Tet Offensive breathed life into the flagging campaign of Senator Eugene McCarthy, who had entered the race in the fall of 1967 as an antiwar candidate. It appeared to legitimate his claims that the United States was making little progress in the fighting and generated a surge in support, volunteers, and money. Prior to Tet, McCarthy was polling in the single digits and appeared to pose no threat to the sitting president. In February, support for McCarthy grew to 18 percent and was climbing, opening up not just the prospect of a significant primary challenge to Johnson from McCarthy but the possibility that Senator Robert F. Kennedy would also enter the race as an antiwar candidate. With the military asking for more troops, opposition to the war growing, economic problems mounting, and a significant primary challenge, Johnson was vulnerable. Still, Nixon had to weigh how much he wanted to criticize the president on the war and from what direction.

Kicking off his campaign in New Hampshire, Nixon began by assailing the Johnson administration on the war in Vietnam, asking what kind of leadership the president was providing when the United States "could not defeat a fourth-rate military power."[9] Although there was no easy solution to the Vietnam War, if the communists were successful "in whole or in part" in Vietnam, the "result will be that they and other Communists in that area will try the same tactics again." Thus, an American victory was vital to peace.[10] In Dover, New Hampshire, on February 12, Nixon stated that the American commitment in Vietnam was "the cork in the bottle of Chinese expansion in Asia." There could be no mistake: "This is a war we cannot lose. For we are fighting in Vietnam, not for Vietnam alone, but for peace in the Pacific. It is this larger cause that makes it essential that our side prevail." If America were to lose, "it is certain that the chances of another and a larger war would be dangerously escalated."[11] Balancing these positions with those of a statesman-like peacemaker, Nixon also returned to the themes of his "Asia after Viet Nam" article to make his case for "preventive diplomacy" to avoid similar wars in the future. A Nixon administration, he declared, would strive to create conditions whereby the United States could help other nations fight but "not fight the war for them." Although he believed it necessary to carry on with the war in Vietnam, Nixon argued that Washington "must look beyond Vietnam. The United States needs some preventive diplomacy to avoid getting into this kind of situation again."[12]

Throughout March, Nixon's rhetoric fluctuated from continued assertion of Vietnam's importance to American interests and credibility and calls for a "military victory" to statements about the need for negotiations. For example, campaigning on March 5 in Nashua, he pledged that the Republicans would provide "new leadership" that would "end the war." Given the failures of the current administration to bring the war to a satisfactory close, the American people should turn to the Republican Party. "If in November this war is not over," Nixon declared, "after all of this power has been at their disposal, then I say that the American people will be justified to elect new leadership." In the type of statement that led to talk of Nixon having a secret plan to end the war, the candidate went on to say that although there was "no push-button technique" to end the war, he was certain that it "[could] be ended" if the United States would mobilize its "economic and political and diplomatic leadership." He went on to say, "I pledge to you the new leadership will end the war and win the peace in the Pacific—and that is what American wants." That evening at a fund-raiser in Washington, DC, he stated that the administration had put too much emphasis on the military side of the war and needed a more balanced approach. In the wake of Tet, the United States needed to "keep the pressure on" militarily, but it also had to look at other avenues to end the war. In particular, he raised the possibility that the United States might have the leverage to get the Soviet Union to use its influence on Hanoi and that this might be the "key to peace."[13] In sum, Nixon's position was that he could end the war quicker than Johnson and the

Democrats, although he could not say exactly how, and that he would prevent the United States from becoming involved in future wars of this type while still protecting US interests, preserving American credibility, and containing communism.

Nixon stood by his pledge that he would "end the war" but maintained he could not provide details about how as that would weaken his bargaining position once he became president. "No one with this responsibility who is seeking office should give away any of his bargaining positions in advance." This was also why he would not be "tied to anything Johnson has said except the commitment [to the war]. Under no circumstances should a man say what he would do next January. The military situation may change, and we may have to take an entirely different look." He did believe "that there is room for negotiation" and continued to note that the Soviet Union was "very possibly the key" to a settlement and that he was open to many new avenues to achieve US goals in Vietnam. He would not, however, support an end to the war that appeared to "indicate that aggression pays—that is why, in my view, a coalition government or another partition would end the war but would lose the peace." Nixon therefore would not "take any positions that [he] would be bound by at a later point. One of the advantages of a new President is that he can start fresh without being imprisoned by the formulas of the past." [14]

In an interview with *US News & World Report*, Nixon focused on the theme of new leadership but combined it with military threats in a manner that provided a glimpse of the actual policy he would follow as president. It was important, he claimed, to "get across to the parties in interest—the Soviet Union and the North Vietnamese—the simple fact that the United States . . . [has] enough power—immense power—that we have never used, that we do not want to use this power, unless necessary, but that if they continue to put pressure on, we shall have to consider other options." Furthermore, he recalled from the Korean War that negotiations were often just a tactic the communists used to gain a military advantage. "When we talk they fight," and "we must never let that happen in Vietnam. I am a firm liner, because I know the Communists, and I know that as far as they are concerned all this talk that we must prove that we are for peace—look, if they were for peace they wouldn't have started the war." [15]

As the campaign shifted from New Hampshire, where Nixon easily won, to Wisconsin, Nixon added further fuel to the claims that he had some sort of secret plan by calling for Eisenhower diplomacy to bring an end to the war in Vietnam. He declared that in 1953, when he became vice president, the United States had been stuck in a stalemate in Korea. Yet Dwight Eisenhower's administration had "ended that war and kept the nation out of other wars for eight years." The inference was clear that he had devised a strategy as he again repeated his promise to end the war in Vietnam. Still, he refused to provide any specifics other than to say that the ultimate objective was to assist South Vietnam in winning the war and "not to fight it for them." If the South Vietnamese did not "assume the majority of the burden in their own defense, they cannot be saved."[16] Having stated he would end the war and fueled speculations that he had a secret plan for doing so—speculation he never denied—Nixon found himself under significant pressure to be more specific about his thoughts on the war and pledge to end it. The demand for more information become so great that Nixon finally announced on March 26 that he would soon deliver a major speech on US-Soviet relations "as they deal with Vietnam."[17]

As Nixon prepared to say more about how he would handle the war if elected, President Johnson preempted his speech. Senator McCarthy had barely lost to President Johnson in the New Hampshire primary and was poised to win the primary in Wisconsin. Moreover, seeing Johnson as politically vulnerable, Robert Kennedy announced on March 16 that he was entering the race, claiming that the Tet Offensive had demonstrated the failure of US policy in Vietnam. On the same day that Nixon indicated he would give a major address on the war, Johnson was meeting with the so-called Wise Men to discuss the state of the war. The news was, for the president, discouraging on all fronts as the group of current and former senior foreign policymakers concluded that the war was a stalemate that could not be broken by further escalation or won in an acceptable time frame and at acceptable costs.

Faced with the disheartening reports on the status of the war and his falling political fortunes, Johnson decided to address the nation and chose the same day Nixon was planning to speak, March 31, for his address. That night, the president announced to the nation that, in an effort to advance negotiations and find an end to the war, he would cap American escalation and place limits on the American bombing in the North. In a surprise ending to his speech, Johnson shocked everyone by stating that he was withdrawing from the race for the presidency.

Nixon cancelled the talk he was to give, one that contained similar proposals to the steps the president set out, and quickly issued a statement that in light of Johnson's actions, he would impose a moratorium on statements regarding the war in Vietnam in order to assist the efforts toward peace. The candidate indicated throughout April that he would maintain his silence "as long as there is hope for successful negotiation," as President Johnson needed "a free hand to negotiate an honorable peace," and that he would not "do anything to undercut [the president] until he's had a chance to bring [peace] about." The next month, in an effort to continue to keep the war out of the campaign while simultaneously criticizing Kennedy's and McCarthy's positions, Nixon stated, "Let's not destroy the chances for peace with a mouthful of words from some irresponsible candidates for the President of the United States." If a candidate were to give the impression that he could give Hanoi a better deal, "it will destroy any chance for the negotiations to bring an honorable end to the war. The enemy will wait for the next man." Nixon continued by adding that, in his view, "no Presidential candidate—of either party—should say or do anything to destroy the fragile hope that has arisen" for peace to be negotiated in Paris.[18]

Nixon's position allowed him the greatest flexibility when it came to the issue of the war, enabling him to appear statesmanlike and more dovish than he was without losing the support of voters who wanted to pursue a military victory in Vietnam. Nixon would, however, occasionally speak on the war over the summer, especially to indicate the difference between his position and that of the Democratic candidates. He criticized as irresponsible Kennedy's and McCarthy's calls for peace through the creation of a coalition government in Saigon and held to the position that the war in Vietnam was necessary to American interests while reiterating that he would seek peace. What the candidate meant when he spoke about peace and how to obtain it were the key points. Ending the war, for Nixon, meant achieving victory in Vietnam—that is, securing the American goal of maintaining a noncommunist government in South Vietnam and upholding American credibility. In an interview published in the July issue of *Good Housekeeping*, Nixon asserted that seeing the fight through to the end was necessary for long-term peace. He declared, "We have to stop it with victory, or it will start all over again in a few years." People calling for an immediate end to the war "are thinking only in immediate terms. By doing so we may save the lives of boys in their twenties, but not of their younger brothers who will have to fight all over again." He understood, he said, the pain of the loss of American lives. Still, he asserted, "there is no alternative to the war going on" besides victory.[19]

On July 26, Nixon met with President Johnson to discuss the Vietnam War. He reiterated his position that he did not wish to do anything as a candidate to harm the negotiations in Paris, that "he did not know what more [the United States] could do" to get Hanoi to engage in serious talks, and that there were no more steps Johnson could take "to prove our good faith" to find peace. The president said he was right. He had authorized five or six bombing halts and made over thirty proposals, but North Vietnam never responded to any of them. Now, Johnson stated, he had stopped the bombing of Hanoi, Haiphong, and about 90 percent of the population and over three-fourths of the territory, and still there was no movement on talks.[20]

Nixon said that he was sure the president knew that he supported the American commitment in Vietnam and that they both understood that the United States was "there in order to try to have peace in the Pacific." If communist aggression was not halted in Vietnam, then the rest of the region would face war in the near future, and "the commitment [was]

very, very important there." He understood further that "there are terrible pressures regarding Vietnam." The public was now losing sight of
the necessity of the fighting and faith in the war, and whole groups
thought the United States "was losing the war, [that] we've already lost."
Thus, the right thing to do for the nation at this point "may be politically
wrong in this country." The reason was clear to Nixon. "You know the
country is running away from us. Frankly, the press, I don't say that in
any mean and bitter sense, but they have begun finally to get through."[21]

Johnson assured Nixon not only that he was correct but also that the
United States was in fact winning the war. The disconnect between public opinion and the necessity of the war in Vietnam, Johnson said, had led
him to his March 31 announcement that he would not seek reelection.
The president stated that one reason he chose not to run was that he
could not get the North Vietnamese "to the Conference table and I had no
chance for peace if I did not, that I could not clean up Vietnam during my
time, doubtful if I ever could but certainly I couldn't between now and
January as a candidate. Now the question was—was it more important
for me to be a candidate and try to take another four years to do these
things, or to drop the candidacy part and try to do them now." Nixon
told the president that the "one thing that I want to assure you of, which I
am sure you know, is we have come to the end of a line and we have got
to look back and nobody at this time wants to make any decision to
prolong this damn war a day longer." At the same time, the war had to be
ended in such a way that there was not "another one in four or five years.
I have always put it in terms of winning the peace—not winning over
North Vietnam. Winning the peace—so that is the thing I am particularly
interested in."[22]

After Secretary of State Dean Rusk joined the meeting, Nixon returned
to his concern with public opinion. "It's too bad we have an election at
this time and they say why not stop the bombing and so on and so forth."
That brought pressure to take actions to buy time. "I think as I said to the
President earlier that our problem here is American public opinion which
really thinks, well, let's go the extra mile and that is, how far can you go
without getting something in return." Yet the United States could not
give up all of its leverage without some movement by North Vietnam in
return. Nixon "wanted to know . . . whether there was any indication that
[Hanoi] would do something. He wanted to know if they were hurting so
much that they might be willing to do something." Secretary Rusk said
that it was impossible to know for sure what made communists back
down. "The fact that the war has been prosecuted against them so effectively brings them to the point that they now might consider trying to
find a way to de-escalate. Let me remind you of something—going back
twenty years. There were no objective reasons why the communists had
to stop the bringing in of guerrillas into Greece. There was no objective
reason why they had to lift the Berlin blockade when they did." The same

was true in Korea, where China could have brought more troops into the war. "In other words, there is a physical capability to continue something of this sort, but long before you get to that there is a possibility that for reasons of their own, which we do not fully understand, they decided that they had better bring it to an end in some fashion." Nixon agreed, stating that "you never know" when you will bring the communists to their breaking point. The implication was that pressure had to be maintained until that moment was reached to force movement by Hanoi in Paris and obtain an acceptable end to the war.[23]

At the same time, Nixon continued, it was vital to maintain American credibility. "Let's suppose that we chickened out basically. Call it any way you want it. It is going to be interpreted that way if we agree to a Coalition Government or any of the others. Let's suppose that happens. . . . The nations in that area are stronger today than they were three years ago because we have kept the cork in the bottle. But let's suppose it happened today. What's going to be the effect on Thailand and Malaysia and Japan, particularly Japan?" The key point was "that we are there for a reason, as I understand it, and I think this is the fundamental point." Nixon was concerned about "what has happened to American public opinion, within a matter of six months starting with the Tet Offensive." There was a weakening of will and perception that "the war is lost. Now if you put it that way, that is what we've got to be concerned about." Secretary Rusk said nobody in South Vietnam believed that the United States was losing. "They don't feel that way out there." Nixon made it clear that this was his understanding as well.[24]

In preparation for the Republican National Convention, Nixon sent a statement to the party regarding its platform on the war. He began with the his standard position that he did not want to say anything that would undercut the effectiveness of the American negotiators in Paris, then immediately switched to a series of criticisms and concerns with the Democrats and their handling of the fighting. All agreed that the war had to end, he stated, but "it must be ended honorably, consistent with America's limited aims and with the long-term requirements of peace in Asia." Nixon rejected the idea that there could be a quick end to the war in Vietnam, noting that to achieve this goal would "require patience." Moreover, to obtain an acceptable peace agreement, the war "must be waged more effectively" than was currently the case, and the United States needed to employ new approaches that went beyond just the military buildup to "a new strategy" that required "a fuller enlistment of our Vietnamese allies in their own defense," a reference back to his *Foreign Affairs* article and what would be termed the Vietnamization of the war.[25]

The presumptive Republican nominee returned to old criticisms of Johnson's handling of the war, claiming that the president had missed an opportunity to deal a decisive military blow at the start of the fighting, instead adopting a policy of gradual escalation that was too little, too late.

"The swift, overwhelming blow that would have been decisive two or three years ago is no longer possible today. Instead, we find that we have been locked into a massive, grinding war of attrition." The implication was that Nixon would change this. His administration, he wrote, would do what the present administration had failed to do and employ "dramatic escalation of our efforts in the economic, political, diplomatic and psychological fronts." This meant better training for Saigon's forces and the development of South Vietnam's capacity to wage war while also providing a clearer explanation of the importance of the war to the American public.[26]

Nixon was proposing de-escalating for political purposes while still pursuing a military victory. The measure of progress, he said, was not in body counts but in "the number of South Vietnamese won to the building and defense of their own country." Vietnam represented "a new kind of war," one that could "actually be waged more effectively with fewer men and at less cost." Thus, the reliance on American troops could be "phased out" as the South Vietnamese replaced them. "The fact is that our men have not been out-fought; the Administration has been out-thought," Nixon declared, and the nation needed new leadership that could "make a fresh beginning free from the legacy of those errors." The policy Nixon was proposing would not only "speed an end to the war in Vietnam, but also . . . lay the groundwork for the organization of a lasting and larger peace. Certainly one of the lessons from the agony of Vietnam is that we need a new diplomacy to prevent future Vietnams."[27]

Arriving in Miami for the convention, Nixon held a news conference in which he effectively presented himself as a man who had evolved from a hard-line anticommunist into a person who sought negotiations. He outlined an approach that would realign American foreign policy from containment through confrontation to containment via negotiation. Communism, he declared, was no longer a monolithic force, and the divisions could be exploited in what he termed a "new era of negotiations with the Soviet Union" and "eventually with the leaders of the next superpower, Communist China." The *New York Times* reported that his comments "tended to confirm the general impression that he had moved to a more dovish position on the war," as he now advocated negotiations and de-escalation by the United States.[28]

Yet the bulk of his comments stressed that he would continue to support Saigon and sought victory in Vietnam. A negotiated settlement had to be reached on "an honorable basis." To allow South Vietnam to fall to communism would mean that the United States would face another war in Asia in the near future. The war was "winnable," and Nixon was determined to see it through to a successful conclusion. He stated, "I certainly do not seek the Presidency for the purpose of presiding over the destruction of the credibility of the American power throughout the world."[29] This is the key to understanding what would become Nixon's policy once he assumed office. The rest of his comments were feints to position himself as a moderate and tactics to win the election.

In his acceptance speech on August 8, Nixon restated the themes from his news conference about entering an era of negotiations, and he repeated the refrain about his hope that the "current negotiations may bring an honorable end" to the war and his willingness to "say nothing during this campaign that might destroy that chance." Yet the record was clear, he insisted: despite the United States' might, "never has so much military and economic and diplomatic power been used so ineffectively"; it was time for new leadership in Washington. He pledged that "the first priority foreign policy objective of our next Administration will be to bring an honorable end to the war in Vietnam"; he would then work to ensure there were no more Vietnams in the future. In the process, he said, he would restore American power and negotiate from a position of strength, not weakness. "What I call for is not a new isolationism. It is a new internationalism in which America enlists its allies and its friends around the world in those struggles in which their interest is as great as ours."[30]

Nixon later turned to an important theme that would shape his policy in Vietnam once he entered the White House: stability and order. "America," Nixon declared, "is a great nation. It is time we started to act like a great nation around the world." It was an age of upheaval and revolution, but the answer to the problems that faced the nation and the world could be found in an earlier revolution—"a revolution that will never grow old, the world's greatest revolution, the American Revolution." The spirit of 1776 was dedicated to progress, but "our founders recognized that the first requisite of progress is order." This is what the United States stood for in the world and what it was fighting to establish in Vietnam, and its success or failure would define American greatness. "When the strongest nation in the world can be tied down for years," Nixon exclaimed, "by a war in Vietnam with no end in sight," it was "time for new leadership" in Washington. To help bring about that change, he called upon what he termed the "forgotten majority" of Americans for support, the "non-shouters, the non-demonstrators" who were the "real voice of America." He would, Nixon declared to his supporters, restore pride in the nation and respect for the United States abroad.[31]

That Nixon continued to prioritize a military solution to the war was evident in his second meeting with Lyndon Johnson in just over two weeks. Visiting the president right after the Republican National Convention, Nixon again told Johnson that he would not criticize the administration on Vietnam unless it "softened" its position on terms for getting negotiations started. In conjunction with the July conversation, in his meeting with Johnson on August 10, Nixon was trying to ensure that the president held firm against a bombing pause—an action Nixon told Johnson on July 26 that he would not advocate himself—or any further reduction of American military action that might get serious negotiation underway in Paris.[32]

After the Democratic National Convention in Chicago at the end of August, Nixon enjoyed a more than twenty-point lead in the race against Humphrey. Although the war was a crucial issue to the electorate, Nixon held to his position that he would not discuss specific ideas about how to end the war so as not to endanger the talks in Paris. This left it up to Humphrey to make the war a campaign issue if he was willing to break with Johnson's positions. On September 21, the Democrat took his first step, announcing that although only the president could currently seek peace, come January, "I will make peace." In early October, Humphrey was more specific, stating that a complete bombing halt was an acceptable risk to try to move negotiations forward.[33] In the wake of these statements, Humphrey's campaign gained momentum and support, making the race a virtual dead heat by the end of the month.

In response, Nixon took aim at Humphrey's new positions while also reasserting his commitment to peace in Vietnam. He claimed that Humphrey's positions were impairing negotiations by promising to reduce US forces and that the Democratic contender was prepared to give away the "only trump card" American negotiators had without receiving any guarantees. At the same time, Nixon claimed that he "strongly recommended" the Democrats' new emphasis on de-Americanizing the war as it represented the best way to lessen the American commitment while still achieving US goals in the war.[34]

If the military situation improved, more could be done in terms of negotiations in the future than could be accomplished at the time, Nixon argued. In avoiding any further specifics, he reminded reporters that Eisenhower "did not indicate exactly in 1952 how he would end the [Korean] war." The Vietnam War was winnable in the sense of achieving "an honorable end to the war" through a negotiated settlement, but that agreement would have to ensure the territorial and political integrity of South Vietnam. Nixon would not support the imposition of a coalition government on Saigon or a pullout of American forces "under any kind of subterfuge" as that would, he claimed, reward aggression, play into the hands of the communist "hard-liners," and invite Moscow and Beijing "to try aggression somewhere else."[35] A coalition government would therefore constitute a "thinly disguised surrender" and was "no solution at all." Any settlement of the conflict, Nixon maintained, had to deter future wars and preserve American credibility.[36]

As the race tightened, Nixon took to defending the war in Vietnam as a necessary sacrifice to contain communism and to provide time for the other noncommunist nations in Asia to build their strength behind the American shield; at the same time he acknowledged the public's opposition to the war. In an October 19 radio address titled "To Keep the Peace," Nixon declared that the nations in Asia "recognize the threat from Communist China," and "they want protection against it. The American commitment in Vietnam has bought time for this to take place." It would be irresponsible to waste that effort, "bought at such terrible cost," by walking away from Vietnam and America's obligations. Rather, it must be "used to insure that any future aggression is held in check without another unilateral American commitment on the pattern of Vietnam." Thus, the United States had to continue to work with the noncommunist nations in Asia to assist their efforts to resist communist attacks. Still, Vietnam had demonstrated the "limits of U.S. power" to achieve this goal without indigenous assistance. A new approach based on regional cooperation and development, assisted by the United States, would not only save American lives but be more effective and recognize that the American public was reluctant to become involved in another war in Asia.[37]

Toward the end of the campaign, as Humphrey continued to gain ground due to his position on bombing, negotiations, and peace in Vietnam, Nixon went to extraordinary lengths to prevent an October peace surprise. Fearful of a breakthrough in Paris, the Nixon camp turned to Anna Chennault, one of the most prominent Asian American women in America. Known for her hostility toward communism, she had excellent connections in the South Vietnamese government and was approached to act as an intermediary between Nixon's campaign and the Saigon government. She first met with Nixon, along with South Vietnam's ambassador to the United States, Bui Diem, in July, when the two urged upon Nixon the need for close relations with Saigon. The future president agreed but wanted the contact to be indirect, through Chennault. Thus, Nixon established a back channel with Saigon that kept him informed about the secret negotiations and allowed him to transmit messages to South Vietnam's president, Nguyen Van Thieu.[38]

In October, at the same time that Humphrey was breaking away from Johnson's position on the war, Henry Kissinger, who had recently been in Paris and met with American negotiators, told John Mitchell, Nixon's law partner and campaign manager, that there was movement in the talks and something big could develop prior to the election. Through Chennault, Thieu made it clear that he opposed the direction discussions were taking; he said he was only participating due to pressure from Washington and would much rather have peace talks after the election. When word began to circulate that Johnson would halt bombing to facilitate negotiations, Nixon feared the decision's impact on voters and began issuing warnings that the Democrats might launch an October surprise to salvage the election.

That fear was realized on October 31. Johnson startled the nation by announcing a bombing halt to get peace talks started in Paris. Nixon's public response was predictable. He stated that he hoped the decision would "bring some progress" to the peace talks and that he would say nothing that might "destroy the chance of peace."[39] Yet, behind the scenes, his campaign continued its efforts to have the Saigon government block any serious negotiations in Paris.

Just prior to Johnson's action, the administration learned of the communications between Saigon and the Nixon campaign. When the president spoke to Humphrey and Nixon about his impending announcement, he issued a veiled warning directed at the Republican candidate: "The fate of our country lies in your hands. . . . There would be serious trouble if anything anyone said were to interrupt or disrupt any progress we are trying to make to bring this war to a halt." Chennault, however, acting in concert with the campaign, continued to urge Thieu to resist any breakthrough in Paris on the promise that Saigon would be better served once Nixon became president. Saigon had to stand firm, Chennault and Bui Diem told Thieu. On November 2, the South Vietnamese president announced he would not attend the negotiations at that time. His boycott meant that no serious talks would begin until well after the American presidential election on November 5.[40]

When confronted by Johnson on November 3, two days before the election, about his involvement with Chennault's contacts with Saigon, an action the president had characterized as "treason" the day before in a discussion with Republican senator Everett Dirkson, Nixon lied, denying any awareness of Chennault's machinations or Thieu's actions. Johnson left it up to Humphrey to decide whether to expose Nixon's deeds. The Democratic candidate decided not to go public for fear damaging efforts to get Saigon to negotiate and worsening the already deep divisions at home.[41]

Thus, Nixon held off Humphrey's surge and narrowly defeated him, in part because the talks in Paris never materialized. The president-elect had broken his repeated pledge not to take any action to upset the chances for negotiations in Paris and peace in Vietnam. At the same time, he racked up an important debt to Thieu for assuring that there would be no breakthrough negotiations when Nixon took office. In the process, Nixon revealed the final aspects of his Vietnam policy: deception, duplicity, and covert action that ran directly counter to his public statements. Along with his discussions of Vietnamization, his hope to use the Soviet Union to pressure North Vietnam, his belief that the war was winnable, his prioritization of a military solution, and his indications that he had new means to achieve these goals, Nixon had set out the main parameters of the policy he would follow during his first two years in office. There was no secret plan for peace. Rather, Nixon would expand and escalate the war militarily in the search for what he called "peace with honor," that is, the preservation of the Thieu regime in Saigon and the maintenance of American credibility.

NOTES

1. Jules Witcover, "Nixon: The Reentry Problem," *New Republic*, June 17, 1967, 12.
2. Robert B. Semple Jr., "It's Time again for the Nixon Phenomenon," *New York Times Magazine*, January 21, 1968, 24.
3. Richard M. Nixon, "Asia after Viet Nam," *Foreign Affairs* 46 (October 1967): 111–25.
4. Nixon, "Asia after Viet Nam."
5. Nixon, "Asia after Viet Nam."
6. "Can the New Nixon Make It?" *Nation's Business* 56 (January 1968): 39.
7. David F. Schmitz, *The Tet Offensive: Politics, War, and Public Opinion* (Lanham, MD: Rowman & Littlefield, 2005).
8. Cronkite quoted in Schmitz, *The Tet Offensive*, 99; see also 111–12.
9. "There May Be Trouble Over Asia in November," *New York Times*, February 11, 1968, E2.
10. "No Quick and Easy Solution to War Discerned by Nixon," *New York Times*, February 12, 1968, 11.
11. "Nixon Sees Vietnam as 'Cork in Bottle,'" *New York Times*, February 13, 1968, 33.
12. "Nixon Developing a Vietnam Stand," *New York Times*, February 14, 1968, 29.
13. "Nixon Vows to End War With a 'New Leadership,'" *New York Times*, March 6, 1968, 11.
14. "Nixon Withholds His Peace Ideas," *New York Times*, March 11, 1968, 1.
15. "Nixon's Views in a Nutshell," *US News & World Report*, March 11, 1968, 44.
16. "Nixon Urges Rise in Allied Soldiers," *New York Times*, March 15, 1968, 26.
17. "Nixon to Give Plan on Soviet War Role," *New York Times*, March 27, 1968, 31.
18. "Nixon Vows Vietnam Silence to Aid Peace Move," *New York Times*, April 20, 1968, 17; "Nixon Sees Peril in War Discussion," *New York Times*, May 4, 1968, 11.
19. *New York Times*, May 4, 1968; "No Alternative, Nixon Says, U.S. Must Continue the War," *New York Times*, June 18, 1968, 37.
20. Department of State, *Foreign Relations of the United States, 1964–1968*, Vol. 6: *Vietnam, January–August 1968* (Washington, DC: Government Printing Office), Document 310 (hereafter *FRUS*, followed by years, volume, and document number).
21. *FRUS, 1964–1968*, Vol. 6: *Vietnam, January–August 1968*, Document 310.
22. *FRUS, 1964–1968*, Vol. 6: *Vietnam, January–August 1968*, Document 310.
23. *FRUS, 1964–1968*, Vol. 6: *Vietnam, January–August 1968*, Document 310.
24. *FRUS, 1964–1968*, Vol. 6: *Vietnam, January–August 1968*, Document 310.
25. "Nixon Asks Easing of U.S. War Role," *New York Times*, August 2, 1968, 1; "Text of Nixon Statement to G.O.P. Platform Panel on the War," *New York Times*, August 2, 1968, 16.
26. *New York Times*, August 2, 1968.
27. *New York Times*, August 2, 1968.
28. "Nixon Says He Has Eased Views on Communist Bloc," *New York Times*, August 7, 1968, 1.
29. *New York Times*, August 7, 1968.
30. Richard M. Nixon, "Acceptance Speech," *Vital Speeches of the Day*, September 1, 1968, 674–77.
31. Nixon, "Acceptance Speech."
32. *FRUS, 1964–1968*, Vol. 6: *Vietnam, January–August 1968*, Document 327. I want to thank Gabrielle Westcott for alerting me to the conversations between Johnson and Nixon on July 26 and August 10.
33. Johns, *Vietnam's Second Front*, 223.
34. "Nixon Says Humphrey Harms Efforts of U.S. in Paris Talks," *New York Times*, September 26, 1968, 1; "Nixon Would Push for a Bigger Role by Saigon in War," *New York Times*, October 1, 1968, 1; "Nixon Hopes Johnson Step Will Aid the Talks in Paris," *New York Times*, November 1, 1968, 1.

35. "Nixon Suggests He Could Achive Peace in Vietnam," *New York Times*, October 8, 1968, 1.

36. "Nixon Would Bar Forced Coalition in South Vietnam," *New York Times*, October 28, 1968, 1.

37. "New Asian Accord is Urged by Nixon," *New York Times*, October 20, 1968, 1.

38. Johns, *Vietnam's Second Front*, 221–31.

39. *New York Times*, November 1, 1968.

40. Johns, *Vietnam's Second Front*, 227.

41. Johns, *Vietnam's Second Front*, 229.

THREE

Nixon Takes Over

Richard Nixon became president during the twentieth-century United States' most turbulent and divisive moment. The postwar consensus had shattered. In 1968, political assassinations, urban rioting, violence at the Democratic National Convention, deepening economic problems, generational divisions, and growing antiwar sentiment were tearing the nation apart. The Vietnam War was at the center of it all, yet no end ,was in sight. After four years of escalation, more than 540,000 troops sent overseas, $30 billion a year spent, and more bombs dropped on Vietnam than during all of World War II, it was a stalemate. The bombing halt had failed to bring any progress in the negotiations in Paris, and the number of casualties rose to over thirty thousand Americans killed. The nation was tired of the war, with a majority deeming it an unwinnable mistake.

On the one hand, this political reality created the opportunity for the new administration, as Nixon would state many times, to do what was popular—to say the war had been a miscalculation by the Lyndon Johnson administration and announce an orderly, unilateral American withdrawal and an end to the US participation in the fighting. Nixon had argued during the campaign that he sought to end the war and implied that he had a plan to bring about peace. To accomplish that, he claimed, demanded an administration uncompromised by the past. Yet the new president had also made it clear on the campaign trail that he deemed the war necessary to stop communist aggression in Asia and that he would not take the route of simply pulling out because he believed how the Vietnam War ended was critical to American credibility. On the other hand, the political opposition to the war demonstrated to Nixon that any course other than the popular one—ending the war through de-escalation and withdrawal—would require great care; therefore, his options were limited as he sought to find a way to maintain the government in

Saigon and uphold American prestige as a great power. Thus, Nixon's initial steps concerning the Vietnam War were a complex set of decisions designed to allow him to pursue an expansion of the war and achieve victory while creating the appearance of seeking peace and de-escalation.

There was no plan to bring the war to a quick end. Nixon's preferred course was escalation and expansion to achieve victory. The president still sought an end to the war on American terms—resulting in an independent, noncommunist South Vietnam (SVN) and the upholding of American credibility—and achieving this was what he meant by peace with honor. Nixon believed that he could take actions that the Johnson administration had resisted and use American force more effectively to break the stalemate and force concessions from Hanoi. These steps, however, had to be taken carefully—and often covertly—in order to avoid political backlash at home. The president knew he had to buy time at home to carry out his plans for winning the war. Thus, the public presentation of his policies and the realities of his actions were contradictory. By discussing peace, initiating a limited American de-escalation of the war through the Nixon Doctrine, indicating a willingness to talk, and implementing modifications to the draft, the president sought to create the impression that he was taking steps toward peace. Moreover, he worked to marginalize the antiwar movement as an ineffective, violent minority that did not represent the views of the middle class, and he vowed not to allow demonstrations to determine his policy. At the same time, he sought to rally support for the war among what he termed the "silent majority." Secretly, he expanded the war to Cambodia through covert air attacks, drew up plans for a further escalation, and issued an ultimatum with a deadline for Hanoi to agree to American terms in Paris or face mass destruction.

The Vietnam War was, Nixon stated, "problem No. 1," and the administration's actions demonstrated this.[1] The key question was why—after four years of escalation, at a cost of more than thirty thousand dead and $30 billion a year, in the wake of the Tet Offensive, the Clifford Task Force, and the Wise Men's finding that the war could not be won in an acceptable time frame or with sustainable costs—Nixon still believed he could achieve victory and impose a settlement on Hanoi by escalating the war. Moreover, he did so despite the findings of National Security Study Memorandum (NSSM) 1, ordered on January 21, 1969, which concluded that despite the significant losses and damage the United States had inflicted on the enemy, the war remained a stalemate.

Both the president and his national security advisor, Henry Kissinger, believed that North Vietnam (NVN) had a breaking point. As Nixon noted at his first meeting with the National Security Council (NSC), he was prepared to rethink how the United States was fighting the war. He did not "want the enemy to assume that we are locked on the same old tracks as the previous Administration." He would change tactics as the situation dictated, Nixon stated, as he "was very much aware of the domestic issues." Still, "he would rather take the heat now and achieve a sound settlement subsequently."[2]

At the next NSC meeting four days later, Nixon expanded on these thoughts. Operating on the assumption that North Vietnam wanted to negotiate a mutual withdrawal and a political settlement at the same time and that Hanoi would both target US public opinion to erode America's willingness to stay the course and use negotiations to bring about the collapse of Nguyen Van Thieu's government, Nixon instructed the NSC to approach the question of Vietnam as a new issue. "Seek ways in which we can change the game. We must know what we want. The gain could take many turns. I visualize that it could take two years to settle this thing." The goal was a limited one of maintaining the noncommunist government in Saigon and, in so doing, preserving American credibility.[3]

Nixon believed that the "best course of action would be to hang on" in Saigon, bring new pressure to bear on Hanoi through military action, and enlist the support of the Soviet Union to break the deadlock. "On the other hand," the president acknowledged, "we do have the internal problem in the U.S. and it will be very difficult to continue without some change. . . . It also means we may have to take more risks in a settlement than we would prefer. While I am optimistic that it can be done, I am worried about our ability to sell it to the American people. In summary, maybe our best course would be to focus on mutual withdrawal." Secretary of State William Rogers added that one means of managing public opinion would be a troop withdrawal. "I think we can expect more from the American people, especially if we could at some point reduce our commitment by perhaps 50,000." Nixon responded that if the administration did this it could possibly "buy time and perhaps some support."[4]

Kissinger raised the question of how the United States could ensure that the enemy understood "that we are determined to settle this issue one way or the other." The Soviets clearly wanted to improve relations, and, Kissinger added, due to Nixon's known, strident anticommunism and stance on the war prior to the campaign, "the Soviets are nervous about you, Mr. President." Nixon responded that he would "need about six months of strong military action, combined with a good public stance which reflects our efforts to seek peace. I feel we must not lose our nerve on this one. We should buy time with negotiations and continue to punish the enemy." That would make clear US resolve and force real negotiations from the other side. A small reduction of American troops would help, added Chairman of the Joint Chiefs of Staff Earle Wheeler, in that it would suggest that the Saigon government was "progressing and their forces are growing." Nixon believed that "this might be the thing to do in four months or so, after the initial negotiations are underway." Nixon stated that he saw little chance of a political settlement at the time. Given this, he summarized his position for the NSC:

The south must know that we are with them. The north thinks they are going to win anyway. . . . The mix of actions should be something like this. We talk hard in private but with an obvious peaceful public stance, seeking to gain time, initially giving the South Vietnamese a chance to strengthen the regime and add to the pacification effort while punishing the Viet Cong (VC). Within three or four months bring home a few troops unilaterally as a separate and distinct action from the Paris negotiations, and as a ploy for more time domestically, while we continue to press at the negotiating table for a military settlement.[5]

Morton Halperin of the NSC staff was one of the officials who urged Kissinger to order NSSM 1. He was worried about the direction the new administration would take in the war and that doubts within the government would not reach the president. Halperin wanted to convince Nixon and Kissinger that the war was a quagmire and that the best option was for the United States to cut its losses and seek a quick end.[6] There were disagreements on many specific points and over data among agencies, but a consensus had formed on a number of the most significant issues. Based on current force levels and strategy, NSSM 1 found that while the position of Saigon had been strengthened in recent months, the Army of the Republic of Vietnam (ARVN) "[could not] now, or in the foreseeable future, stand up to both the VC and sizable North Vietnamese forces"; that the Saigon government remained weakest, and the VC and the National Liberation Front (NLF) strongest, in rural areas; and that it was "not clear whether the GVN [government of South Vietnam] and other non-communist groups would be able to survive a peaceful competition with the NLF for political power in South Vietnam."[7]

Moreover, despite the fact that the enemy had suffered high losses due to the Tet Offensive, "they have not changed their essential objectives and they have sufficient strength to pursue these objectives. We are not attriting enemy forces faster than they can recruit or infiltrate." Although "Soviet and Chinese supplies have enabled the enemy to carry on despite our operations," they had limited influence as Hanoi operated independently of Moscow and Beijing. This was in large part because the "enemy basically controls both sides' casualty rates," and they still had the capacity to "launch major offensives, though not with 1968 Tet effectiveness or impact." Most importantly, NSSM 1 concluded, "The enemy is in Paris for a variety of reasons, including a desire to pursue his objectives at lower costs. He is not there primarily out of weakness, but rather from a realization that a military victory is not attainable as long as U.S. forces remain in SVN, yet a victory in the political area is very possible."[8]

Nixon rejected the withdrawal option. Rather than being dissuaded, the president saw the document as proof of the weakness of the Johnson administration and the need to bring a dramatic change in American strategy. Nixon believed he could obtain a military victory and impose a settlement on Hanoi and the NLF through escalation. He therefore asked what the options were for escalation. There was no such option in NSSM 1 because Halperin, who wrote the summary memorandum, did not believe there was a military means to the victory the president sought.[9] Yet Nixon was determined not to become "the first American President to lose a war, and he was not prepared to give in to public pressures which would have that practical consequence."[10] The president was convinced that a military victory was possible and that winning the war was necessary to maintain American credibility, deter further wars of national liberation, and provide him with leverage over the Soviet Union and China.

Nixon faced a difficult problem in pursuing escalation. The American public wanted an end to the war and expected the administration to achieve that goal through negotiations in Paris and not greater military effort. Nixon therefore designed his policies to get around this obstacle. He believed that through a covert expansion of the war into Cambodia, escalation of the bombing through his "madman strategy," implementation of the Nixon Doctrine and the policy of Vietnamization, and successful manipulation of public opinion, he could gain the political time necessary to force concessions from Hanoi militarily and bring about an end to the war that achieved his goals. A small de-escalation of American troops would reduce the number of American casualties, create the impression that the president was starting to wind the war down, and retain American public support for the administration's policy.

The first steps were to present the president as doing all he could to achieve peace in Vietnam while portraying the enemy as intransigent. In his first press conference, Helen Thomas immediately asked Nixon what his peace plan for Vietnam was now that he was president. Nixon responded indirectly that the administration was off to a "good start" in Paris. The United States had set out its terms for an agreement based on "things which we believe the other side should agree to and can agree to: the restoration of the demilitarized zone [DMZ] as set forth in the Geneva Conference" as a clear international border; "mutual withdrawal . . . of forces by both sides; the exchange of prisoners." The direction of talks from that point "depends upon what the other side offers in turn." In response to another question at the end of the news conference, Nixon noted that the substantive issues were "whether we are going to have mutual withdrawal, whether we are going to have self-determination by the people of South Vietnam without outside interference." This, he stated "is going to take time," but "it will have my personal attention."[11]

At a March 4 news conference, Nixon was asked what impact the recent communist offensive in Vietnam would have on the peace talks. The president stated that it was too early to say as they needed to determine the purpose of the offensive—whether it was an effort to break the will of Saigon, "directed against public opinion in the United States to put more pressure on the administration to move more in the direction of North Vietnam's position at the Paris peace talks," or an effort at a military victory over Saigon—and then the appropriate response. The president did declare that the offensive had failed no matter what its objective. Moreover, he emphasized that although the United States had not "moved in a precipitate fashion," the fact that he had "shown patience and forbearance should not be considered a sign of weakness." The president also signaled that there was a limit to his patience and that he would not "tolerate attacks which result in heavier casualties to our men at a time that we are honestly trying to seek peace" in Paris.[12] Ten days later, Nixon stated that if Hanoi wanted to de-escalate the fighting, he would respond in kind, as the United States was "trying to do everything that we can in the conduct of our war in Vietnam to see that we can go forward toward peace in Paris."[13]

Finally, in April, he told the nation at another news conference that since he had taken office, "the chances for peace in Southeast Asia have significantly improved." There were a couple of reasons for this, the president opined. The first was the growing effectiveness of the South Vietnamese forces. They were now "far better able to handle themselves militarily, and that program is going forward on a much more intensive basis than it was when this administration came into office." Second, there was greater political stability in South Vietnam to go along with an improved military situation. Given this, the president was "feeling somewhat optimistic, although we still have some hard ground to plow." He rejected any idea of a unilateral withdrawal of American forces and would only start bringing troops home when the security status of South Vietnam allowed it. "Looking to the future, I would have to say that I think there are good prospects that American forces can be reduced," but there needed to be more progress in the training of the ARVN, a drop in the level of fighting, and movement in negotiations in Paris on the part of the enemy.[14]

While publicly presenting himself as seeking peace through de-escalation and negotiations, Nixon was covertly escalating the war in an effort to force concessions from Hanoi. He set out to prove to North Vietnam that he would stop at nothing, including bombing cities and irrigation dikes and using nuclear weapons, to achieve "peace with honor." As he told his chief of staff, H. R. "Bob" Haldeman, part of his plan for victory rested on what he called the "madman theory." He wanted "the North Vietnamese to believe I've reached the point where I might do *anything* to stop the war. We'll just slip the word to them that 'for God's sake, you know Nixon is obsessed about Communists. We can't restrain him when he's angry—and he has his hand on the nuclear button,' and Ho Chi Minh himself will be in Paris in two days begging for peace."[15] The idea came from how Dwight Eisenhower had ended the Korean War: he had informed China that he was willing to use nuclear weapons if the armistice talks did not make progress. There was a difference, however, between 1953 and 1969, and Nixon was well aware of that fact. When Eisenhower issued his threat, the United States had the capacity strike China, whereas the Soviet Union could not deliver a nuclear attack on the United States. Now, Moscow could hit anywhere in North America, and Soviet leaders would have to consider their own credibility with their allies and the need to retaliate should the United States escalate the war to this level. It would therefore be necessary to have the Kremlin in agreement about the necessity of an end to the Vietnam War.

To make the threat credible, as well as to try to break the stalemate in the fighting in the South, Nixon initiated the "secret" bombing of Cambodia. The administration believed that the intensified fighting in Vietnam that began right after Nixon took office indicated that Hanoi "seemed to want to test the Administration's resolve to maintain its commitment to the South Vietnamese." Under these circumstances, the United States needed "to demonstrate U.S. resolve and put North Vietnam on notice that military action and major attacks in population centers . . . could not be pursued with impunity."[16] Planning for the use of American B-52s against North Vietnamese and NLF sanctuaries in Cambodia began in early February with a recommendation from General Creighton W. Abrams, commander of the US Military Assistance Command, Vietnam (MACV), to launch raids against the suspected location of the headquarters of North Vietnam's Central Office for South Vietnam (COSVN) in the so-called Fishhook area on the Cambodian border with South Vietnam. Abrams was instructed to establish a back-channel communication on this issue in order to bypass the embassy and State Department. At a February 18 meeting, Kissinger, Secretary of Defense Melvin Laird, Deputy Secretary of Defense David Packard, General Wheeler, and senior military advisor to Kissinger Alexander Haig recommended to President Nixon that Abrams be instructed to prepare for a covert bombing of select areas in Cambodia by commencing bombing right up to the South Vietnam–Cambodian border. Abrams was to continue planning for an operation in Cambodia while waiting for military action in the Fishhook area to serve as a pretext for heavy bombing. This would allow American officials to claim, should the operation be exposed, that the bombing was an accident. If intense fighting did not develop, the plan would be reconsidered in March.[17]

The president approved the operation on February 22. Laird and Wheeler assured him a few days later that they believed the "proposed strikes [could] be executed effectively," but they worried about leaks and advised the president to wait on launching the bombing near the border until there were more intensive attacks by the enemy against American forces. Given the State Department's awareness of Abrams's original recommendation, they feared that "by virtue of the presumed widespread knowledge of this possible mission, it would be difficult to claim, and make credible, an operational error. Equally difficult, in view of the moderate scale thus far and the currently diminishing level of enemy activity, would be the forthright approach of admitting an attack against an alleged enemy headquarters in a neutral nation."[18]

In early March, Nixon was provided with an opportunity to initiate the bombing operation in response to a series of rocket attacks on Saigon and other South Vietnamese cities. The president ordered the bombing of Cambodia, code-named Breakfast, on March 15, and the first B-52 runs began on March 18. The Breakfast campaign allowed for strikes against North Vietnamese Army (NVA) base areas up to ten miles into Cambodia. According to Kissinger's notes from a telephone conversation, the president told him that he wanted "everything that will fly . . . to get over to North Vietnam. . . . He will let them know who is boss around here."[19] Kissinger reviewed for the president the strategy and justifications for the attack the next day. "Failure to take action," he wrote Nixon, "in response to Saigon/Hue shellings—especially after repeated Presidential warnings—would appear to Hanoi as a demonstration of weakness" and "encourage Hanoi to use shellings and other military pressures in an effort to force major concessions at the Paris negotiations." Moreover, the national security advisor valued the bombing for its potential to portray the president as irrational and volatile, in line with Nixon's madman theory. "Retaliatory action," Kissinger wrote, "if combined with a proposal for private talks, will serve as a signal to the Soviets of the Administration's determination to end the war. It would be a signal that things may get out of hand."[20]

To provide cover for the bombings, North Vietnamese "military concentrations in the DMZ will be attacked 12 hours prior to Breakfast Plan. This attack, in response to currently well publicized NVN buildup in the DMZ, will be acknowledged as the 'appropriate response' to the shelling of Saigon and Hue. This would have the following advantages: (a) it would indicate a response; (b) it would divert public attention; (c) it would therefore enable Cambodia to play down the Breakfast Plan and; (d) it would still show restraint." Breakfast would be described "as a routine military operation within the framework of our current military actions in Cambodian territory and not publicly or in any messages identified as a retaliatory action against the shelling of Saigon and Hue. Hanoi is likely to recognize the action as our response, without a public statement."[21]

Nixon took the action because, he believed, "the state of play in Paris is completely sterile. I am convinced that the only way to move the negotiations off dead center is to do something on the military front. That is something they will understand." Moreover, the bombing had benefits in Saigon as it would signal clearly to Thieu that "we really mean business," making it much easier to get South Vietnam to cooperate on talks. Right after the first of the covert bombings of the sanctuaries, Kissinger believed that "if they [the North Vietnamese] retaliate without any diplomatic screaming, we are in the driver's seat. Psychologically the impact must have been something." General Wheeler reported that North Vietnamese MiGs were recalled to China, "and they are in a high state of alarm." Kissinger responded that this action threw all of Hanoi's plans off course as it caught them by complete surprise.[22] Secrecy was so paramount that "the military developed special double accounting procedures" in order to keep track of ammunition expenditures and official operations as well as the actual covert sorties over Cambodia.[23]

The press guidance regarding Operation Breakfast was explicit on the cover story to be used if any questions arose regarding Cambodia. If asked "whether or not U.S. B-52s have struck in Cambodia, U.S. spokesmen will confirm that B-52s did strike on routine missions adjacent to the Cambodian border" but add no further details. As anticipated, neither Hanoi nor Phnom Penh protested the strikes because the former did not want to acknowledge its use of Cambodia for camps and logistical operations, and the latter would accept the strikes as long as they were contained to areas of NVA operations. When the *New York Times* finally ran a story on the bombings, the Pentagon acknowledged that it was conducting operations in South Vietnam near the Cambodian border with B-52s but stated that reports of strikes inside Cambodia were "speculative."[24]

The secrecy was necessary to prevent political controversy at home, but it was also seen as part of the effectiveness of the operation. Cambodian leader Prince Norodom Sihanouk had indicated he was growing worried about the sizeable North Vietnamese military presence in his nation; furthermore, Washington had begun a dialogue with Phnom Penh that "was proceeding favorably" and that the administration did not want to disrupt. "Against this background, had we officially made public our operation, Sihanouk would be forced to protest." The secrecy allowed Sihanouk to ignore the bombing and raised doubts in Hanoi about the Cambodian leader's intentions. This advantage was increased in July when Sihanouk renewed diplomatic relations with the United States, which had been broken off in 1965.[25]

The same was true with Moscow. "A covert 'accidental' strike against COSVN Headquarters," Kissinger told Nixon, "had the advantage of showing the Soviets that we are serious about the war, without forcing them to take a public stance against our attacks." This would add to the pressure on Hanoi and provide an advantage to the United States in negotiations. "A secret attack which would not become public would clearly signal our resolve to the North Vietnamese without putting them in a public position of seemingly negotiating under pressure—a position which in all likelihood would have forestalled any movement toward serious talks," explained Kissinger.[26]

In an effort to exploit what the administration now saw as an advantage, planning began for massive military strikes designed to deliver the type of decisive blow envisioned by the madman theory and bring an end to the war if Hanoi did not heed Nixon's March warning and demonstration of his willingness to escalate the conflict. Every option was on the table, including an invasion of North Vietnam, the bombing of its cities and dikes, the mining of Haiphong Harbor, and the use of nuclear weapons. In the development of what came to be called Operation Duck Hook, Hanoi was warned that it had to change its negotiating position or prepare for "measures of great consequence and force."[27]

In addition, the "secret" bombing of Cambodia was expanded into Operation Menu (Breakfast, Lunch, Dinner) as the scope and duration of the campaign grew well beyond the initial parameters of the Breakfast plan. By the end of August, the strikes averaged eighty-six sorties per week against six base camps, and the Menu campaign would continue until May 26, 1970.[28] Kissinger favored the extension of the bombing to other parts of Cambodia "because it represents a forceful U.S. action" and because of the "message it conveys to the Soviets" regarding American resolve in Vietnam.[29] Secretary of Defense Laird agreed that continuing to escalate the fighting beyond what the previous administration had done would send the right message. He believed that the "follow-on strikes . . . could intensify any alarm the enemy might feel concerning the possibility of continuing strikes in what have been heretofore sanctuary areas."[30] Haldeman noted that the operations were designed to back up Kissinger's negotiations by demonstrating America's resolve to Moscow in order to enlist Soviet support in pressuring Hanoi.[31] The secret bombings of Cambodia appeared to Kissinger and Nixon to have the desired impact. With the exception of a few stories in the *New York Times*, which the administration successfully deflected, the bombings remained secret, and there was no political backlash.

More significantly, the willingness to bomb Cambodia demonstrated the administration's ability to take unexpected actions. The purpose of Operation Lunch was to "reinforce the message to Hanoi and Moscow that the U.S. will not always react within established ground rules and is willing to take certain risks." There was some concern that these operations could be "exposed—either by a U.S. press leak or Cambodian/Hanoi protest" and "lead to domestic criticisms of escalating the war," but this was deemed an acceptable risk due to the perceived value of warning the enemy that Nixon was willing to use unconventional and unpredictable measures to gain the upper hand in the war.[32] By the end of April, Kissinger reported to Nixon that all sources indicated that the bombing was having "both military and psychological impact" on the enemy and that Hanoi now knew that its "Cambodian logistical base and troop sanctuaries no longer enjoy[ed] immunity."[33] Operation Menu should continue, General Wheeler advised, because the strikes continued to have the value of hitting "base areas posing the highest military threat to US and Allied forces" and because of "their additional value in providing a signal to the North Vietnamese and the Soviets of US resolve."[34]

Along with the Menu bombings and the threat of further escalation, Nixon pursued his madman strategy through another avenue, the Kremlin. He believed pressure could be brought to bear on Hanoi through Moscow. This effort to get the Soviet Union to use its influence to force concessions by North Vietnam in the negotiations was a key piece of Nixon's war policy. The president believed that the Soviet Union wanted to ease tensions and improve relations with the West, particularly in the areas of arms control and trade. In addition to serving as a threat to Hanoi, the madman strategy was designed to make the Kremlin worry about the direction in which Nixon would take the Cold War and anxious to find ways to work with Washington to avoid direct conflict. This, along with growing Soviet-Chinese tensions, seemed to provide, Nixon and Kissinger believed, an opening that the administration could exploit. The Soviets had helped bring about the peace talks, and the president was sure that Moscow had enough leverage to make Hanoi soften its negotiating position.

In early April, the Soviet ambassador to the United States, Anatoly Dobrynin, came to see Kissinger on the pretext of discussing European matters, but the significant conversation was about Vietnam. The ambassador asked for Kissinger's assessment of the war and developments since coming to office. The national security advisor confidently replied that he and Nixon "knew what we were doing and would not be deflected by public protest." Dobrynin wanted to know, given this, if the United States had "any intention of expanding the war." Kissinger merely noted that "the President was determined to end the war one way or the other," that the administration meant what it said when Nixon warned Hanoi not to escalate, and that he "hoped Hanoi kept Moscow fully informed of everything that was going on."[35]

The conversation turned to the negotiations, and Kissinger told Nixon that at this point he "decided to play fairly tough" with Dobrynin, stating that Washington would want to discuss military issues first. The ambassador asked if there was any chance of replacing Thieu, to which Kissinger said no. The national security advisor returned to the question of American escalation. Kissinger stated, "It would be too bad if we were driven in this direction because it was hard to think of a place where a confrontation between the Soviet Union and the United States made less sense." He claimed that American and Soviet interests in Vietnam "were quite compatible." The ambassador replied, "Our interests in Vietnam are practically identical. We might want a slightly more neutral South Vietnam than you, but it is not an issue of consequence."[36]

In a telephone conversation two days later, Nixon told Kissinger that, given Hanoi's statements that the American military policy in Vietnam was failing, he believed that MACV "ought to go ahead and crack them pretty hard" with further bombings in Cambodia. Kissinger agreed. Referring to his conversation with Dobrynin, he claimed that "the Soviets

[were] getting edgy" and looking for a way to interject themselves into the negotiations, which might allow them to act. Given this, Nixon said it was time "we hit them again." "Say we crack them next week," Kissinger stated. The "week after, we approach Dobrynin" and let him know that Hanoi's strategy of waiting for the United States to weaken would not work. Nixon thought this was a good approach. "The necessity for the North Vietnamese to know that there's still a lot of snap left in the old boys is very important," the president stated. "And I don't know any other way to do it." A military strike was necessary, Kissinger concurred, but the enemy also needed a forum to respond. Thus, they would have to turn to the talks in Paris.[37]

On April 14, Kissinger met again with Dobrynin to make the American threat clear. The president, he stated, was tired of Hanoi's stalling in Paris. He had therefore "decided to make one more direct approach on the highest level before drawing the conclusion that the war could only be ended by unilateral means." The Soviets had to understand that Nixon was determined "not [to] be the first American President to lose a war, and he is not prepared to give in to public pressures which would have that practical consequence." Moreover, "the President is convinced that it is in no one's interest to have an outcome that would encourage Mainland China's aggressive drive." If a final effort at negotiations failed, then other measures would be taken, and "these measures could not help but involve wider risks. U.S.-Soviet relations are therefore at a crossroad."[38]

Reading from his talking points, Kissinger told Dobrynin that Nixon "views this point in history with the utmost gravity, especially since he is eager to move into an era of conciliation with the Soviet Union on a broad front. He is willing to begin talks on strategic arms limitations. He has agreed not to threaten the status quo in Europe. He is willing to consider meetings at the highest levels." All of this was jeopardized by the continuation of the war.

> The President believes that an acceptable settlement to the Vietnamese conflict is the key to everything. Therefore, concurrently, the President proposes to designate a high-level representative to meet with a North Vietnamese negotiator at any location, including Moscow, designated by the Soviet Union to seek agreement with a designated North Vietnamese negotiator on a military as well as a political settlement. The President visualizes that this negotiation would be conducted distinct from the existing Paris framework in order to avoid the sluggish and heretofore cumbersome mechanisms that have evolved in Paris.

The United States, Kissinger stated, would give this peace effort just six weeks to succeed.[39]

Dobrynin inquired whether this meant that unless the war in Vietnam was ended, there would be no strategic arms talks or discussions on other important issues. Kissinger stated that Washington was willing to continue to talk but "would take measures which might create a complicated situation." Asked if these measures might place Soviet ships in danger, Kissinger replied that "many measures were under intensive study. In dealing with the President, it was well to remember that he always did more than he threatened and that he never threatened idly." The Soviet ambassador emphasized that Moscow was in a difficult position. No matter what happened in Vietnam, the Kremlin wished to continue talking with the United States. Yet Washington had to "understand the limitations of Soviet influence in Hanoi." While Moscow "might recommend certain steps, it would never threaten to cut off supplies." In addition, "Communist China was constantly accusing the Soviet Union of betraying Hanoi. The Soviet Union could not afford to appear at a Communist meeting and find itself accused of having undermined a fellow Socialist country. On the other hand, the Soviet Union had no strategic interest in Southeast Asia. The chief reasons for its support of North Vietnam have been the appeals of a fellow Socialist country." It was China's intention, Dobrynin stated, to provoke a conflict between the United States and the Soviet Union, and an escalation of the fighting in Vietnam would only serve China's interests. Kissinger stated that he and the president agreed. "It was, therefore, incumbent on the Soviet Union to help us remove this danger," Kissinger concluded. "We felt that in this period, the great nuclear powers still have the possibility of making peace." [40]

For his covert actions to be effective and to secure victory, the president had to continue to buy time politically by creating the appearance that his policy was one of peace and disengagement. With the madman policy enacted, Nixon turned his attention back to managing public opinion. Nixon knew, as he told the NSC at the end of March, that in terms of public opinion, "the reality is that we are working against a time clock." He wanted "to move in a deliberate way, not to show panic. We cannot be stampeded by the likes of [Senator William] Fulbright." The president estimated that he had six to eight months for his madman policy to work and expected he would have "to play a strong public game" to carry this off while gaining ground in South Vietnam. [41] When Nixon took office, he had two advantages over the opponents of the war. First, there was the traditional honeymoon period of allowing a new administration time to set its course and implement its policies. Second, and more significantly, the antiwar movement was in disarray in the wake of the debacle at the Democratic National Convention in August 1968 and the arrest and prosecution of a group of radical antiwar leaders known as the Chicago 8.

Nixon sought to keep his opponents on the defensive and off balance through his public diplomacy for peace. In March 1969, he supported the withdrawal of federal grants for students found guilty of crimes "in connection with campus disorders" during protests, and in April he declared to the US Chamber of Commerce that "there can be no compromise with lawlessness and no surrender to force if free education is to survive in the U.S." Furthermore, "it is time for faculties, boards of trustees, and school administrators to have the backbone to stand up against this kind of situation." Other administration officials labeled student protestors as "new barbarians" who were "ideologically criminal."[42]

On May 14, the president gave his first speech to the nation on the Vietnam War. He began by noting that some believed his first act in office should have been to remove all American troops from Vietnam. "This would have been the easy thing to do," Nixon stated. "It might have been the popular thing to do." But it would have "betrayed" his responsibilities to the nation as president. He declared that he wanted "to end this war" but that he must do so in a responsible manner so that Americans would not "have to fight in the future in another Vietnam someplace else in the world." Thus, he said, he had taken many actions in the past four months in the quest for peace. His administration had undertaken an extensive review of all American policies, blunted an enemy offensive in late February and March, established a strong, collaborative relationship with Saigon, and accelerated the training of South Vietnamese forces.[43]

Nixon emphasized that the United States was in Vietnam to maintain the independence of South Vietnam and to preserve American credibility. To abandon the war at this point would lead to the fall of Saigon, "risk a massacre that would shock and dismay everyone in the world who values human life," and "threaten our long-term hopes for peace in the world. A great nation cannot renege on its pledges. A great nation must be worthy of trust." If the United States were to leave Vietnam now, "the cause of peace might not survive the damage that would be done to other nations' confidence in our reliability." It would strengthen the forces of aggression in the communist world and increase the danger of a larger war in the future. "If we are to move successfully from an era of confrontation to an era of negotiation, then we have to demonstrate—at the point at which confrontation is being tested—that confrontation with the United States is costly and unrewarding."[44]

In pursuing the "essential objective in Vietnam," to allow for true self-determination in Saigon "without outside interference," Americans had to understand that peace "cannot be achieved overnight." Still, Nixon declared, a settlement could be reached on "very simple" basic terms: "mutual withdrawal of non–South Vietnamese forces from South Vietnam and free choice for the people of South Vietnam." He then set out a list of specific measures to bring an end to the war: a twelve-month staged withdrawal of outside forces, with the remaining forces moving into designated areas and prohibited from combat operations; final mutual withdrawal under international supervision; supervised elections in South Vietnam; exchange of prisoners; and an agreement to observe the 1954 Geneva Accords.[45]

Nixon portrayed his peace program as "generous in its terms" and open to a consideration of other options. Nonetheless, he warned that "no greater mistake could be made than to confuse flexibility with lack of resolution" and that a needless dragging out of the talks and fighting or an escalation of the war would "affect other decisions." The president stated that he believed reports that "indicate that the enemy has given up hope for a military victory in South Vietnam, but is counting on a collapse of American will in the United States. There could be no greater error in judgment." Nixon continued, "Let me be quite blunt. Our fighting men are not going to be worn down; our mediators are not going to be talked down; and our allies are not going to be let down." He concluded by stating that all his past and current policies were consistent with his campaign pledge "to end this war in a way that would increase our chances to win true and lasting peace in Vietnam, in the Pacific, and in the world. I am determined to keep that pledge."[46]

On June 4, while speaking at the commencement exercises at the Air Force Academy, Nixon took on the critics of the war while setting out his fundamental assumptions concerning the US role in the world. He termed those who sought a unilateral American withdrawal from Vietnam "new isolationists" who, believing that "the United States is as much responsible for the tensions in the world as the adversaries we face," called for a retrenchment of American commitments and reduction of the nation's military strength. Nixon exclaimed that such actions "would be disastrous" and would only bring "the kind of peace that suffocated freedom in Czechoslovakia." Rather, "I say that America has a vital national interest in world stability, and no other nation can uphold that interest for us. We stand at a crossroad in our history. We shall reaffirm our destiny for greatness or we shall choose instead to withdraw into ourselves." Only "a resurgence of American idealism can bring about . . . a world order of peace and justice." Having cast the United States as the indispensable nation, he stated that America would "continue to be a source of world leadership, a source of freedom's strength, in creating a just world order that will bring an end to war."[47]

Four days later, Nixon met with President Thieu on Midway Island to discuss the war and unveil another part of his strategy to buy time for his effort at victory in Vietnam. Both Thieu and General Abrams informed him "that the progress of the training program and the equipping program for South Vietnamese forces had been so successful . . . he could now recommend that the United States begin to replace U.S. combat forces with Vietnamese forces." As a result, Nixon announced that he had ordered the immediate withdrawal of approximately twenty-five thousand troops to be completed by the end of August. Furthermore, he stated that he would continually review the criteria he established for the deescalation of American forces, the training of ARVN forces, progress in the peace talks, and the level of the enemy threat and make further withdrawals as warranted. He emphasized that "no actions will be taken which threaten the safety of our troops and the troops of our allies," and no step would be taken that "endangers the attainment of our objective, the right of self-determination for the people of South Vietnam."[48] As the president told Thieu in private, his goal was to end the war prior to the 1970 congressional elections, as he realized that the "U.S. domestic situation is a weapon in the war."[49] Nixon believed the announcement would "break the stride of those elements . . . pressing for large and immediate withdrawal of U.S. forces" and that the confidence shown in Saigon would bolster Thieu's standing in Saigon and Washington.[50]

The policy was termed "Vietnamization." Nixon sought to turn more of the fighting over to South Vietnamese forces while withdrawing US troops. In May, NSSM 19 concluded that "an adequate GVN internal security capability is essential for an effective political struggle with the VC," and it was "particularly urgent at this time because of the need for the GVN to improve significantly their capabilities before a negotiated settlement in SVN." The stronger Saigon became, it was believed, the more willing Hanoi would be to reach a political settlement.[51] Secretary of Defense Laird endorsed the plan to begin a phased withdrawal of American troops with no set timetable. This would strengthen Saigon, force North Vietnam to reevaluate its strategy in consideration of that change, and encourage moderates at home to continue to support the administration's policy.[52]

Vietnamization was also part of Nixon's broader policy to reduce the costs of the Cold War. The United States would continue to supply money, arms, advice, intelligence, and, most importantly, airpower, but it would reduce its role in the daily fighting of the war. Nixon hoped that this approach would allow him to continue the war without facing domestic opposition from the antiwar movement or charges of abandoning Vietnam to the communists. Upon his return to the United States, the president stated that his policies had brought the war to "the point where we can begin to bring Americans home from Vietnam" and had "opened wide the door to peace." He emphasized, in response to former secretary of defense Clark Clifford's suggestion that America should have all of its troops out of Vietnam by the end of 1970, that his administration was "on the right road in Vietnam," having started the withdrawal of American forces, and he said he hoped "we could beat Mr. Clifford's timetable."[53]

On July 25, 1969, during a news conference on Guam, the president first set out what he would later call the Nixon Doctrine. Expanding on the idea of Vietnamization, the Nixon Doctrine reaffirmed the US commitment to Asia and the policy of containment but stated that the goal of American policy was to avoid direct American intervention and significant troop commitments abroad. The president believed that Asia "poses . . . over the long haul, looking down to the end of the century, the greatest threat to the peace of the world, and, for that reason, the United

States should continue to play a significant role." But this did not mean that America would find itself in future Vietnam-type wars. Rather, "we should develop a policy that would avoid other Vietnams." In helping nations defend themselves from communism, the United States should provide support and assistance to equip other countries to fight, but it should not fight for them. Washington would "keep the treaty commitments that we have," but concerning how to defend nations, "we must avoid the kind of policy that will make countries in Asia so dependent upon us that we are dragged into conflicts such as the one we have in Vietnam." Having reaffirmed US treaty commitments with Asian allies, Nixon stated, "as far as problems of internal security are concerned, as far as the problem of military defense, except for the threat of a major power involving nuclear weapons . . . the United States is going to encourage and has a right to expect that this problem will be increasingly handled by, and the responsibility for it taken by, the Asian nations themselves." This was to be the principle of American "policy generally throughout the world." [54]

As Nixon would note in a conversation with Kissinger the following January in preparing his State of the Union address, the Nixon Doctrine represented not a withdrawal from the world but rather the best means to keep the United States in Asia and to allow Washington to continue to defend its allies and prevent further aggression. "The Nixon Doctrine is not a retreat from our world responsibilities. It is a method—a new way. . . . You might give it a historical slant. As we enter the '70s more than 25 years have passed since WWII—we made a new policy to deal with the new situation. For 25 years the US had to assume the major responsibility. We are for negotiation rather than for confrontation." [55]

In his memoirs, the president stated that the Nixon Doctrine was often misinterpreted as signaling a new isolationism in which the United States reduced its commitments to the world. In his view, "the Nixon Doctrine was not a formula for getting America out of Asia, but one that provided the only sound basis for America's staying in and continuing to play a responsible role in helping non-communist nations and neutrals as well as our Asian allies to defend their independence." [56] He did not believe the American public would support another Vietnam-type war. The Nixon Doctrine, therefore, was an attempt to continue American intervention in the Third World without costing American lives.

Upon arriving in Saigon on July 30, Nixon summarized his policy by stating that during his first six months in office he had "gone the extra mile in behalf of peace." His administration had not resumed the bombing of North Vietnam, had begun to withdraw troops, and had made a peace offer "as generous as any ever made in the history of warfare." The door was now open, and it was time for America's adversaries to respond. Setting up the rationale for a future escalation, the president declared that if there was no movement by Hanoi, "the other side must assume the responsibility" for the continuation of the war.[57] In their private discussions with Thieu, Nixon and Kissinger elaborated on how the Nixon Doctrine fit into the administration's overall Vietnam strategy and madman approach. Kissinger told the South Vietnamese leader that the president's position on negotiations "had put the doves in the U.S. on the defensive." This gave them time to carry out their policy while also allowing for a strong military response if the other side launched an offensive. Nixon then told Thieu that he was planning "to issue a warning in the near future to Hanoi about the course they were following." He explained that he had in mind that which had allowed him to claim back in June that Clark Clifford's "formula was not optimistic enough if we issue a warning to the enemy and then have to act on it."[58]

As the president delivered his comments, the administration was preparing to deliver the terms of the president's threat in secret to the North Vietnamese. Operation Duck Hook was designed to expand the concept of the madman theory from Cambodia to North Vietnam. It called for decisive military blows against the cities and dikes of North Vietnam, a possible land invasion of the North across the DMZ, the mining of Haiphong Harbor, and the possible use of nuclear weapons. Meeting in Paris on August 4 with Xuan Thuy, head of the Democratic Republic of Vietnam's delegation to the Paris peace talks on Vietnam, and Mai Van Bo, the Democratic Republic of Vietnam's delegate general in France, Kissinger began by stating that the United States had a great deal of "respect for the courage and dignity of the Vietnamese people" and that he and President Nixon "sincerely wanted peace and were approaching it with an attitude of good will, but he was also there to tell them how the situation appeared to [Washington]." In the past year, the United States had made significant moves toward peace, including ending the bombing of the North, unilateral withdrawal of twenty-five thousand troops, a plan for peace based on self-determination in the South, and a willingness to discuss the other side's proposals. Specifically, the United States was "willing to withdraw all of its forces without exception from Vietnam as part of a program for the removal of all outside forces from Vietnam" and to "accept any outcome of a free political process." It was important to note that Washington realized that "neither side can be expected to give up at the conference table what had not been conceded on the battlefield" and that a "fair political process must register the existing relationship of political forces." Finally, the administration was prepared to discuss all of the North's and the NLF's proposals, together with Nixon's plan, and to "show our good will in the period between now and November 1, we will withdraw somewhat larger forces than we have already withdrawn and reduce our B-52 and tactical air operations by 10%."[59]

At the same time, November 1, 1969, would mark the one-year anniversary of the bombing halt, and the United States was dismayed, despite all it had done, with the lack of progress in the negotiations. What they had now, Kissinger stated, were "plenary discussions . . . in which the speeches made are not distinguished by their novelty." Given this, Kissinger was instructed to tell his counterparts "in all solemnity that if by November 1, no major progress has been made toward a solution, we will be compelled—with great reluctance—to take measures of the greatest consequences." A strategy of just putting forth rhetoric and depicting the conflict as "Mr. Nixon's War" would not serve Hanoi's interests. "If it is Mr. Nixon's War," Kissinger countered, "he cannot afford not to win it." Kissinger continued by stating that "in fairness and respect he must tell them that we cannot continue to accept the procedures that have characterized our contacts in the last 15 months after November 1," and while "no one knows what the final result would be of such a sequence of events," the United States believed "that such a tragic conflict to test each other can be avoided."[60]

Kissinger reported back to Nixon that he was pleased that "Xuan Thuy did not hit back hard at my statements about the necessity for us to take actions of gravest consequence if there is not major progress by November 1." While Xuan Thuy did indicate that an agreement had to meet the terms Hanoi and the NLF had put forward—unconditional US withdrawal and the removal of Thieu—or "they will have no choice but to continue to fight," "he did not press this point strongly." Moreover, "although he 'explained' the communists' ten points to me, he did not do so very aggressively. He stated that he did not regard them as the 'ten commandments' after I said that we did not so regard them." Most notably, "Xuan Thuy for the first time hinted at some linkage between the withdrawal of our forces and theirs (points two and three of their ten points). While he was vague on specifics, the message was clear and significant."[61]

With the madman policy fully enacted, Kissinger was concerned that American public opinion would not allow the administration to carry it out successfully. Regarding the November 1 deadline, the national security advisor worried whether, on the one hand, Hanoi would respond and, on the other, the administration could carry out its ultimatum through Operation Duck Hook in the face of domestic opposition. On September 10, he sent Nixon a memo that set out the contradictions and problems inherent in the administration's policy in Vietnam. He began by noting, "I have become deeply concerned about our present course on Vietnam" due in large part to the pressures of time. "While time acts against both us and our enemy, it runs more quickly against our strategy than against theirs. This pessimistic view is based on my view of Hanoi's strategy and the probable success of the various elements of our own." The United States was pursuing a policy that sought "to solve the problem of Vietnam on three highly interrelated fronts: (1) within the U.S., (2) in Vietnam, and (3) through diplomacy. To achieve our basic goals through diplomacy, we must be reasonably successful on both of the other two fronts." In other words, the administration had to hold off opposition to the war long enough to allow its military strategy and threats to force concessions in Paris if it was to achieve the goal of maintaining the Thieu government in Saigon.[62]

Kissinger's pessimism was due to the domestic "front." "The pressure of public opinion on you to resolve the war quickly will increase—and I believe increase greatly—during the coming months." The current support for the administration's policy was thin and could evaporate quickly. "The plans for student demonstrations in October are well known, and while many Americans will oppose the students' activities, they will also be reminded of their own opposition to the continuation of the war." Vietnamization, in this context, was a double-edged sword. It was popular and strengthened the president's position that he was working toward peace, but it also raised expectations and created the conditions that would increase the pressures to end the war. "The result of the recrudescence of intense public concern must be to polarize public opinion. You will then be somewhat in the same position as was President Johnson. . . . You will be caught between the Hawks and the Doves." The impact would be greater pressure on the administration to take action, and "statements by government officials which attempt to assuage the Hawks or Doves will serve to confuse Hanoi but also to confirm it in its course of waiting us out."[63]

The state of the war in Vietnam did not offer a solution to this dilemma. The Menu bombings had not forced a change in the stalemate on the battlefield or in Hanoi's negotiating position in Paris. Kissinger did not "believe that with our current plans we can win the war within two years, although our success or failure in hurting the enemy remains very important." Nor did Vietnamization provide a military solution, as the national security advisor was "not optimistic about the ability of the South Vietnamese armed forces to assume a larger part of the burden than current MACV plans allow. These plans, however, call for a thirty-month period in which to turn the burden of the war over to the GVN. I do not believe we have this much time."[64]

Kissinger had reached the crux of his analysis. "Withdrawal of U.S. troops will become like salted peanuts to the American public," he warned the president. "The more U.S. troops come home, the more will be demanded. This could eventually result, in effect, in demands for unilateral withdrawal—perhaps within a year." Moreover, as the United States removed its forces, "Hanoi will be encouraged—they are the last people we will be able to fool about the ability of the South Vietnamese to take over from us. They have the option of attacking GVN forces to embarrass us throughout the process or of waiting until we have largely withdrawn before doing so (probably after a period of higher infiltration)." The final problem was the South Vietnam government. "The present GVN cannot go much farther towards a political settlement without seriously endangering its own existence; but at the same time, it has not gone far enough to make such a settlement likely."[65]

With these realities facing Washington, "there is not . . . enough of a prospect of progress in Vietnam to persuade Hanoi to make real concessions in Paris. Their intransigence is also based on their estimate of growing U.S. domestic opposition to our Vietnam policies. It looks as though they are prepared to try to wait us out." American military actions had hurt enemy forces and made them incapable of sustaining the initiative on the battlefield. General Vo Nguyen Giap had therefore adopted "a low-cost strategy aimed at producing a psychological, rather than military, defeat for the U.S." Hanoi's strategy to allow time to wear down American will, Kissinger surmised, "fits both with its doctrine of how to fight a revolutionary war and with its expectations about increasingly significant problems for the U.S." Thus, he concluded, "I do not believe we can make enough evident progress in Vietnam to hold the line within the U.S. (and the U.S. Government), and Hanoi has adopted a strategy which it should be able to maintain for some time—barring some break like Sino-Soviet hostilities. Hence my growing concern."[66]

Kissinger's concerns were also prompted by the upcoming NSC meeting to discuss options about the war and a forthcoming announcement by Nixon, in an effort to hold opponents of the war at bay, of further troop withdrawals. The subsequent NSC meeting on September 12 featured a discussion of how, given that Hanoi had yet to respond to the threat of Operation Duck Hook, the administration should proceed. The president wanted to discuss ways that he could act militarily to force North Vietnam's hand. Secretary of State Rogers proposed an invasion of North Vietnam, while Nixon asked if hitting all new targets, such as Haiphong, or destroying the dikes would bring change. General Abrams cautioned that no short-term actions could hurt the enemy. Given that Hanoi had plenty of supplies, "it would not be an overwhelming disaster, even if we knock out their power plants." Kissinger asked, "There is nothing that can hurt them?" Abrams replied, "They can carry on," and General Wheeler added that there was "no fatal blow through seeking a no-holds-barred solution in a couple of weeks."[67]

It was seen as crucial that the announcement of troop withdrawals be interpreted not as weakness and bugging out but as part of Vietnamization. Nixon said it was necessary to hit the North even though that would open the administration up to domestic criticism. There was, however, a limit, he said, to how much the administration could do to appease his critics. "They will never be satisfied. Next we give a ceasefire, then it could be dump Thieu. We will only lose the war on the third front—at home." The president asked Rogers his opinion about this, and the secretary of state wanted to know if Nixon meant the views as represented by the *New York Times* and *Washington Post*. Nixon responded, "You can't separate them from Congress, they are largely the same." He expected opposition from the columnists, but the war, he claimed, had had public support until the Tet Offensive. His administration, Nixon contended, had done well since coming to office in staying ahead of the opposition due to the May 14 speech and July meetings. The president was apparently still convinced he had enough support to pursue victory. But if the tide turned, he stated, "once they get you on the run, it will move fast against us. Then we lose our position with North Vietnam and the confidence of the GVN." Thus he had to make sure he continued to rally support for his policies through positive polarization. "What I am saying is, you either favor or oppose the President's conduct of the war. I think you can buy time."[68]

Kissinger sought to break the deadlock he had identified by turning to Operation Duck Hook. He convened a small group of senior officials to look at the military options the administration could use. Hanoi, he was convinced, did not believe in the US determination to win the war, and the upcoming fall demonstrations showed that the time for Nixon's madman policy was running out on the domestic side. The national security advisor told the group that American concessions had not brought any change in the enemy's position, and new options were needed. "I refuse to believe," Kissinger exclaimed, "that a little fourth-rate power like North Vietnam does not have a breaking point." He asked his advisors to "examine the option of a savage, decisive blow against North Vietnam." The final plan called for an initial four-day attack beginning on November 1, with bombings of key North Vietnamese targets and the mining of ports and harbors. This would be followed by a brief pause to allow Hanoi to assess the situation, then an additional series of attacks over the course of four day, which could include an invasion of the North, the bombing of dikes, and possibly the use of nuclear weapons, followed by pauses. A presidential speech was drafted, and the Joint Chiefs of Staff prepared to make the plans operational.[69]

The anticipated presidential statement on troop removal came on September 16. Nixon announced that he was reducing the troop ceiling to 484,000 by December 15 (it had been 549,500 in January 1969). That meant, given the earlier de-escalation, that a minimum of thirty-five thousand troops would leave Vietnam over the next three months. Nixon cast the decision as a clear example of the progress being made in Vietnam in training ARVN forces and as part of his ongoing effort to find a peaceful resolution to the conflict. "The time for meaningful negotiation," he declared, "has therefore arrived," and "the time has come to end this war."[70]

Three days later, in a further effort to gain the upper hand on opponents of the war, the president announced that due to his reduction of forces in Vietnam, the upcoming draft calls in November and December, totaling fifty thousand men, were cancelled and that the October draft calls would be phased out over the final three months of the year. Moreover, Nixon stated that if Congress did not act quickly on his proposals to change the draft, made back in May, he would enact the new procedures by executive order. Nixon's new draft rules included a shift to a system in which only nineteen-year-olds would be called and the order would be determined by a lottery of birthdays and not local draft boards. These changes would eliminate much of the uncertainty and arbitrariness of the draft, key issues to antiwar protestors.[71]

As was the case with almost all of his press conferences, the first question to the president on September 26 was about the war, in this case the recent withdrawal of troops and whether there was a set end date for the American military presence in Vietnam. Nixon stated that he thought setting an arbitrary target was a defeatist measure that would undercut his policy and destroy any chances at a negotiated peace. Hanoi could just wait for the date to arrive and achieve its goal. Nonetheless, he believed that he could still achieve his aim of "ending the war before the end of 1970 or before the middle of 1971," the two most common dates suggested in Congress. In response to a question about the upcoming October Moratorium and student protests, Nixon stated that he was well aware of the opposition to the war on college campuses. "However, under no circumstances will I be affected whatever by it." He ended the meeting with reporters by restating his optimism that his administration was "on the right course in Vietnam . . . to end this war." That end would come much sooner if he could have "a united front behind very reasonable proposals. If we have that united front, the enemy will begin to talk."[72] Responding to critics of his statement, Nixon sent a letter to a Georgetown student that he released to the public to further clarify his position. If he were to respond to the demonstrations, he stated, "it would give the decision, not to the majority, and not to those with the strongest arguments, but to those with the loudest voices."[73]

These actions and arguments, however, did little to resolve the dilemma of Nixon's policy and inability to break the stalemate in Vietnam or rally greater support at home. Nixon and Kissinger were similarly frustrated in their efforts to make the covert side of the madman policy work. With the plans for Duck Hook being finalized, the administration sought to use Dobrynin again as a conduit of its threat and to have the Kremlin apply pressure on Hanoi. Kissinger met with the Soviet ambassador on September 27 to inform him that Vietnam was the most important issue in US-Soviet relations. Nixon had instructed Kissinger in advance that it was "very important to leave no illusions on the decision he has made on the whole Southeast Asia area. It is very important for everyone to realize the whole situation is changed. We would have been delighted to have nice personal relations [with the Soviet Union], but that boat is gone by now, and that is that." The president wanted "to be sure this is understood; and that we reached this conclusion reluctantly."[74]

The American leaders had prearranged that Nixon would call during the meeting, and Kissinger would use that opening to deliver the warning to Dobrynin. When Kissinger hung up with Nixon, he told the ambassador that Moscow "should also have no illusions about the seriousness with which we took Hanoi's attempt to undermine the domestic position of the President." It was, Kissinger stated, "a pity that all our efforts to negotiate had failed. The President has told me in his call that the train has just left the station and was now headed down the track."[75] In alignment with these threats, Nixon ordered a secret nuclear alert for mid-October. He hoped it would provide credibility to the threats against Hanoi and his November 1 deadline, push the Soviets to force Hanoi to make concessions, and allow him to bring an end to the war on American terms.[76]

On October 2, Kissinger presented Nixon with the current plan for Duck Hook. The memorandum, titled "Contingency Military Operation against North Vietnam," stated that the primary objective was "to give Hanoi incentive to negotiate a compromise settlement through a series of military blows." Thus, the plans were designed to "persuade the North Vietnamese, through effective military action, and an explicit willingness to repeat it, that the alternative to compromise is unacceptable damage to their society." At the same time, it would be made clear to the enemy "that our goal is not the total destruction of the country or the regime, which would invite major outside intervention." The actions had to be calibrated so as not to provoke a Soviet or Chinese military response; yet they had to be "effective and firm enough to forestall circumvention and promote their eventual influence on Hanoi to compromise." Therefore, the goal was to "impose a substantial physical isolation of North Vietnam and destroy vital targets sufficient to confront Hanoi with military and economic disruption and deprivation, involving costly and time-consuming restoration or countermeasures. Our immediate military objective would be significant impact on North Vietnam as a society—not simply a resumption of bombing aimed at reducing their support of the war in the south."[77]

At the same time, showing that the president was not swayed by public pressure would be crucial to the success of Duck Hook. The administration's "political posture had to demonstrate that it was clearly immune to all likely pressures against continuing the action so long as Hanoi refuses to compromise." The statement being made would be that "the NVN demands for our unconditional surrender are utterly unacceptable," that the administration was willing "to go to almost any lengths to end the war quickly," that the president had "decided to give NVN incentives to end the war by compromise sooner, rather than later," and that the United States was willing to "keep the negotiating avenue open, essentially on the basis of our May 14th . . . proposal."[78]

October proved to be a pivotal moment in the war as the contradictions in Nixon's policy, as set out by Kissinger, came to a head. With the November 1 deadline fast approaching, Nixon tried his best to build support for the war. The upcoming October Moratorium on October 15 and the November 13–15 Mobilization against the War demonstrations caused a great deal of worry within the administration. The October Moratorium represented the effort by antiwar forces to regroup and respond to the shattering of many organizations and the discrediting of their tactics in the eyes of the public after Chicago. Organized by the Vietnam Moratorium Committee, headed by Sam Brown Jr., a former campaign organizer for Eugene McCarthy, the initial focus was on college campuses. The moratorium's appeal was that it represented a new, decentralized approach to expressing opposition to the war. People were asked to do something different during the day from their normal routine to demonstrate their opposition. Rather than massive rallies in major cities, local groups promoted activities in communities and towns all across the country, such as candlelight vigils, teach-ins, silent witnessing, church services, and gatherings with like-minded people in public areas. This approach gained the support of numerous religious, civic, and civil rights organizations and rallied the former supporters of McCarthy and Robert Kennedy. Thus, the moratorium represented the more moderate, middle-class opponents of the war rather than students or radicals.

"My real concern," Nixon wrote in his memoirs, "was that these highly publicized efforts aimed at forcing me to end the war were seriously undermining my behind-the-scenes attempts to do just that."[79] The president urged the public on September 30 to back his efforts toward peace. "The peace that we will be able to achieve will be due to the fact that Americans, when it really counted, did not buckle and run away, but stood fast, so that the enemy knew that it had no choice except to negotiate—negotiate a fair peace."[80] Nixon told Kissinger that he would not yield to any public pressure because if he did there would be no "line of demarcation" to stop aggression. He "did not want the enemy to think that we are affected by them [the protestors]."[81] The United States had to achieve its goal in Vietnam, the president told Sir Robert Thompson, the British counterinsurgency expert, because at stake was "not only the future peace of the Pacific and the chances for independence in the region, but the survival of the US as a world power with the will to use this power. . . . In fact, the domino theory would apply."[82]

Nixon still believed he could escalate the war if it meant victory because he thought "that the people were not so much anti-war as tending to feel that the US should get in or get out. They did not like the idea of the greatest power in the world being made to back down by a little country." This, he believed, made the "option to the right," Operation Duck Hook, viable.[83] The dilemma was how to mobilize that support when so much of the military policy was covert and the administration's public position was that it was reducing the US role in the war.

In an effort to discredit the protests, the administration highlighted the support the demonstration received from North Vietnam's premier Pham Van Dong, who termed the upcoming event a "timely rebuff" of Nixon's policies. Vice President Spiro Agnew called upon its organizers to "repudiate the support of a totalitarian government which has on its hands the blood of 40,000 Americans."[84] By challenging the protest leaders to deny the connection to Hanoi, the administration was implying that one existed. If anything, the administration's effort backfired. As Daniel Patrick Moynihan, counselor to the president for urban affairs, noted, the moratorium was a tremendous success for its organizers as it was large, peaceful, and able to gain new recruits and prestige because the "young white middle-class crowds were sweet tempered and considerate." The administration's attack on their patriotism meant that the "middle-class, academic, and intellectual world [would] now be solidly with them."[85] Just as significantly, Hanoi's message of support signaled that it would not be changing its negotiating position in response to the president's ultimatum.

The size and positive reception of the demonstrations shook the administration and led the president to abandon Operation Duck Hook. "Although publicly I continued to ignore the raging antiwar controversy," Nixon recalled, "I had to face the facts that it had probably destroyed the credibility of my ultimatum to Hanoi." It was clear after the moratorium that "American public opinion would be seriously divided by any military escalation of the war."[86] Having decided to shelve the planned massive attacks, Nixon still wanted Moscow and Hanoi to know he would reconsider the option. Meeting with Dobrynin on October 20, the president berated the ambassador for what he saw as the Soviet Union's lack of effort in putting pressure on North Vietnam and told him the lack of progress in Paris made it very difficult to improve US-Soviet relations. The United States now "would have to pursue its own methods for bringing the war to an end." It could not allow Hanoi to drag out the negotiations without taking action. "The humiliation of a defeat was absolutely unacceptable." Nixon acknowledged that the "Soviet leaders were tough and courageous, but so was he," and he reiterated his point that if the war dragged on, "the U.S. would find its own way to bring it to an end."[87]

That night, Nixon told Kissinger that in his meeting the next day with Dobrynin, the national security advisor should "shake his head and say 'I'm sorry, Mr. Ambassador, but he [Nixon] is out of control. Mr. Ambassador, as you know, I am very close to the President, but you don't know this man—he has been through more than the rest of us put together.' He's made up his mind and unless there is some movement just shake your head." The president speculated that Dobrynin would ask, "What does this mean? Are you threatening me?" Kissinger's response should be no, the United States just needed some movement by Hanoi. Kissinger told Nixon that if the Soviets "ignore what you said this afternoon, they either believe that your freedom of action is so circumscribed that you can't do anything or Hanoi is out of control." Nothing came of Kissinger's follow-up meeting with the Soviet ambassador, and he concluded in a memorandum to Nixon that it remained "essential to continue to back up our verbal threats with military present moves."[88]

Nixon also had to convince Thieu that his decision not to implement Operation Duck Hook did not mean a lessening of his commitment to the survival of the Saigon regime. Ambassador Ellsworth Bunker reported on October 22 that he had delivered the president's reassurance "that U.S. policy on the war will not change, that the president intends to hold firm in accordance with his discussions with Thieu, and that the protests will not alter that course." The change was portrayed as a tactical rather than a policy decision, and Bunker noted that he was able to assuage Thieu's concern that the president was intending to announce a unilateral US cease-fire proposal in his upcoming speech. The following week the ambassador provided a follow-up message in which he noted that the "most unsettling factor" in the effectiveness of the Saigon government was the "apprehension about the intentions of the United States" due to public statements in Congress advocating American withdrawal. He believed, however, that "Vietnamization can and will work if it is carried out prudently and pragmatically and with enough flexibility to enable us to counter enemy moves."[89] Thus, he recommended making sure the administration had enough time to stay the course.

Having abandoned the November 1 deadline, Nixon had to recast his planned November 3 speech to announce the launching of Operation Duck Hook. Instead, in what became known as his "Silent Majority" speech, the president set out the principles of the Nixon Doctrine, elaborated on the policy of Vietnamization, and implemented his ideas on positive polarization of the American public in an attempt to buy time to salvage his policy and win the war in Vietnam. Nixon decided it was time to directly engage the antiwar movement to rally support for his policy and demonstrate to Hanoi that it could not count on American public opinion to soften his positions. Positive polarization was designed to mobilize support for the president, place the blame for failure at the feet of the antiwar movement and Nixon's critics, and free the administration from the restrictions of public opinion.

At the beginning of his talk to the nation, the president outlined the difficult situation he had inherited and how he could have taken the popular course, withdrawn, and blamed the defeat on Johnson. This, he insisted, would have been "a disaster not only for South Vietnam but for the United States and for the cause of peace." It would have rewarded the aggression of North Vietnam and led to a massacre in the South by the communists. "For the United States, this first defeat in our Nation's history would result in a collapse of confidence in American leadership, not only in Asia but throughout the world." A nation, Nixon opined, "cannot remain great if it betrays its allies and lets down its friends. Our defeat and humiliation in South Vietnam without question would promote recklessness in the councils of those great powers who have not yet abandoned their goals of world conquest." The result would be more wars, not peace.[90]

The question before the nation, Nixon declared, was "How can we win America's peace?" He repeated the proposal he had made on May 14 and listed other steps taken to reach a peaceful end to the war, but he had to report that no progress had been made. To blame, the president stated, "is the other side's absolute refusal to show the least willingness to join us in seeking a just peace. And it will not do so while it is convinced that all it has to do is to wait for our next concession, and our next concession after that one, until it gets what it wants." For these reasons he had embarked on another plan, in conjunction with the Nixon Doctrine, "which not only will help end the war in Vietnam, but which is an essential element of our program to prevent future Vietnams."[91]

The Nixon Doctrine, the president reminded the public, rested on three principles to guide American foreign policy. The United States would keep all of its treaty commitments, "provide a shield if a nuclear power threatens the freedom of a nation allied" with the United States "or of a nation whose survival we consider vital to our security," and, in cases of other forms of aggression, "furnish military and economic assistance when requested in accordance with our treaty commitments. But we shall look to the nation directly threatened to assume the primary responsibility of providing the manpower for its defense." Stopping aggression and defending freedom, Nixon said, was "everybody's business—not just America's business." He was therefore changing the direction of American policy in Vietnam. "In the previous administration, we Americanized the war in Vietnam. In this administration, we are Vietnamizing the search for peace."[92]

Vietnamization had begun in March when the president ordered increased training of ARVN forces. In July, the president revealed to the nation, he had told General Abrams that the primary mission of American forces was to prepare the South Vietnamese to take over the fighting of the war. This, Nixon stated, had allowed the first withdrawals of American forces, which would reach over sixty thousand men by the middle of the next month without any loss of effectiveness on the battlefield. The ultimate goal was the complete removal of American troops. Hanoi, however, should not misinterpret these actions as weakness; nor should it try to take advantage of the program, Nixon warned. If it did, he was prepared "to take strong and effective measures to deal with" any increase in enemy force that endangered American soldiers.[93]

The choice, Nixon claimed, was defeat or a just peace. Nixon used the end of his speech to rally support for the war. Protestors, he stated, wanted an immediate end to the war. "But as President of the United States, I would be untrue to my oath of office if I allowed the policy of this Nation to be dictated by the minority who hold that point of view and who try to impose it on the Nation by mounting demonstrations in the street." World peace and freedom rested with U.S. decisions. "Let historians not record that when America was the most powerful nation in the world we passed on the other side of the road and allowed the last hopes for peace and freedom of millions of people to be suffocated by the forces of totalitarianism. And so tonight—to you, the great silent majority of my fellow Americans—I ask for your support."[94]

Nixon concluded by recalling his campaign pledge to "end the war in a way that we could win the peace"; he claimed that his plan put the nation on that course. "The more support I can have from the American people, the sooner that pledge can be redeemed; for the more divided we are at home, the less likely the enemy is to negotiate at Paris. Let us be united for peace. Let us also be united against defeat. Because let us understand: North Vietnam cannot defeat or humiliate the United States. Only Americans can do that."[95]

The speech represented both a concession to the political reality at home that the American public would not accept a dramatic escalation of the war and an effort to change the political calculus in the country. It was quickly followed by attacks against the antiwar movement and the media by Vice President Agnew as well as an administration-orchestrated series of pro-war rallies, manufactured letter-writing campaigns of support, and demonstrations of patriotism. Agnew's particular target was television news, which he complained had immediately, after Nixon's speech sought to "rally the American people to see the conflict through to a lasting and just peace in the Pacific," subjected the president's policies "to instant analysis and querulous criticism." As *Time* magazine succinctly stated, "The Administration now seems committed to the politics of polarization. Viet Nam is the touchstone of division, the litmus test of loyalty. Nixon's aim is to demonstrate to Hanoi that the protestors do not speak for the American public, and so gain time and leverage" for his Vietnam policy. The president was counting on people being more annoyed with the protestors than tired of the war.[96]

Seeking to divert attention from the protests and to highlight support for the war, on the first day of the November demonstrations Nixon took the highly unusual step of visiting both houses of Congress to thank members for their backing of his policies and to promise that he would achieve a just peace in Vietnam. In the House, he noted that over three hundred members had signed and sent a resolution to Paris in support of his November 3 speech, and he called for a return to the bipartisan consensus that was the hallmark of American foreign policy after World War II.[97]

Although polls showed a high level of approval for Nixon's speech and displeasure with the tactics of the antiwar movement, public support for the war did not increase, and a majority of Americans disagreed with the president's portrayal of protestors as irresponsible and disloyal.[98] The November demonstrations in Washington, DC, were large, peaceful, and powerful events, with participants, *Time* magazine observed, "moved by the spirit of Woodstock—a mingling of festive mood and soulful reflection." The protest began with the somber, silent "March against Death," with demonstrators processing in single file from Arlington National Cemetery, past the White House, where each person carrying a candle and a placard with the name of a soldier killed in Vietnam read the name out loud, and then proceeded to the Capitol, where they placed the signs in a coffin. The culminating demonstration on November 15 was the largest ever, with approximately five hundred thousand people gathered on the Washington Mall and millions more participating in other cities throughout the nation.[99]

The following week, news of the March 1968 My Lai massacre broke. It served to remind the nation of the costs of the war to the Vietnamese and the moral ambiguities that surrounded the American effort. The disturbing pictures of villagers killed by American troops and testimonies by soldiers raised difficult questions about the conduct of the war, American policy, and the US role in Vietnam. There were no easy answers, but a month that began with President Nixon seeking to rally support for the war ended with the administration on the defensive against a revitalized antiwar movement and extensive debates about the correctness of the war it sought to continue.

In an effort to regain control over the debate on the war, Nixon spoke to the nation again on December 15 to deliver what he called a progress report on Vietnam. He said that, regrettably, there had been no movement in the Paris negotiations since his November 3 speech. The enemy continued to insist on a unilateral American withdrawal of forces, "imposition of a Communist government on the people of South Vietnam against their will, and defeat and humiliation for the United States. This we cannot and will not accept." There was, Nixon declared, positive news regarding Vietnamization and the training of ARVN forces. All the reports he was receiving, including one from Sir Robert Thompson, whom the president had asked to go to South Vietnam to evaluate the situation, were "cautiously optimistic" about South Vietnam's future. He characterized Thompson as being impressed with the improved "security situation, both in Saigon and in the rural areas" and quoted him as stating that a "winning position in the sense of . . . maintaining an independent, non-Communist South Vietnam has been achieved." Now the confidence and will to complete the job were necessary.[100]

On the basis of this analysis, Nixon announced another withdrawal of fifty thousand American soldiers by April 15, 1970. This would bring the total reduction of troops since he took office to 115,500 men. This decision, he stated, was another step in his Vietnamization policy and plan for peace. It demonstrated the progress being made in Saigon and his willingness "to bring an end to the war and to achieve a just peace." The president continued to insist that North Vietnam's hope "that division in the United States would eventually bring them the victory they cannot win over our fighting men in Vietnam" was an empty one and that it was time for Hanoi to "abandon its dreams of military victory" and negotiate.[101]

Nixon knew, however, that he was the one racing against the clock to achieve a military solution against the very growing pressure to end the war that he dismissed. Given his strategy since January, he had to continue, as Kissinger predicted in September, to withdraw American forces while still searching for the military blow that would force Hanoi to yield to Nixon's peace plan. As noted in NSSM 80, sent to Kissinger on December 24, 1969, there was "no sign of a change in the other side's intransigent attitude which would permit the Paris talks to move forward." The only hope was that, to the extent that the enemy became convinced "that our replacement program will succeed, the incentive for them to negotiate seriously will increase." In such a circumstance, Hanoi would face "a choice between a negotiated settlement on terms other than their demands and an indefinitely prolonged conflict" with a Saigon that was "increasingly able to defend itself without outside assistance." Thus, without a knockout military action, Vietnamization was the only hope the administration had for achieving its long-standing goals of preserving the noncommunist government in Saigon and American credibility. Yet, NSSM 80 concluded, "the Communist leaders have accepted the challenge of Vietnamization and will try hard to upset our timetable," and those efforts would intensify as "the U.S. combat presence diminishes."[102] This would test America's will and ability to see the program and Nixon's policies through to success. With the stalemate continuing after one year in office, Nixon was still in search of a plan to win the war.

NOTES

1. Kimball, *The Vietnam War Files*, 11.
2. "Minutes of the First Meeting of the National Security Council," January 21, 1969, NSC Institutional (H) Files (hereafter NSCH Files)/Minutes of Meetings, Box H120, Richard Nixon Presidential Library (hereafter RNPL), Yorba Linda, California.
3. "Minutes National Security Council Meeting," January 25, 1969, NSCH Files/ Minutes of Meetings, Box H120, RNPL. It is likely that the president said "game" rather than "gain" as recorded in the minutes.
4. "Minutes National Security Council Meeting," January 25, 1969.
5. "Minutes National Security Council Meeting," January 25, 1969.

6. Morton Halperin, oral history, RNPL; National Security Study Memorandum 1 (hereafter NSSM, followed by number) 1, January 21, 1969, NSSMs, RNPL.

7. *FRUS, 1969–1976*, Vol. 6: *Vietnam, January 1969–July 1970*, Document 44.

8. *FRUS, 1969–1976*, Vol. 6: *Vietnam, January 1969–July 1970*, Document 44.

9. Halperin, oral history, RNPL.

10. Larry Berman, *No Peace, No Honor: Nixon, Kissinger, and Betrayal in Vietnam* (New York: Free Press, 2001), 49.

11. *Public Papers of the Presidents: Richard Nixon, 1969* (Washington, DC: Government Printing Office, 1970), 15–23.

12. *Public Papers of the Presidents: Nixon, 1969*, 182–84.

13. *Public Papers of the Presidents: Nixon, 1969*, 209–11.

14. *Public Papers of the Presidents: Nixon, 1969*, 298–300.

15. H. R. Haldeman, *The Ends of Power* (New York: Times Books, 1978), 83 (emphasis in the original).

16. "The Cambodian Bombing Decision," Henry A. Kissinger Office Files/HAK Administrative and Staff Files: Cambodia—Cambodian Bombing Decision (3 of 4), Box 11, RNPL.

17. *FRUS, 1969–1976*, Vol. 6: *Vietnam, January 1969–July 1970*, Document 22.

18. *FRUS, 1969–1976*, Vol. 6: *Vietnam, January 1969–July 1970*, Documents 23 and 25.

19. *FRUS, 1969–1976*, Vol. 6: *Vietnam, January 1969–July 1970*, Document 39. The president meant North Vietnamese bases in Cambodia.

20. Kissinger to Nixon, March 16, 1969, Memorandum for the President, National Security Council Files (hereafter NSC Files)/Vietnam, Subject Files: Breakfast Plan, Box 89, RNPL.

21. Kissinger to Nixon, March 16, 1969, Memorandum for the President.

22. *FRUS, 1969–1976*, Vol. 6: *Vietnam, January 1969–July 1970*, Document 41.

23. "Cambodian Bombing: (B-52 Menu)," undated (June 1970), Henry A. Kissinger Office Files/HAK Administrative and Staff Files: Cambodia—Cambodian Bombing Decision (1 of 4), Box 11, RNPL.

24. Kissinger to Rogers, March 17, 1969, "Breakfast Plan Press Guidance"; Kissinger to Nixon, March 19, 1969, "Reaction to Breakfast Plan"; Fazio to Kissinger, May 9, 1969, NSC Files/Vietnam Subject Files: Breakfast, Box 103, RNPL.

25. "The Cambodian Bombing Decision"; Kissinger to Nixon, February 19, 1969, Memorandum for the President, NSC Files/Vietnam Subject Files: Planning for Strikes Breakfast, Lunch, Dinner, Box 104, RNPL.

26. "The Cambodian Bombing Decision"; Kissinger to Nixon, February 19, 1969, Memorandum for the President.

27. Nixon, *RN, The Memoirs of Richard Nixon* (New York: Grosset and Dunlop, 1978), 394.

28. Laird to Nixon, March 24, 1970, "Assessment of MENU Operations," NSC Files/Vietnam Subject Files, Box 105, RNPL; Kissinger to Nixon, March 27, 1970, "B-52 Operations in Cambodia," NSC Files/Vietnam Subject Files, Box 105, RNPL.

29. Kissinger to Nixon, April 22, 1969, Memorandum for the President, NSC Files/Vietnam, Subject Files: Breakfast Plan, Box 103, RNPL.

30. Laird to Nixon, April 11, 1969, Memorandum for the President, NSC Files/Vietnam, Subject Files: Breakfast Plan, Box 103, RNPL.

31. H. R. Haldeman, *The Haldeman Diaries: Inside the Nixon White House* (Santa Monica, CA: Sony Electronic Publishing Co., 1994), 52.

32. "Operation Lunch," undated memo (April 1969), NSC Files/Vietnam Subject Files: Lunch, Box 105, RNPL.

33. Kissinger to Nixon, April 29, 1969, "Summary of Operations Breakfast Bravo and Coco and Lunch," NSC Files/Vietnam, Subject Files: Breakfast Plan, Box 103, RNPL.

34. Wheeler to Laird, June 23, 1969, "Menu Operations," NSC Files/Vietnam, Subject Files: Lunch Coco, Dinner Coco, Dessert Snack, Box 105, RNPL.

35. *FRUS, 1969–1976*, Vol. 6: *Vietnam, January 1969–July 1970*, Document 53.

36. *FRUS, 1969–1976*, Vol. 6: *Vietnam, January 1969–July 1970*, Document 53.

37. *FRUS, 1969–1976*, Vol. 6: *Vietnam, January 1969–July 1970*, Document 55.

38. *FRUS, 1969–1976*, Vol. 6: *Vietnam, January 1969–July 1970*, Document 60.

39. *FRUS, 1969–1976*, Vol. 6: *Vietnam, January 1969–July 1970*, Document 60.

40. *FRUS, 1969–1976*, Vol. 6: *Vietnam, January 1969–July 1970*, Document 60.

41. "Minutes National Security Council Meeting," March 28, 1969, NSCH Files/ Minutes of Meetings, Box H121, RNPL.

42. *Public Papers of the Presidents: Nixon, 1969*, 336; "The Campus Upheaval: An End to Patience," *Time*, May 9, 1969, 22–23.

43. *Public Papers of the Presidents: Nixon, 1969*, 369–75.

44. *Public Papers of the Presidents: Nixon, 1969*, 369–75.

45. *Public Papers of the Presidents: Nixon, 1969*, 369–75.

46. *Public Papers of the Presidents: Nixon, 1969*, 369–75.

47. *Public Papers of the Presidents: Nixon, 1969*, 432–37.

48. *Public Papers of the Presidents: Nixon, 1969*, 443–44.

49. Memorandum of Conversation, June 13, 1969, NSC Files, Box 1026, RNPL.

50. Kissinger to Bunker, May 21, 1969, NSC Files/Vietnam Subject Files: Backchannel (2 of 2), Box 65, RNPL.

51. "National Security Study Memorandum 19," May 1969, NSCH Files, Box 135, RNPL.

52. Laird to Nixon, June 2, 1969, "Vietnamizing the War (NSSM 36)," NSCH Files, Box 142, RNPL.

53. *Public Papers of the Presidents: Nixon, 1969*, 450–51, 471–72.

54. *Public Papers of the Presidents: Nixon, 1969*, 544–56.

55. *FRUS, 1969–1976*, Vol. 1: *Foundations of Foreign Policy, 1969–1972*, Document 50.

56. Nixon, *RN*, 395.

57. *Public Papers of the Presidents: Nixon, 1969*, 585–87.

58. Memorandum of Conversation, July 30, 1969, NSC Files, Box 1023, RNPL.

59. *FRUS, 1969–1976*, Vol. 6: *Vietnam, January 1969–July 1970*, Document 106.

60. *FRUS, 1969–1976*, Vol. 6: *Vietnam, January 1969–July 1970*, Document 106.

61. *FRUS, 1969–1976*, Vol. 6: *Vietnam, January 1969–July 1970*, Document 106.

62. Kissinger to Nixon, September 10, 1969, "Our Present Course on Vietnam," NSCH Files/Special NSC Meeting 9–12–69 Vietnam, Box O24, RNPL.

63. Kissinger to Nixon, September 10, 1969, "Our Present Course on Vietnam."

64. Kissinger to Nixon, September 10, 1969, "Our Present Course on Vietnam."

65. Kissinger to Nixon, September 10, 1969, "Our Present Course on Vietnam."

66. Kissinger to Nixon, September 10, 1969, "Our Present Course on Vietnam."

67. "Minutes National Security Council Meeting," September 12, 1969, NSCH Files/ Minutes of Meetings, Box H109, RNPL.

68. "Minutes National Security Council Meeting," September 12, 1969.

69. *FRUS, 1969–1976*, Vol. 6: *Vietnam, January 1969–July 1970*, Document 129; Kimball, *Nixon's Vietnam War*, 163–64. See also *FRUS, 1969–1976*, Vol. 6: *Vietnam, January 1969–July 1970*, Document 134.

70. *Public Papers of the Presidents: Nixon, 1969*, 718.

71. *Public Papers of the Presidents: Nixon, 1969*, 731.

72. *Public Papers of the Presidents: Nixon, 1969*, 748–58.

73. *Public Papers of the Presidents: Nixon, 1969*, 799.

74. *FRUS, 1969–1976*, Vol. 6: *Vietnam, January 1969–July 1970*, Document 125.

75. *FRUS, 1969–1976*, Vol. 6: *Vietnam, January 1969–July 1970*, Document 125.

76. Jeffrey Kimball, *Nixon's Vietnam War* (Lawrence: University Press of Kansas, 1998), 164.

77. *FRUS, 1969–1976*, Vol. 6: *Vietnam, January 1969–July 1970*, Document 129. See also *FRUS, 1969–1976*, Vol. 6: *Vietnam, January 1969–July 1970*, Document 134.

78. *FRUS, 1969–1976*, Vol. 6: *Vietnam, January 1969–July 1970*, Document 129.

79. Nixon, *RN*, 401.

80. "President Leads Attempt to Mute Criticism of War," *New York Times*, October 1, 1969.

81. *FRUS, 1969–1976*, Vol. 6: *Vietnam, January 1969–July 1970*, Document 135 (brackets in the source text).

82. *FRUS, 1969–1976*, Vol. 6: *Vietnam, January 1969–July 1970*, Document 137.

83. *FRUS, 1969–1976*, Vol. 6: *Vietnam, January 1969–July 1970*, Document 137.

84. "Hanoi Calls Moratorium 'Timely Rebuff' to Nixon," *New York Times*, October 15, 1969; Nixon, *RN*, 402.

85. Moynihan to Nixon, October 16, 1969, NSC Files, Box 357, RNPL.

86. Nixon, *RN*, 401–2; see also Melvin Small, *Johnson, Nixon, and the Doves* (New Brunswick, NJ: Rutgers University Press, 1989).

87. *FRUS, 1969–1976*, Vol. 6: *Vietnam, January 1969–July 1970*, Document 139.

88. *FRUS, 1969–1976*, Vol. 6: *Vietnam, January 1969–July 1970*, Document 139 (brackets in the source text).

89. Bunker to Kissinger, October 22, 1969, and Bunker to Nixon, October 29, 1969, NSC Files/Vietnam Subject Files: Backchannel October 1969, Box 65, RNPL.

90. *Public Papers of the Presidents: Nixon, 1969*, 901–9.

91. *Public Papers of the Presidents: Nixon, 1969*, 901–9.

92. *Public Papers of the Presidents: Nixon, 1969*, 901–9.

93. *Public Papers of the Presidents: Nixon, 1969*, 901–9.

94. *Public Papers of the Presidents: Nixon, 1969*, 901–9.

95. *Public Papers of the Presidents: Nixon, 1969*, 901–9.

96. "The Politics of Polarization," *Time*, November 21, 1969, 16–22.

97. "Nixon, in a Visit, Thanks Congress for War Support," *New York Times*, November 14, 1969, 1.

98. Kimball, *Nixon's Vietnam War*, 175.

99. "Parades for Peace and Patriotism," 23–26.

100. *Public Papers of the Presidents: Nixon, 1969*, 1025–28. See *FRUS, 1969–1976*, Vol. 6: *Vietnam, January 1969–July 1970*, Document 153, for more information on Thompson's report; and Abrams to Wheeler, November 24, 1969, NSC Files/Vietnam Subject Files, Box 66, RNPL, for an example of other optimistic reports.

101. *Public Papers of the Presidents: Nixon, 1969*, 1025–28.

102. Brown to Kissinger, December 24, 1969, "NSSM 80—Vietnam Portion," NSCH Files, Box 165, RNPL.

President Nixon and Vice President Nguyen Cao Ky of South Vietnam, April 1, 1969, Washington, D.C.

President Nixon, General Creighton Abrams, General Earle Wheeler, and Secretary of Defense Melvin Laird, Oval Office, White House, discussing situation in South Vietnam, May 12, 1969.

President Nixon and President Nguyen Van Thieu of South Vietnam, Midway Island, June 8, 1969.

President Nixon and President Nguyen Van Thieu of South Vietnam, Midway Island, June 8, 1969.

President Nixon and meeting of the National Security Council to discuss the Vietnam War, September 12, 1969.

President Nixon delivering the "Silent Majority" speech from the Oval Office, November 3, 1969.

President Nixon in House Chamber, U.S. Capitol, November 11, 1969.

President Nixon pointing to map of Cambodia while delivering a televised address on American involvement in Cambodia, April 30, 1970.

President Nixon signing wage and price freeze for construction industry, San Clemente, California, March 30, 1971.

President Nixon giving a televised speech on troop withdrawals, with chart labeled "Authorized Troop Level in South Vietnam," April 7, 1971.

President Nixon, National Security Advisor Henry Kissinger, and U.S. Ambassador to South Vietnam Ellsworth Bunker, June 16, 1971.

President Nixon announcing the end of the U.S. ground offensive role in Vietnam, and the withdrawal of 45,000 more troops, November 12, 1971.

President Nixon and American troops of the First Infantry Division in Dian, South Vietnam, July 30, 1971.

President Nixon greeting troops on the Magical Mystery Tour tank of the First Infantry Division in Dian, South Vietnam, July 30, 1971.

President Nixon pinning Distinguished Service Cross medals on soldiers of the
First Infantry Division in Dian, South Vietnam, July 30, 1971.

FOUR

Expansion and Crisis

The beginning of 1970 found President Richard Nixon frustrated by the lack of progress in Vietnam and the growing opposition at home to his quest for victory. His efforts to force concessions from Hanoi in Paris through the secret bombing of Cambodia, the madman policy, Operation Duck Hook, and pressure from Moscow had all failed, and the war was still a stalemate. The North Vietnamese remained defiant in sticking to their peace terms: unilateral American withdrawal and the establishment of a coalition government in Saigon that did not include President Nguyen Van Thieu. Similarly, the policies designed to buy time at home—the announcement of the Nixon Doctrine and Vietnamization, the first drawdown of American forces, and changes to the draft laws—along with strategies to rally support for the war through positive polarization and the "Silent Majority" speech, did not yield the results sought. By the end of 1969, a larger, more moderate, and more middle-class antiwar movement was determined to bring an immediate end to the war.

The fundamental dilemma of Nixon's policy persisted. The pursuit of victory by covert escalation had failed to break the stalemate on the battlefield. This led to increased pressure at home for the removal of American forces, further fueled by the president's public position that he was winding down the war. In an effort to break the deadlock in the fighting and stay ahead of the political pressures at home, Nixon again turned to Cambodia as the place to carry out his expansion and escalation approach to victory. Nixon still believed he could take an action that President Lyndon Johnson had resisted and use it as a decisive military blow to turn the tide of the war and negotiations. However, his chosen course of action—the invasion of Cambodia, launched on April 30, 1970—could not be undertaken covertly. Determined to prove his resolve, demonstrate American credibility, and defeat the enemy, Nixon took on the political risks of escalation and confrontation with the anti-war movement. Buoyed by overly optimistic reports of military progress in South Vietnam and improvements in Saigon, the president gambled that a "bold move"[1] would change the dynamic of the war and bring about peace with honor.

Instead, the invasion generated the political backlash the administration feared when it had shelved Duck Hook the previous October. Protests erupted throughout the nation, Congress moved to restrict the power of the president, and political divisions deepened at home. In Vietnam, the military faced a crisis of discipline, and Nixon was forced to curtail the Cambodian operation. The president tacked back to Vietnamization as the only option to try to salvage the war. The failure of the invasion marked the collapse of the madman policy and the end of Nixon's quest to secure a military victory in Vietnam. Moreover, the costs at home mounted as the war sent the economy into a recession, further restricting the president's actions and signaling the end of the "American Century." The Cambodian campaign proved a decisive turning point in the war, though not in the direction Nixon had intended.

From the administration's point of view, in an analysis remarkably similar to the Johnson administration's in the fall of 1967, the war was a paradox.[2] All studies and analyses showed progress against the enemy, improvements in the performance of the Army of the Republic of Vietnam (ARVN), and greater political support for Saigon. For example, Military Assistance Command, Vietnam (MACV) reported toward the end of 1969 that enemy strength had dropped by over forty thousand troops since the beginning of the year. This was due to a high number of combat losses, desertions by National Liberation Front (NLF) cadres through the Chieu Hoi Program that welcomed them to the South Vietnamese side, and difficulties in recruiting new troops. This was leading, General Creighton W. Abrams claimed, to "morale and discipline problems among enemy forces" and conflicts between the North Vietnamese Army (NVA) and NLF personnel. On the other side, he proclaimed, ARVN forces continued to improve, putting greater pressure on the enemy in the field and leading to increased logistical problems and greater losses of supplies. The result was "a reduction in the intensity of the enemy's offensive activity," cancelled military operations, and longer lulls in the fighting.[3]

A February 1970 National Security Council study, titled "Enemy Manpower Situation in Vietnam," reached similar conclusions. While the "enemy has, to a large extent, been able to control his losses by increasing or decreasing the aggressiveness of his forces," NVA and NLF strength had significantly declined during 1969 by forty to fifty thousand men. Thus, "the current enemy manpower situation is not bright," and if recent trends continued, "the enemy will continue to suffer a slow attrition in the strength of his military forces." Hanoi could only reverse the decline and rebuild by limiting combat operations while increasing infiltration and recruitment. "However, the most likely prospect is that the enemy's force strength will continue to slowly decline."[4]

In an end-of-the-year review of the war, it was reported that the United States had achieved success on the battlefield and in its implementation of the policy of Vietnamization. The administration's policies, National Security Study Memorandum (NSSM) 80 asserted, had led to a series of victories. "The enemy's attempted major offensive in February and March was defeated at great cost to him," rendering him unable to sustain momentum in any operations for the rest of the year. In addition, the NVA and NLF suffered significant casualties, including nearly 160,000 killed, leading to a reduction in overall combat strength. Vietnamization, with the goal of strengthening ARVN forces so they "could defend themselves against the current enemy threat, including the North Vietnamese," in order to allow the United States to withdraw its forces, was on the right course. During enemy operations in May and June, it was pointed out, "one of these attacks provided a significant and successful test of Vietnamese capability to defeat major North Vietnamese elements without U.S. ground support." The report concluded that examples such as this one, together with the increased aggressiveness of South Vietnamese troops, had "justified the risk in undertaking this program." Looking ahead, the ARVN now had the numbers, equipment, and training "to take over their own defense." As long as Saigon was assured of US assistance, "the people of Viet-Nam will be able to defend themselves until the other side finally agrees to a negotiated settlement or abandons the effort."[5]

Moreover, "while countering the enemy's offensives," Saigon was extending "its influence and services to the population." The pacification program was critical to long-term success. The Thieu government was aggressively working to build trust with the peasants, most notably by improving security in the villages through the creation of "a volunteer Peoples' Self-Defense Force" that numbered over three million by the end of the year. Due to this, NSSM 80 claimed that over 90 percent now "lived in relatively secure hamlets." This, in conjunction with ARVN improvement, was giving the people confidence in the future of South Vietnam. The positive changes in rural Vietnam in such a short period were remarkable, NSSM 80 concluded, and "there for all to see." Thieu was now "widely known and generally respected throughout the countryside," as security was bringing "a significant re-emergence of village life." The NLF was losing members, and refugees were returning to their villages. "Perhaps the best measure of this success is the fact that the VC [Viet Cong] are so concerned by the steady erosion of their population base that the pacification program itself is now a major target."[6]

A Vietnam Special Studies Group (VSSG) paper titled "The Situation in the Countryside" reached similar conclusions, and Henry Kissinger sent its analysis to the president, stating that it "accurately described" the conditions in rural South Vietnam. As the study noted, the war was a conflict for the control of the villages. The best measure of what the report termed "the control war" was the "level of combined political and military strength within the population that *when possessed by one side excludes effective strength by the other side.*" Employing this criteria, it was argued that prior to the 1968 Tet Offensive, the NLF had had the upper hand with control over 35 percent of the rural population; Saigon had had only 20 percent, and the remaining 45 percent had been contested by both sides. During the Tet Offensive, "GVN [government of South Vietnam] control fell by 5% and VC control rose by about 7%," although Saigon was able to gain some of that back by the end of the year. By September 1969, the VSSG stated, the situation had changed dramatically: Saigon now "controlled about 55% of the rural population," and the "VC controlled only 7%," leaving 38 percent of the villages still influenced by both sides.[7]

The most critical factors that caused this shift in the control war were the actions taken by the Saigon government. Prior to 1969, "it was *the vigorous offensive activity of U.S. forces more than ARVN forces which gave the Allies the upper hand in the main force war.*" In the wake of Tet, "it was principally U.S. units which applied relentless pressure on the enemy throughout the following year." This made gains possible, but it did not bring them about. Rather, "the principal proximate cause of the improved control situation in the past year was *the great shift in the relative strength and effectiveness of GVN and VC local security forces.*" As ARVN strength grew, "VC guerrilla strength fell by 40% and the infrastructure was also weakened." The enemy had *"lost the initiative in the control war to the GVN,"* and its effort to reverse this "trend through a new protracted war strategy" was failing. The "decisive factors in changing the control situation," the VSSG concluded, were the effectiveness of US main force units after Tet that provided the context for Saigon's increased effort and effectiveness in the face of a weakened enemy in rural Vietnam.[8]

In December 1969, North Vietnamese defense minister General Vo Nguyen Giap published a series of articles on the war's progress that prompted a great deal of analysis in the United States. Providing a summary of the commentary, Kissinger wrote Nixon that "Giap's article is [*sic*] probably the clearest evidence yet that the Communists no longer seriously believe they can win the war by direct military means against the present allied military lineup in South Vietnam, with its heavy complement of U.S. combat forces. This comes through in Giap's call for the development of an enemy force thoroughly capable of protracting the conflict, of playing for time, of holding ground, and, hopefully, of consolidating it until the day enough Americans are gone to allow a more even challenge of the GVN's armed forces."

In addition, Kissinger argued, Giap's call for a stronger effort in the countryside "would seem to be an implicit admission of the danger Hanoi sees in continued GVN expansion of its foothold in the rural area via the pacification and Vietnamization programs. Thus, Giap appears to be acknowledging the effectiveness of these programs so far." The national security advisor concluded that there would be no unanticipated change of communist tactics or offensive in 1970. Rather, the United States could expect "a continuation . . . of the Communist effort to test the success of Vietnamization" and a strategy of trying to wait for further American troop reductions.[9]

All the optimism included cautions, and there were indications of an enemy buildup in preparation for a winter-spring campaign. New forces were being sent to the South from the North, supplies were arriving in North Vietnam in larger quantities from the Soviet Union and China, improvements were being made to the transportation and distribution system along the Ho Chi Minh Trail, and NVA main force units were being repositioned and concentrated in areas of the South considered vulnerable. Overall, MACV reported, it had to be recognized that Hanoi "retains a significant capability for continued offensive action." Enemy forces, military commanders in Saigon agreed, had many options: continuing the war at the present level to inflict casualties and demonstrate that they could wage a protracted war to force an American withdrawal; launching limited offensives to increase Allied casualties in an effort to gain political concessions in Paris; attempting another Tet-size offensive to try to gain significant ground militarily and capture population centers; and reducing the level of the conflict to strengthen NLF forces. Abrams, less optimistic than the others, anticipated stepped-up fighting that sought to inflict maximum casualties and disrupt Vietnamization and Saigon's pacification efforts. The "primary obstacle" to the enemy's goal of overthrowing the Saigon government was still the "continued presence of large U.S. forces." Therefore, all military efforts were designed to hasten their removal.[10]

Continued improvement in the control war was reported from September, when the first VSSG analysis concluded, to the end of 1969, with Saigon now said to be in charge of over 61 percent of the population. Still, after a team visit to Vietnam in January, the VSSG found that the rate of increased rural security had slowed because "the enemy's effort and capabilities to counter pacification are increasing." While the achievements of 1969 were impressive, they stemmed mainly from a decline in NLF operations. "The odds," the VSSG concluded, "are at best about even that the GVN will survive and the GVN control in the countryside will be maintained or improved during the period of American troop withdrawal." In the coming year, however, it was "far more likely that the GVN will lose control than it is that they will significantly increase it." This was because "there is no sign that the enemy has given up." The VSSG team found that the NLF had adjusted its approach and, it appeared, was following *"a protracted war strategy with infrequent high points targeted on pacification and ARVN."* The enemy appeared willing to wait for further reductions of American forces so that it could then exploit the "many serious shortcomings" of the GVN: its lack of support among the peasants, corruption, and dependence upon the United States for "logistic, combat, and advisory support." This meant that as the United States withdrew more troops, *"we can expect to reach the point where control gains . . . will have to be sacrificed. In other words, the GVN cannot win the war militarily there in the near future."* [11]

Nonetheless, Nixon and Kissinger gave more credence to the optimistic analysis and could not understand why success on the battlefield was not yielding compromises in the negotiations in Paris or greater support at home. Concluding that Hanoi was employing a strategy of waiting the United States out, the president searched for a breakthrough that could bring victory in 1970. He ruled out any further American concessions as a sign of weakness that would play into the communists' hands. It was time for a hard line, he told Kissinger on January 14. Ruminating about the end of World War II, Nixon argued that the problem then had been that Stalin did not yield while the United States was trying to find a middle ground, and that had led to failure in Eastern Europe. The US negotiating position in Paris had to be "either they talk or we are going to sit it out. I don't feel this is any time for concession." If the North Vietnamese bring up points such as a coalition government, Kissinger should just "close the book and walk out." [12]

Kissinger concurred, noting that if Washington's analysis was "correct[,] they are in trouble." That did not mean they could not strike with force, "but that will be their last shot." "I agree," the president responded. "They may hit us but they haven't got a lot to hit us with. . . . They don't have the forces to mount any kind of sustained thing." Furthermore, Nixon said that he was "hearing some good reports about the South Vietnamese forces" and did not think they would be overrun in any attack. Given this, Kissinger said, the "smart thing" for the enemy "to do would be to wait until we draw down more forces and wait until next year. If they hit us this year it will mean our analysis is correct and they are losing." [13]

The Central Intelligence Agency's (CIA) assessment, titled "Vietnamization: Progress and Prospects," strengthened this understanding of the war. It concluded that "the real test of Vietnamization will probably not come until at least the end of 1970, by which time the Communists anticipate a substantial further reduction of US ground forces." This posed a significant problem for American policy as "it is clear that the ARVN, especially, still has a considerable way to go in developing both the technical skills and the will to fight necessary to cope with a threat of the magnitude currently posed by enemy forces." Despite "sound evidence that the territorial forces (regional and popular units) have greatly improved over the past year in all the standard indicators of efficiency . . . it must be recognized . . . that the improvement is based on a very poor performance base originally, and that further gains will come harder." Finally, while top ARVN commanders had expressed optimism the previous year on Vietnamization, a more recent "survey revealed a growing pessimism with concern centered around the fear of an overly hasty American withdrawal which would leave the ARVN badly vulnerable to renewed Communist main force pressures."[14]

Nixon and Kissinger concluded that Hanoi's waiting-out strategy meant it was important to take decisive action that year. Nixon dispatched Secretary of Defense Melvin Laird and Chairman of the Joint Chiefs of Staff Earle Wheeler to South Vietnam in February to assess the situation firsthand. Laird's report confirmed the belief that steady progress was being achieved in terms of Vietnamization and that the adroit use of American airpower had brought a decline in the enemy's force level. It was expected, the secretary of defense told the president, that the strength of both the NVA and NLF would "continue to decline" for the foreseeable future. This, combined with extensive air operations to disrupt Hanoi's logistics and supply systems, meant that MACV did not expect a major offensive that year. Most importantly, Laird stated that Vietnamization was working and had placed North Vietnam in a bind. In the American command's view, "the dilemma for Hanoi must be severe. If the enemy waits to test Vietnamization in the field, he stands to lose ground, both militarily and politically. If he tests Vietnamization in the foreseeable future, he stands to take massive military losses. The best the enemy can hope for, therefore, is some localized and short-term tactical military success."[15]

Still, there was need for caution. Laird praised the work of Ambassador Ellsworth Bunker and General Abrams but noted that "while the progress made in the military aspects of Vietnamization is impressive, the work remaining is of monumental proportions." This was "a reflection of the scope and depth not only of the communist threat but also of the US involvement over the past few years." Yet, Laird declared, the "trip confirmed for me again that we are pursuing a proper and valuable objective in pressing for self-determination in South Vietnam. The uniform view of the US civilian and military leaders in Vietnam and of the GVN leadership is that we are on a proper course towards that objective. The best characterization of the atmosphere among top US and GVN officials in South Vietnam is one of cautious optimism." It was clear that "we now have and can retain sufficient strength to keep the enemy from achieving any kind of military verdict in South Vietnam" and that Saigon was "making satisfactory progress in Vietnamization, especially on the military front."[16]

A special national intelligence estimate titled "Factors Affecting North Vietnam's Policy on the Vietnam War" reached a similar conclusion regarding Hanoi's military strategy and posited that the NVA would not launch any large-scale military operations. The enemy's course of action in 1970, therefore, would be "to pursue prolonged war tactics much along present lines. The North Vietnamese will continue to try to maintain sufficient military pressure to impose U.S. casualties, to inflict setbacks on Vietnamization and pacification and perhaps to engage in major tests of Vietnamization." The "Communists are in trouble in South Vietnam, and they recognize it themselves. They fear that they have overemphasized military action and neglected the political and subversive base. They are now making a great effort to restructure their apparatus in South Vietnam and enhance its staying power." At the same time, Hanoi was not ready to negotiate a settlement in Paris and was instead "counting on the odds swinging in its favor once the U.S. withdrawal has become militarily significant." Hanoi still believed it would "prevail over the South Vietnamese Government structure over the long run," but it "cannot be certain of this so long as U.S. forces are in the South." Vietnamization presented a challenge as it could mean "an indefinite American presence, and they thus see themselves faced for the first time with an allied strategy designed to challenge their fundamental assumption." Thus, enemy actions would be geared to attacking the pacification program and disrupting Vietnamization.[17]

Kissinger, following Laird's and Saigon's analysis, told Nixon that he found the National Intelligence Estimate "valid" but that it "glosses over . . . the real dilemmas which Hanoi currently faces." If the enemy did set out to "challenge the pacification program it must commit its main force units which it has been holding in the base areas along the Cambodian and Laotian borders; however, these units when committed run the risk of heavy losses and military defeat." Yet it must act, because holding back would only allow further gains by Saigon in the control war as enemy "infrastructure in the countryside continues to suffer under the pacification program." In other words, delay just made the military situation worse in the South, "always the key element in Hanoi's calculations. Meanwhile, by stalling on the negotiations, Hanoi permits the U.S. to carry out Vietnamization at its own pace." This meant that the pressure was building in the North "for some movement" in Paris.[18]

Kissinger intended to find out if there was the possibility of progress in Paris at his upcoming secret meetings with Le Duc Tho and Xuan Thuy. After two meetings over the next month, the national security advisor reported to the president that there were finally some indications of change from the North Vietnamese. It was still too early to know if this meant Hanoi was moving toward a negotiated settlement or was merely delaying to "reduce our military pressure so they can continue the conflict at length." Still, Kissinger found Hanoi's concessions to be "very real." Its negotiators were willing to engage in secret talks without pre-conditions, "scrapped the ten points" as the only basis for talking, "abandoned their refusal to discuss their own withdrawal . . . [and] agreed to discuss our proposals as well as theirs." The last point was most important, the "one issue to which all others are subordinate—*reciprocity* in the withdrawal of non–South Vietnamese troops from South Vietnam (and foreign troops from Laos and Cambodia)." The primary US objective was to reach an agreement on that point. If it did, that meant the North would have "given up their claim of moral superiority" or that its forces participated in the war "on a different moral and legal basis than ours. This would be a quantum jump in the negotiations."[19]

Nixon, however, did not believe he could wait for Hanoi to change its position on troop withdrawals, and developments in Vietnam and Cambodia were pushing him toward another escalation of the war. On March 18, Lon Nol, Sirik Matak, and the Cambodian army overthrew Prince Norodom Sihanouk. Washington welcomed the change of power in Phnom Penh. Kissinger wrote Nixon that Lon Nol saw the presence of North Vietnamese forces in Cambodia as a threat that he wanted to address and that "this will create serious problems for the VC/NVA, which will have considerable reason to take a more hostile line toward Cambodia." Nixon immediately noted that he wanted the CIA to "implement a plan for maximum assistance to pro-U.S. elements in Cambodia."[20] The proposed CIA actions were delivered to the president on March 23. The main component was to covertly "work to support and sustain the present Cambodian Government by supporting its military effort against the Viet Cong in Cambodia and shoring up its position by the provision of covert economic and political support" against the anticipated effort by North Vietnam to unseat the new regime.[21] Nixon approved the plan. He also ordered that the "Menu operations continued at a high level," that plans for joint American–South Vietnamese attacks on the sanctuaries be developed by MACV, and that the administration "dust off the seven-day plan for attacks in North Vietnam."[22] The latter referred to the escalation options in Operation Duck Hook.

For the next month, military operations were developed to ensure the survival of the Lon Nol regime. Kissinger, the Joint Chiefs of Staff, and American leaders in Saigon all supported the continuation of the Menu bombings and an attack on the sanctuaries as the centerpieces of this effort. Ambassador Bunker and General Abrams termed the B-52 strikes "one of the most telling operations in the entire war." While they came with some political risk, the Joint Chiefs concluded that in balance the "value remains . . . in our favor" because the bombings "produced extensive damage to enemy facilities and losses of enemy troops and materials," reduced the level of combat activity, had "a direct bearing on the success of Vietnamization," and "may have played a significant role in the recent political changes in Cambodia."[23] Bunker and Abrams believed that planning for cross-border operations would "signal to the enemy that we are not prepared to stand idle if they pursue a policy of military or insurrectionary pressure against the Lon Nol government"; it would also demonstrate faith in Saigon and "give encouragement to the Lon Nol government at a time when they are most in need of it."[24] Furthermore, Kissinger informed Nixon that it was the consensus of senior officials in the administration and the Pentagon that the communist forces in Cambodia would be able to defeat Lon Nol's government should Hanoi decide to attack and that such action was considered likely because "Hanoi cannot tolerate the loss of its Cambodian sanctuaries, and must do something to remove the Lon Nol government or force a change in Phnom Penh's policies."[25]

As the situation in Cambodia continued to deteriorate, Nixon delivered a planned address to the nation on April 20 to announce a further reduction of 150,000 American forces by the spring of 1971. Although the president did not tell the public, the bulk of these troops would be removed in early 1971. Nixon's decision and the size of the reduction, despite opposition from the military and Kissinger, was in keeping with his efforts to stay ahead of domestic opposition to continue to buy time to prosecute the war.[26] Prior to his speech, Nixon met with Admiral John McCain and Kissinger to discuss developments in Cambodia and potential South Vietnamese and US military action against NVA sanctuaries. McCain told Wheeler that Nixon emphasized "the need for speed in view of the 'precarious situation' in Cambodia." Nixon told Kissinger that "Cambodia is important and we will have to do it fast. I need to know how soon the [South Vietnamese] can get going over there." Kissinger concurred that "the United States could not stand by and watch Cambodia collapse and ultimately cause the collapse of the U.S. effort in Vietnam."[27]

The April 20 speech was an odd mix of optimistic analysis of the situation in Vietnam combined with threats against the enemy. Nixon declared that he was able to announce the significant drawdown of forces because of the success being achieved in training the South Vietnamese army, the reductions in enemy forces, and the progress in pacification in the countryside of South Vietnam. Yet he acknowledged recent enemy buildups and activity in Cambodia and that his decision "clearly involves risks." He repeated the warning he had delivered in his "Silent Majority" speech that should Hanoi use the American action as an opportunity to escalate the war, he would not "hesitate to take strong and effective measures to deal with that situation." Still, the president said his decision to withdraw more forces meant that "we finally have in sight the just peace we are seeking. We can now say with confidence that pacification is succeeding," as was Vietnamization. The enemy had failed to win in Vietnam because they had misjudged America and "thought they could win politically in the United States. This proved to be their most fatal miscalculation." Washington, he stated, had proven its resolve and fidelity to history. "America has never been defeated in the proud 190-year history of this country," Nixon concluded, "and we shall not be defeated in Vietnam."[28]

The president's decisions over the next week and half reflected the fundamental contradiction between the speech and his policy. Although he was announcing de-escalation, he was planning to expand the war into Cambodia despite knowing that doing so would provoke intense criticism at home, raise questions about the sincerity of his administration's peace efforts in Paris, and challenge its credibility concerning the achievements in South Vietnam. Two days later, after receiving an intelligence report suggesting "that the enemy [was] moving to isolate Phnom Penh" in order to "bring military pressure on it from all sides, and perhaps, ultimately, to bring Sihanouk back," he authorized the final planning that led to the invasion of Cambodia.[29]

Nixon wanted decisive action and cast his support for the new government in Phnom Penh in Cold War terms. "I think we need a bold move in Cambodia," he wrote Kissinger on April 22, "to show that we stand with Lon Nol. I do not believe he is going to survive. There is, however, some chance that he might and in any event we must do something symbolic to help him survive." The United States had been "taken in with the line" that by aiding Phnom Penh "we would destroy [Cambodia's] neutrality" and give Hanoi an excuse to intervene. "Over and over again we fail to learn that the Communists never need an excuse to come in," as demonstrated by Hungary in 1956 and Czechoslovakia in 1968. He continued by stating that the North Vietnamese "are romping in there and the only government in Cambodia in the last 25 years that had the guts to take a pro-Western and pro-American stand is ready to fall." He also instructed Kissinger that day to contact the Soviets and give them "a flat warning that in the event the Communists do move on Phnom Penh we shall react," as the fate of Cambodia "involves our interests in Vietnam and . . . we shall not stand by."[30]

Kissinger set out for Nixon what he saw as the numerous and dire consequences if Cambodia fell to the communists. It would lead to "a profound psychological shock in South Vietnam" as it became "completely surrounded by hostile territory." North Vietnam's military capabilities would improve as its operations from Cambodia would become overt and larger, and it would have the ability to recruit new units of ethnic Vietnamese who lived in Cambodia, along with guaranteeing consistent supplies of food and military equipment to the NLF from secure territory. Moreover, "Vietnamization would be impossible to carry out" if Cambodia was lost, as South Vietnam "could not preserve itself against pressure from all sides without a very large continuing presence of U.S. forces." Finally, American credibility would be shattered because "in the rest of Asia, there would be a feeling that Communism was on the march and we were powerless to stop it."[31]

To address the crises, the president was advised that the United States was continuing the B-52 bombings on a weekly basis, providing covert shipments of arms and money to Lon Nol's government, and supporting the ARVN's "shallow" operations along the South Vietnam–Cambodian border designed to "harass the enemy and tie down some of his forces" but "insufficient to limit his offensive operation in Cambodia." The military was also developing plans for either "deeper penetrations" that would extend the area ARVN forces could advance up to ten miles into Cambodia. US artillery and airpower would back the operation in order to disrupt "enemy logistical support and [sow] confusion which would take some pressure off Cambodia." The final option was "massive operations" that combined air, artillery, and divisional-size units of American and South Vietnamese forces "seeking to permanently deny the sanctuaries to the enemy."[32]

Clouding the picture was uncertainty about how the American public would respond to an overt military operation in Cambodia. This led to a debate over whether the cross-border attack should be limited to the current bombing and shallow probes, as supported by Laird and Secretary of State William Rogers, who both worried primarily about domestic reaction, should entail a "deeper penetration" attack using only ARVN forces, with the United States providing tactical support but no troops, the option Kissinger favored, or should involve a large-scale joint American–South Vietnamese attack, which the military sought. On April 22, the president approved Kissinger's middle option but left room for a change prior to issuing a final order.[33] H. R. "Bob" Haldeman noted that Nixon and Kissinger still believed the United States could win the war "this year, if we keep enough pressure on, and don't crumble at home."[34]

At a follow-up meeting two days later, Nixon excluded Laird and Rogers due to their opposition to US participation in a cross-border operation. The president wanted to discuss the "feasibility of a combined U.S.-ARVN attack against the Fishhook sanctuary to complement the South Vietnamese attack on the Parrot's Beak" area of Cambodia. The Joint Chiefs and the CIA both strongly supported this option, and Kissinger instructed Abrams after the meeting to begin to "act on the assumption that the operation might be ordered." Wheeler also told Abrams to prepare for an attack on Cambodia. The president, Wheeler stated, was worried he would be criticized in the same manner that President John F. Kennedy had been in the wake of the Bay of Pigs if the attack on Cambodia failed. Nixon therefore wanted his military commanders to "have an aggressive frame of mind and a determination to achieve success."[35] Later that day, Nixon told Kissinger on the phone that he had to "seize the opportunity" to deliver a decisive blow, noting that "on November 3, [1969,] we said all that and didn't do anything. This time they won't be expecting [it]."[36]

By Sunday, April 26, the president had decided on the military's "massive operations" option. A meeting was held that night to discuss planning in order to provide the appearance that the president was still listening to options and providing everyone with an opportunity to express his or her view. To Nixon's and Kissinger's surprise, Laird and Rogers "fell in with the charade [that] it was all a planning exercise and did not take a position."[37] Immediately afterward, the president and national security advisor drafted National Security Decision Memorandum 57, authorizing "the conduct of ground operations by U.S. forces or by US/GVN forces into identified North Vietnamese/Viet Cong sanctuaries in Cambodia up to a depth of 30 kilometers," along with American tactical air, helicopter, and artillery support.[38]

Laird and Rogers did not remain complacent once they realized a decision had already been reached. In a meeting they requested the next day, the secretaries of defense and state made clear their resentment that the decision was made without full consultation, and they thought it would come at a great cost to the United States without much gain. Nixon agreed to suspend the order for a day to allow Rogers to testify in the Senate that afternoon that no US troops were being sent into Cambodia. He also wanted Abrams and Bunker to provide their input on the decision. Once that was received, the president said, they would meet again, and he would let them know his decision. In a last-ditch effort to change the president's mind, Laird sent a detailed memo after the meeting to Nixon setting out his concerns.[39]

At the meeting in the Oval Office on the morning of April 28, Nixon set out his decision without any further discussion. He acknowledged the opposition of the secretaries of defense and state to the employment of US troops in Cambodia but noted that the Saigon embassy, MACV, CIA, and Joint Chiefs of Staff all supported a joint US-South Vietnamese operation. The president therefore reaffirmed his earlier decision to authorize the cross-border attacks by ARVN and American forces because it "was necessary in order to sustain the continuation of the Vietnamization Program" and could help with the negotiations in Paris. Nixon stated that he had also "taken into consideration . . . the probable adverse reaction in some Congressional circles and some segments of the public."[40] Admiral Thomas Moorer, acting chair of the Joint Chiefs of Staff, instructed Abrams that it was President Nixon's desire that he "employ maximum feasible military strength against the remaining base areas in Cambodia which you consider important to enemy operations" and that these operations "be carried out through a bold and aggressive approach" in order to "hit the enemy the hardest blow possible and destroy as much of the enemy's base areas" as can be done in the next thirty days. This was the "number one priority" of all military operations.[41]

Nixon had told Kissinger prior to the meeting that he knew they would "take heat" but that "you take the heat if you don't do anything. . . . If we lose the whole thing, what will they say?" They will say that "Vietnamization is a failure," Kissinger said. "We are not going to lose that way," the president replied.[42] In line with the president's argument, Kissinger recommended changes to the president's upcoming speech to make the point on Vietnamization more explicit. He inserted new language in order "to reconcile our statements that Vietnamization is making encouraging progress with our view that recent Cambodian events threaten the program."[43]

Speaking to the nation only ten days after he had outlined his plan to withdraw 150,000 Americans from Vietnam in the next year, Nixon announced on Thursday, April 30, his decision to escalate the war by sending American and South Vietnamese forces into Cambodia "to clean out major enemy sanctuaries on the Cambodian-Vietnam border." He stated that he was backing up his earlier warning from April 20 that he "would not hesitate to take strong and effective measures" if there was increased enemy activity. The incursion into Cambodia, as he termed it, was being undertaken "to protect our men who are in Vietnam and to guarantee the continued success of our withdrawal and Vietnamization programs." After consultation with senior military and civilian advisors, the president "concluded that the time has come for action." In the last ten days, enemy operations clearly endangered "the lives of Americans who are in Vietnam now and would constitute an unacceptable risk to those who will be there after withdrawal of another 150,000."[44]

The president disingenuously claimed that since the 1954 Geneva Accords, "American policy . . . has been to scrupulously respect the neutrality of the Cambodia people." In contrast, North Vietnam had established sanctuaries in Cambodia along its border with South Vietnam, and "they are used for hit-and-run attacks on American and South Vietnamese forces." Nixon described these sanctuaries as containing "major base camps, training sites, logistics facilities, weapons and ammunition factories, airstrips, and prisoner-of-war compounds." Continuing to dissemble with the public, the president declared that the United States and South Vietnam had not previously "moved against these enemy sanctuaries because we did not want to violate the territory of a neutral nation." Now, with enemy forces concentrating in the area for a massive offensive, and with North Vietnamese troops moving deeper into Cambodia and threatening Phnom Penh, the president was responding to a Cambodian request for assistance.[45]

Confronted with this crisis, Nixon claimed he had no choice but "to go to the heart of the trouble. That means cleaning out major North Vietnamese and Vietcong occupied territories." As part of the operation, allied forces, Nixon declared, "will attack the headquarters for the entire Communist military operation in South Vietnam." This was not, the president insisted, anticipating the criticism to come of his decision, "an invasion of Cambodia." The territory to be attacked was "completely occupied" by enemy forces, and once they were driven out, the United States would withdraw back to South Vietnam. "We take this action," Nixon claimed, "not for the purpose of expanding the war into Cambodia but for the purpose of ending the war in Vietnam and winning the just peace we all desire." The operation would hasten that goal. At the same time, it would serve as a warning to Hanoi not to escalate the fighting because the United States "will not be humiliated. We will not be defeated. We will not allow American men by the thousands to be killed by an enemy from privileged sanctuaries." If he permitted this, the president stated, "the credibility of the United States would be destroyed in every area of the world where only the power of the United States deters aggression." [46]

The president cast his decision in historic terms. Recalling his coda to the "Silent Majority" speech, Nixon warned, "My fellow Americans, we live in an age of anarchy, both abroad and at home. We see mindless attacks on all the great institutions which have been created by free civilizations in the last 500 years. Even here in the United States, great universities are being systematically destroyed. Small nations all over the world find themselves under attack from within and from without." Action was imperative, he believed. "If, when the chips are down, the world's most powerful nation, the United States of America, acts like a pitiful, helpless giant, the forces of totalitarianism and anarchy will threaten free nations and free institutions throughout the world." [47] Nixon continued,

> It is not our power but our will and character that is being tested tonight. The question all Americans must ask and answer tonight is this: Does the richest and strongest nation in the history of the world have the character to meet a direct challenge by a group which rejects every effort to win a just peace, ignores our warning, tramples on solemn agreements, violates the neutrality of an unarmed people, and uses our prisoners as hostages? If we fail to meet this challenge, all other nations will be on notice that despite its overwhelming power the United States, when a real crisis comes, will be found wanting.

Only through a bold act could he honor the pledge he had made to end the war and win a just peace. [48]

Nixon placed his decision on par with other great decisions reached in the Oval Office of the White House to deter aggression and end wars. "In this room," Nixon instructed the public, "Woodrow Wilson made the great decisions which led to victory in World War I. Franklin Roosevelt made the decisions which led to our victory in World War II. Dwight D. Eisenhower made decisions which ended the war in Korea and avoided war in the Middle East. John F. Kennedy, in his finest hour, made the great decision which removed Soviet nuclear missiles from Cuba and the Western Hemisphere." [49]

Nixon realized his decision would be divisive and that he would be criticized from many sides. But, he said, he rejected the popular and easy path of unilateral withdrawal for the reasons he had outlined and because it would reward aggression. "I know that a peace of humiliation for the United States would lead to a bigger war or surrender later." If this made him a one-term president, he was prepared to pay that price as it was "insignificant compared to whether by our failure to act in this crisis the United States proves itself to be unworthy to lead the forces of freedom in this critical period in world history. I would rather be a one-term President and do what I believe is right than to be a two-term President at the cost of seeing America become a second-rate power and to see this Nation accept the first defeat in its proud 190-year history." Too much was at stake, Nixon claimed, for him to abandon his effort "of winning a just peace in Vietnam and in the Pacific." He therefore asked for "support for our brave men fighting tonight halfway around the world—not for territory—not for glory—but so that their younger brothers and their sons and your sons can have a chance to grow up in a world of peace and freedom and justice." [50]

Nixon's argument was firmly rooted in Cold War assumptions, fears, and ideology as he sought to rally support for his decision. This line of thinking, which had been used so effectively in the 1960s to justify American intervention in Vietnam, no longer held the same sway in 1970. The bipartisan consensus on containment had been shattered in 1968, and the president's use of this rhetoric in a speech to a public disillusioned with the war only served to anger his political opponents as much as his decision to invade Cambodia.

The negative reaction was immediate and more extensive than the administration had feared. For many, as Tom Wicker wrote in the *New York Times*, it confirmed that Nixon "does not have and never has had a 'plan to end the war.'" Instead, he had expanded it to another country and appeared determined to fight for a military victory. [51] On Friday, May 1, protests erupted on college campuses across the nation as students expressed their opposition to a wider war. The White House claimed that calls and telegrams regarding the president's speech were running six to one favorable, but the administration's actions indicated great concern. Visiting the Pentagon for a military briefing, Nixon stopped to talk with civilian employees and compared American troops and college students. As reported in the *New York Times*, he called the soldiers in Vietnam "the greatest." "They stand tall and they are proud." In contrast, "you see these bums, you know, blowing up the campuses." They are fortunate to be in college, but "here they are burning up the books, storming around about this issue. You name it. Get rid of the war, there will be another one." [52]

On the following Monday, May 4, the demonstrations at Kent State University devolved into tragedy as four students were killed and eleven others wounded by the Ohio National Guard, which had been brought onto campus after a weekend of unrest. That afternoon, Nixon told Kissinger on the phone about the killings, noting that Kent State "had been bad for quite some time—it has been rather violent." Kissinger worried that the administration would be blamed for the event and that thirty-three university presidents were calling for an American withdrawal from Vietnam. The president feared student strikes because "out of classes they'll be able to raise hell." Kissinger opined that the "university presidents are a disgrace," whereas Nixon was concerned with all the bad publicity their statements brought. He told Kissinger, "We have to stand hard as a rock. . . . If countries begin to be run by children, God help us."[53] Publicly, the administration placed the blame for the deaths squarely on the students. Press secretary Ronald Ziegler read a statement on behalf of the president that the shootings at Kent State "should remind us all once again that when dissent turns to violence, it invites tragedy." Nixon hoped it would serve to bring administrators, faculty, and students "to stand firmly for the right which exists in this country for peaceful dissent and just as strongly against the resort to violence as a means of such expression."[54]

In the wake of the Kent State shootings, demonstrations and student strikes spread, leading to the shutdown of approximately five hundred colleges and universities and to protests on the weekend of May 8 to 10 in Washington, DC. Rogers stated, "These student protests are greater than any of us anticipated." The growing unrest had, according to Haldeman, a "profound impact" on the administration, which took numerous steps to try to diffuse the building tension. Kissinger met on May 6 with students and faculty from Stanford, and subsequently with nine other student groups during the month, to discuss US policy in Vietnam. Nixon also met with students from Kent State on May 6 and with eight university presidents the following day.[55] Nixon asked the college leaders what the government should be doing about campus unrest. He realized that the Cambodian announcement had sparked turmoil but defended his decision. He stated that "he was not asking the support of the college presidents for his action in Cambodia, an action that he had to take, ironically, for the very reason that the demonstrations" were being held—to bring peace to Vietnam. Toward that end, he said "that when the Cambodian action is completed in early June, he will have bought at least ten months more time. Our actions in Cambodia avoid either complete capitulation on the one hand or leaving our forces indefensible on the other." Nixon insisted that he had no intention "to fight in Cambodia or Laos, and that this summer should well bring the best news out of the Viet Nam war."[56]

In response to his meetings, Nixon ordered a Justice Department inquiry and a staff report on Kent State and how to avoid future tragedies; he also announced that he was naming G. Alexander Heard, chancellor of

Vanderbilt University, as a special adviser for the next two months to assist the administration in understanding the issues on campuses. He noted the concerns that many had over the current turmoil and stated that it was "a time for communication rather than violence and above all for mutual understanding."[57]

On the night of Friday, May 8, the president held a news conference to answer questions about Cambodia and campus unrest. Nixon made it clear that while he understood the protestors wanted peace, he would not allow their actions to change how he went about achieving their shared goal. He would not withdraw precipitously, as that would "allow the enemy to come into Vietnam and massacre the civilians there by the millions, as they would." Furthermore, "if we do that, let me say that America is finished insofar as the peacekeeper in the Asian world is concerned." Regarding his use of the term "bums," the president did not back down. Nixon stated that it was not meant to apply to those who engaged in legitimate protest. But when "students on university campuses burn buildings, when they engage in violence, when they break up furniture, when they terrorize their fellow students and terrorize the faculty, then I think 'bums' is perhaps too kind a word to apply."[58]

Early the next morning, Nixon surprised demonstrators by making an early-morning visit to the Lincoln Memorial with his valet, Manuel Sanchez. Most of the discussion was a rambling discourse by the president about travel, foreign nations, and different people, but Nixon did briefly address the war in Vietnam. He repeated to the students what he had said the night before, that he shared their desire for peace and that his "goal was not to get into Cambodia . . . but to get out of Vietnam." He did not want "their hatred of the war" to turn into "a bitter hatred of our whole system, our country and everything that it stood for." Nixon said he knew most of them "think I'm an S.O.B., but I want you to know I understand just how you feel." When young, he had thought Neville Chamberlain was great man for keeping the peace and that Winston Churchill "was a madman." He was wrong then, of course, and it was an important lesson to remember.[59]

An even greater challenge to the administration's policy emerged in the Senate. On May 1, Senator Frank Church (D-ID) declared that it was time for the Nixon administration to "acknowledge the futility of our continued military intervention in Vietnam" and admit "the impossibility of sustaining at any acceptable cost an anticommunist regime in Saigon, allied with, dependent on, and supported by the United States." It was, the senator concluded, "war without end." Moreover, Church stated that it was time "for Congress to draw the line against an expanded American involvement in this widening war" and to begin "to put an end to it."[60] He, along with Senator John Sherman Cooper (R-KY), introduced the Cooper-Church Amendment to restrict American military operations in Cambodia by mandating the removal of all American troops from Cambodia by June 30 and requiring explicit Senate approval to use any American forces in Cambodia in the future. It was designed to force a true de-escalation of the fighting by reversing Nixon's policy in Cambodia and limiting the president's ability to escalate the fighting and expand the war. At the same time, Senators George McGovern (D-SD) and Mark Hatfield (R-OR) introduced an "end the war" amendment calling for the removal of all American troops from Vietnam by the end of 1970.

While the Nixon administration adamantly opposed both congressional measures, it did not believe the McGovern-Hatfield Amendment would pass. It therefore mounted its attack against Cooper-Church because Nixon and Kissinger feared both the immediate implications of the restrictions on their actions in Cambodia and that it would, as Kissinger wrote to Nixon, present "an unnecessary restriction on your Constitutional authority as Commander-in-Chief."[61] It was the position of the administration that Congress only had the authority to limit the civilian acts of the president. Constitutionally, Kissinger wrote to Nixon in preparation for meetings on May 4 with members of Congress, the operation in Cambodia was not a new war but rather a response to the needs of the current war in Vietnam. Therefore, "the action in Cambodia should not be viewed as an independent use of the U.S. armed forces involved in the general question of the President's responsibility to Congress under the power to 'declare war.' It should be defended as a Presidential action under his Constitutional authority to take all reasonable action to protect our troops which were already committed in a conflict long under way when this Administration took office and to bring about the withdrawal under circumstances contributing to a durable peace." With regard to the Cooper-Church Amendment, "only the President is constitutionally empowered to deploy American forces in the field on the basis of his evaluation of military necessities." Regarding the critics' claim that the United States had violated another country's neutrality, Kissinger wrote, the legal "basis under international law for the present actions on Cambodian territory by the armed forces of the United States and South Vietnam is the right of collective self-defense against an armed attack recognized in Article 51 of the United Nations Charter."[62]

Furthermore, the White House worried that the passage of Cooper-Church would make it appear that the removal of American troops from Cambodia resulted from the Senate's forcing the president to act. The administration claimed that the amendment would tie the hands of the commander in chief at a time when American troops were under fire, thereby endangering the lives of American soldiers. Haldeman noted that the administration's strategy was to "attack Senate doves—for knife-in-the-back disloyalty—lack of patriotism."[63] Speaking on Cambodia, the president claimed the incursion was a great success, as it had bought important time for Vietnamization to move forward with the training of ARVN forces and saved thousands of American lives.[64] On May 14, Kissinger, Laird, and Undersecretary of State Elliot Richardson all lobbied senators to reject the Cooper-Church Amendment. Kissinger argued that it would signal a lack of confidence in the president, critically impair Nixon's ability to effectively secure a just peace, and damage relations with the nation's allies, who would see this action as a sign that America's assurances could not be trusted.[65]

These efforts were coordinated with Republican and Democratic senators who supported the war. They offered a series of proposals and objections ranging from the claim that the amendment would place American forces under the command of Congress to assertions that it crippled the military's effectiveness in the field, undercut the president's negotiating options, and harmed the policy of Vietnamization. The most significant challenge came in the form of Robert Byrd's (D-WV) amendment, which would allow the president to ignore the restrictions imposed by Cooper-Church if necessary to protect the lives of American forces in Vietnam.[66]

In the face of the likely passage of the Cooper-Church Amendment and the growing protests against his policy, Nixon began to remove American force from Cambodia, announcing that they would all be removed by June 30, thereby rendering the amendment moot. However, Nixon was determined to portray the Cambodian incursion as a tremendous success. A talking paper for a White House strategy session emphasized that "we must sell strongly the success of the operation—not the defensive line that 'we'll be out by June 30.'" It was necessary to attack the opposition and hit Cooper-Church hard. "We've got to pull out all the stops on this," as the administration could not allow the Senate to "get credit" for the removal of American forces.[67]

On June 3, Nixon proclaimed that the Cambodian invasion was "the most successful operation of this long and very difficult war." The joint US-ARVN forces "have captured and destroyed far more in war material than we anticipated; and American and allied casualties have been far lower than we expected." In the process, the incursion had "eliminated an immediate danger to the security of remaining Americans in Vietnam," "won some precious time for the South Vietnamese to train and prepare themselves to carry the burden of their national defense," and ensured the continued withdrawal of American forces.[68]

For its supporters, Cooper-Church was still necessary regardless of whether Nixon withdrew all troops by June 30. The amendment, Church stated on the day of the president's announcement, was the first step to extricating the United States from Vietnam by "setting the outer limits . . . to American involvement" and to demonstrating the extent of congressional opposition to the continuation of the war.[69] On June 30, after seven weeks of debate and the defeat of all of the administration-sponsored amendments, the Senate passed Cooper-Church by a vote of 58–37. Although the House of Representatives did not approve a modified version of the amendment until December, the Senate's passage of the Cooper-

Church Amendment marked a milestone. It was the first time Congress had restricted the deployment of troops during a war and voted in opposition to a president's policy on Vietnam. When asked the next day about his reaction to Cooper-Church, the president said that he, not the senators, held the responsibility for the 440,000 men in Vietnam and that he intended to do whatever was necessary to protect them. Other than that, he would wait to see what happened when the House acted. He believed the joint action of the House and Senate would "be more responsible" as he hoped the House would modify the restraints to allow the loophole proposed in the Byrd amendment.[70]

Despite the passage of Cooper-Church, the administration continued to see the Cambodian operation as a triumph. Kissinger, in a note to the president concerning an upcoming meeting with military leaders, stated that "we have already paid the price domestically . . . for the decision to attack the sanctuaries." It was crucial that the United States "inflict maximum damage on the enemy" prior to June 30 as it must be remembered "that the wisdom of the decision to strike Cambodia will be judged not in terms of the immediate problems it has generated in the U.S. but rather in terms of the overall long-term success it achieves."[71] A key element of that long-term success, for the administration, was the belief that the Cambodian operation would demonstrate the validity of the madman theory and force changes in Hanoi's negotiating position. In an evaluation of the incursion, Deputy National Security Advisor Alexander Haig wrote Kissinger that its dual purpose had to be kept in mind. "The operations were not undertaken merely to inflict logistical punishment but, more fundamentally, to signal to Hanoi that their expansion of the conflict in the face of the President's repeated warnings could not be tolerated and that our leadership is willing to move decisively when blatantly challenged."[72]

Deputy Assistant to the President Richard Kennedy reiterated this point in a three-week report titled "Allied Operations against Communist Bases in Cambodia." He stated that the United States had attacked the sanctuaries to "assure continued progress in our Vietnamization program" and to shorten the war by making it clear "to the enemy that they cannot repeatedly ignore our warnings and escalate their attacks in Indochina as they have in Laos, Cambodia, and within Vietnam." The United States, Kennedy wrote in summary, had "struck hard at the enemy's offensive capability. We have reduced the capability of his main force units to threaten our forces in Vietnam. We have limited his ability to interfere with the progress of pacification in South Vietnam. And we have seen a tremendous boost in the morale and confidence of the South Vietnamese armed forces." Thus, the president had taken big strides toward his goals of achieving peace with honor and upholding American credibility. The Cambodian operation would "hasten the day when all American forces can safely return home" and made it "clear to all adversaries that the US will not hesitate to take firm action when its interests are at stake."[73]

Kissinger shared Kennedy's understanding and believed that the Cambodian operation was placing increased pressure on Hanoi. In a memorandum to the president, he stated that North Vietnam "cannot now be certain what the U.S. will do under any given set of circumstances. They had not expected our move into Cambodia." This was compounded by the military setback the enemy had suffered, having "lost a huge quantity of stores and valuable base areas. The loss will require considerable time to make up." As a result, and in conjunction with Hanoi's loss of control of the strategic border area known as the Parrot's Beak, "Communist operations against South Vietnam will be much restricted. They are faced with an extension of the war at a time when they were already under pressure."[74]

On the other hand, Kissinger recognized that the operation had not completely eliminated the threat posed by North Vietnam. "The North Vietnamese still retain considerable assets," including "the best army and the best political organization in Southeast Asia." Hanoi also believed "that recent demonstrations in the U.S. have placed some limits on our freedom of maneuver and that we may therefore not be able to react quite as firmly again." Finally, "the Cambodian government is still very weak and the GVN is beset with severe political and economic difficulties." Overall, however, Kissinger thought that the developments in Cambodia "have probably complicated the options for Hanoi and compelled it to face some difficult decisions. It remains to be seen, perhaps in a month or two, what the leadership will decide to do."[75]

As the deadline for the removal of US troops approached, the Nixon administration encouraged South Vietnamese forces to continue operations in Cambodia, noting that the "restrictions which apply to U.S. forces after June 30 do not . . . apply to SVN [South Vietnamese] forces."[76] Kissinger asked the president "to support continued ARVN operations: to continue clearing out the base areas; to prevent re-establishment of the base areas; and to deter broader enemy attacks against Phnom Penh or Cambodia's southern ports."[77] The national security advisor believed this was necessary "to take advantage of the success of our Cambodian operations to keep the enemy's bases and logistic routes disrupted, and to attack his units in South Vietnam. We have authorized tactical air in Cambodia, are using it importantly in Laos and may provide some support to ARVN operations in Cambodia. Moreover, we should not decrease air activity in a way which could have the effect of lessening Hanoi's incentive to negotiate." Therefore, "ARVN operations should continue in order to take advantage of the gains made in our sanctuary operations and to prevent the enemy from reestablishing his base areas and logistics and communications routes, which could threaten our forces and impede Vietnamization."[78]

Nixon provided a triumphant report on Cambodia to the nation on June 30. It began by declaring, "The Armed Forces of the United States have just completed successfully the destruction of enemy base areas along the Cambodian–South Vietnam frontier," and assured the public that the operation would save American lives, ensure the progress of Vietnamization, and "enhance the prospects for a just peace." The document reviewed the president's prior efforts to negotiate a peace agreement, the implementation of Vietnamization and the beginning of the removal of American troops, and the reasons for the Cambodian operation before providing an extensive list of the perceived military achievements, similar to those enumerated in his June 3 interim report. Looking forward, it stated that South Vietnam was prepared to make sure that the enemy did not reestablish its bases in Cambodia and that the United States would continue to provide aid to Cambodia so that it could defend itself from North Vietnam. Most importantly, the report concluded, the operation should have demonstrated to Hanoi that it was time to negotiate. "In Cambodia, the futility of expanded aggression has been demonstrated." The enemy "cannot impose its will through military means." It was time for North Vietnam to realize the failure of its war in the South and to reach a negotiated peace that allowed the people of South Vietnam "the opportunity to shape their own future." [79]

The next night, the president appeared on television for an interview with the three major television networks. Asked for his justification for continuing to fight in Vietnam, Nixon reiterated statements he had made many times before. He sought a "just peace" in Vietnam, which meant the preservation of the Saigon government and "the right of the people of South Vietnam to determine their own future without having us impose our will upon them, or the North Vietnamese." He speculated that some might say that saving South Vietnam from a communist takeover was not worth the cost and that the United States could withdraw immediately and achieve peace, but that course of action would have "a catastrophic effect on this country and the cause of peace in the years ahead." Those who said the domino theory was obsolete, Nixon opined, had not "talked to the dominoes." A humiliating American retreat would discourage free Asia and "be ominously encouraging to the leaders of Communist China and the Soviet Union who are supporting the North Vietnamese. It will encourage them in their expansionist policies in other areas." If there were elections, however, the president was confident that the communists would lose because the people of South Vietnam were aware of the bloodbath that would result if a communist government came to power. [80]

When asked why he would not set a timetable for the withdrawal of American troops and why he thought Hanoi would now negotiate, a claim made many times before, Nixon stated that "one of the positive benefits of the Cambodian operation is that it has changed the military balance." Only time would tell if it was enough. But if the enemy knew ahead of time when the United States was leaving Vietnam, it would have no reason to negotiate. On the other hand, if the "enemy feels that we are going to stay there long enough for the South Vietnamese to be strong enough to handle their own defense, then I think they have a real incentive to negotiate" to bring an end to the war. Yet, he was asked, what distinguished this escalation from those in the past that also had been described as decisive? "It is my view," Nixon rejoined, based on the amount of supplies captured, the number of enemy killed, and the favorable position it placed the South Vietnamese moving forward, that the incursion into Cambodia was one of "the most decisive actions in terms of damaging the enemy's ability to wage effective warfare that has occurred in this war to date."[81]

By now, this all sounded very familiar, both from earlier claims by Nixon and Kissinger about progress and putting the enemy in a position where it had to negotiate and as an echo of the Johnson years. The perceived progress was an illusion. For the past eighteen months, every time the administration took what Nixon termed a "bold move," it believed it had placed Hanoi on the defensive and in a position that would force it to negotiate. The lack of progress in Paris was therefore a paradox in Washington's view. The North Vietnamese could not win on the battlefield, so why did Hanoi refuse to budge in negotiations?

The answer was because the American analysis rested on a set of false assumptions—most notably, that the war was a case of international aggression, an invasion of South Vietnam by North Vietnam. This led Washington to believe that Hanoi measured success the same way the Nixon administration did, primarily in terms of casualties, kill ratios, and the control war. Furthermore, American policymakers believed that in response to threats and escalations that drove up the costs of the war and denied them victory, the North Vietnamese would acknowledge their inability to win and seek to cut their losses. North Vietnam, however, did not use the same analytical framework as the United States. For Hanoi, the war was a continuation of the revolution and struggle for independence that began in 1945. It saw Saigon not as a legitimate government but rather as a neocolonial regime, as demonstrated by its dependence upon the United States. As North Vietnamese leaders made clear, they knew that eventually the United States would have to leave Vietnam, at which point they would achieve their goal of a unified, independent Vietnam.

Yet the administration would continue to hold onto the view that progress was being made even as the evidence and its own analyses showed that the war remained a stalemate. A meeting of Nixon, Kissinger, American military leaders from South Vietnam, and senior Pentagon officials brought out a number of problems that the United States continued to face despite claims of success in Cambodia. After a summary of achievements that led the president to conclude, "You could say that the operation has given us greater confidence in the Vietnamization program," continuing difficulties were identified. Nixon argued that they had to find some means to keep the military pressure on after the removal of American forces from the sanctuaries "so that the enemy doesn't assume that Cambodia was our last gasp." It was acknowledged that the government in Phnom Penh was weak and could not provide much resistance to the North Vietnamese, making any gains vulnerable in the future. General Abrams reminded the group that "this is a tough enemy."[82]

The only way to keep the war going, Secretary Laird noted, was to "win politically as well as militarily." That meant keeping the momentum of troop withdrawals going to maintain congressional funding. Nixon agreed and stated that this was "why we must continue to draw down our forces." The catch-22 of the situation became apparent. The more the United States withdrew its forces, the more it depended on the ARVN. The more dependent the war was on ARVN efforts, the worse the military situation became. Moreover, "what happens," the president asked, "if Cambodia falls? I want you to put the air in there and not spare the horses." Kissinger stated, "We now have an advantage." The problem was, "Do we exploit this advantage or succumb to husbanding resources?" Nixon agreed with this concern. "That is a real problem," he said. "We will hang on. I will avoid any decision which throws away what we have accomplished. I will be judged on Vietnamization, U.S. casualties and the outcome of Cambodia. We cannot change this but decisions which are not realistic won't do. We have got to stretch the South Vietnamese." But could the ARVN do more? The consensus was no; Saigon was already stretched too thin. Still, the stakes were high, Nixon stated. "The effect of this worldwide will be whether or not we have succeeded. At the same time, we have a political problem involving the Congress and we must get the money."[83]

No one had a solution to the dilemma of wanting to apply more pressure but lacking the capacity to do so at that time. Despite the consensus that the Cambodian operation "was a very sound decision" and the enemy must wonder what was next, there was no plan for how to move forward and win. "If we sit around and just dribble out our power, it is bound to have some effect on the enemy," Nixon stated, but wondered to what end. He said it was important to "continue to play a strong confident game." Laird noted, however, that there would be "some setbacks. We must not be too optimistic here at home" and raise hopes that could not be fulfilled. Nixon realized the problem. "We have got to make a decision best designed to disengage us but still succeed."[84] The president stated the central problem: time had run out not only on his madman strategy but on the idea that the United States could continue to withdraw troops without having a negative impact on the course of the war.

The bad news kept coming. In a June meeting with Anatoly Dobrynin, Kissinger was disappointed by what he learned. The Cambodian operation made Soviet leaders "doubt our motives for a possible summit." Moreover, "while we had made some military gains, Chinese influence in the region had been bolstered and prospects for a settlement set back." The Soviet ambassador posited that Washington had misread Hanoi. *"The North Vietnamese care about a political settlement, not about the rate of our withdrawals,"* Dobrynin said, "and elections were unacceptable to Hanoi." It was North Vietnam's view that the United States was being rigid in Paris, and he "saw little chance for negotiating movement now, but the situation might change after June 30."[85]

Kissinger reported to the president that "there are a number of indications that Hanoi, after a period of indecision following the Cambodian coup and our actions against the sanctuaries, has decided to emphasize military effort over the intermediate term. Hanoi's preparations in the military field and in diplomacy, together with statements by major figures, have given clues to this decision." Intelligence analysis also showed "that Hanoi will demand continued major sacrifices from its people and cooperation from Communist states." Infiltration of men was increasing, and the North Vietnamese had augmented the level of fighting in the northern provinces of South Vietnam and in Cambodia. Hanoi had made it clear "that it expects no serious work to be done in Paris in the intermediate future."[86]

Moreover, General Giap had recently spoken of "protracted war," a sign, American officials believed, "that Hanoi has decided that it must now emphasize long-run military pressure rather than hope for an early victory or early settlement." Giap dismissed the reversals in Cambodia as "temporary" and called for "a general step-up in military pressure, particularly against the pacification program," as well as "intensified Communist actions" against the ARVN. He also "pledged that the North Vietnamese would fight 'shoulder to shoulder' with the Lao and Cambodians and would 'lead the national liberation undertaking of the Indochinese peoples to complete victory.'"[87]

The military and diplomatic stalemate led Kissinger to take stock of where the United States stood after it withdrew its forces from Cambodia. In preparation for a July 21 meeting of the NSC, the national security advisor reviewed the administration's strategy and its negotiating position. "The fundamental question," Kissinger wrote Nixon, "which we will need to answer in the coming months is—what strategy should we pursue?" The talks in Paris remained stalled. The North Vietnamese had not budged despite all US efforts and "continued to demand as the price for negotiations (1) a guaranteed and accelerated schedule for complete U.S. withdrawal and (2) an abandonment of the present South Vietnamese government." In essence, Hanoi wanted to dictate American withdrawal plans. "Clearly, however, both the pace and scope of our withdrawal are matters for us to decide unilaterally. The other side in effect also is saying that negotiation for a settlement cannot proceed unless we are willing to dump the present South Vietnamese government." If the United States agreed, Kissinger asked, "what is there left to talk about at that point?"[88] These were positions the United States rejected. Washington still sought the mutual withdrawal of American and North Vietnamese forces and an arrangement that left the Thieu government in power to conduct future elections. Acceptance of Hanoi's terms meant defeat.

The choices facing the administration were to disengage militarily and "leave the question of political settlement entirely to the North and South Vietnamese," to concentrate on "a political settlement and hinge our withdrawals on this objective," or to "continue on a middle course, withdrawing while attempting to build South Vietnamese strength and meanwhile seeking a political resolution." There was a problem, Kissinger noted, with the administration's preferred option. "If we continue to follow the middle course we will be able to keep our options open for a time. But we must recognize that at some point we will face a decision to move to one or the other of the remaining courses—the point will come when our withdrawals are no longer a major bargaining card. We will have proceeded so far with withdrawals that there will be little incentive left for the other side to respond on political issues to further withdrawal proposals of ours."[89]

Perhaps seeking to soften the analysis, Kissinger told Nixon that his Vietnam policy had witnessed some success. "There has been military and pacification progress, we have transferred an increasing combat burden to the South Vietnamese, and we have maintained substantial American support with our troop reductions and negotiating proposals." But, he informed the president, the policy was reaching the end of the line. "If we stick to our present negotiating stance there will probably be no breakthrough in Paris. The other side might not really insist on both its conditions of unilateral U.S. withdrawal and coalition government, but it will not budge without concessions on at least one of them," Kissinger opined. "Thus at some point our present policy will turn into either negotiations, with our withdrawal schedule part of the bargaining, or into a unilateral withdrawal, with the pace non-negotiable. We will have to choose either to seek actively a settlement while our remaining forces can be used as leverage, or to leave the political settlement strictly to the South Vietnamese, whether by negotiation or force of arms, while we withdraw more or less unilaterally."[90]

As Kissinger noted, the administration's "prime objective is a rapid negotiated settlement to end the war, while our Vietnamization/withdrawal policy is a less preferred course in the absence of progress in Paris. Indeed, Vietnamization is designed to induce the enemy to negotiate by posing the prospect of a gradual American disengagement that maintains our domestic support while successively strengthening the

South Vietnamese forces." Meanwhile the various American proposals "were meant to persuade the enemy that we are ready to make genuine compromises at the conference table."[91] In effect, Vietnamization had become American policy by default. Nixon had to continue the troop withdrawals to satisfy public opinion and maintain the appearance of progress as Hanoi stalled in the negotiations and waited for more troop removals.

"While we have made substantial progress toward disengagement," Kissinger observed, "we have made little concrete advance in the negotiations. . . . The basic problem has been that to date the enemy has been able to calculate that we have greater problems than they do, that protracted struggle is preferable to real negotiations to accomplish their objectives. They thus stick with their two demands of unconditional unilateral American withdrawal and the overthrow of the Saigon regime." The United States could achieve its objectives in Vietnam only through negotiations, not unilateral withdrawal. A "gradual disengagement without a settlement carries its own fundamental danger: at some point we could reach a crunch point where we are caught between an ally that cannot withstand any further American withdrawals and a public that will not stand for any further involvement."[92] This was the same dilemma Kissinger had recognized in September 1969 in his "salted peanuts" memorandum.

"If this were our judgment," Kissinger said, "we might decide to go for a negotiated settlement while our position is strong and while our troop presence is still large enough to be an effective negotiating tool. We should then conduct withdrawals at the slowest pace our domestic structure can stand for bargaining purposes and search for new political formulas to induce negotiating movement." There were, Kissinger noted, "major risks in this strategy." North Vietnam could "swallow our proposals and sit back and wait for further concessions. To the extent that we inject ourselves directly in the political negotiations, we cut across our thesis that the South Vietnamese should shape their own political future. We could undermine GVN confidence and morale by appearing to bargain away its future."[93]

The alternative was to hope that Vietnamization would work. "The basic premise for pursuing this course," Kissinger stated, "would be that we are convinced that the other side has no intention of negotiating seriously. Their track record of intransigence in Paris supports this view. So does the memory of 1954—in retrospect they believe they threw away at the conference table their chance for reunification which they had all but won on the battlefield." Moreover, Hanoi "may well look at anti-war pressures in this country and calculate they can sit tight until progressive American withdrawals or political concessions undermine the GVN. Time is on their side—the U.S. exodus from the South is irreversible and the GVN can never stand on its own." Following this option, the United

States "would hold fast on our substantive positions. We would proceed with Vietnamization and withdrawals, keying our pace to South Vietnamese readiness and American public opinion."[94]

In the end, given that there were no viable alternatives, Kissinger could only recommend to the president that he "continue our present policy." The national security advisor had no way out of the dilemma and no new strategy to offer. Although not an admission of defeat, this cast a very dim light on the future as all options led to the same place—the unilateral withdrawal of American forces with little to show for the war. The United States, Kissinger counseled, should fight and talk, hoping to extract concessions from the North Vietnamese. "Hanoi has its share of problems, compounded," he believed, "by the Cambodian operations." The United States should see if that brought about any change. It was unwise, Kissinger continued, to establish a fixed schedule for withdrawal "to impress Hanoi or our domestic critics," as it "would cause a collapse of will in South Vietnam." At the same time, "a schedule long enough for GVN survival would cause us more problems than benefits at home." Either way, "the North Vietnamese are likely to reject a proposal now, either because they believe we are making it out of weakness and to appease domestic opinion; or because they don't wish to negotiate shortly after suffering the setbacks of our Cambodian operations; or for both reasons." But time was running out. Kissinger concluded, "Somewhere down the road—probably no later than next April when the present slice of withdrawals nears completion—we will have to choose."[95]

At the July 21 NSC meeting, even the success in Cambodia was questioned. The CIA cautioned that the gains in Cambodia were merely temporary. Richard Helms told the National Security Council that while US action had caught Hanoi by surprise, it "did not alter Hanoi's determination to increase its activity in Cambodia. The domestic reaction in the U.S. convinced Hanoi that our actions would be restricted." The enemy would therefore "continue their long-haul, low-profile activity" and increased attacks in the northern provinces and Laos. "There is a new consensus in the Hanoi leadership," Helms stated. "They look to the long haul but they are confident they eventually will win." The North Vietnamese "see their difficulties as great but they are willing to take it. They are willing to accept the privation and the manpower losses." They will continue to play Moscow and Beijing off against each other for influence, and this "rivalry for leadership between the USSR and China makes it difficult for either one to reduce its aid to Hanoi." In addition, the CIA had concluded that North Vietnam's "manpower losses are actually not overwhelming."[96]

In terms of the negotiations in Paris, the North Vietnamese believed "that if they wait long enough we will negotiate on grounds that they can accept." Helms stated that he "would expect little movement in negotiations generally or in Paris in particular for some months. They haven't looked at the Cambodia balance sheet yet. The political situation is not favorable in South Vietnam now to the Communists and major concessions are unlikely. Hanoi appears convinced that the U.S. won't negotiate unless it means an evident North Vietnamese defeat. Their demands will still be our withdrawal."[97]

No new ideas or strategies were proposed. The best the president could offer was the logic of the madman theory. He wanted "to create as much doubt in the minds of the enemy about what we will do in Laos and Cambodia and complete doubt as to what South Vietnam will do. We won't be pinned down on what interdiction is. I want to be sure we give no signal to the enemy. We will continue the bombing in North and South Laos. . . . Leave the enemy concerned." Nixon concluded the meeting by acknowledging the fundamental problem he faced while trying at the same time to deny it. "There is one weakness in our position now," Nixon stated. "The enemy assumes our divisions will bring us down. They are wrong. My position is I won't. Secondly, the restrictions they think Congress will impose they believe will hurt our ability to respond." The president remained defiant but also understood the dilemma he faced. "The bombing of the North will be ended in exchange for something. Our responses in retaliation have been successful in the past. If as we now go into significant withdrawal they sharply step up their attacks imperiling our remaining forces, we will have to take action. Their assumption that we cannot is wrong. It will be difficult but we will act if necessary."[98]

Time was running out on this approach and the president's ability to take new military actions. A year and a half of additional fighting, expansion of the war to Cambodia, threats, and escalation had not deterred Hanoi's willingness to continue to fight. Nor had it brought any movement in its negotiating position. The only change was that there were fewer American soldiers in Vietnam and at home troop withdrawals were expected to continue. Although Nixon would continue to return to it as a panacea, the madman strategy had failed. The year 1970 was to Nixon's Vietnam policy what 1968 had been to Johnson's, and Cambodia was his Tet Offensive. This decisive year saw the first actual limit placed on presidential power, a collapse of the madman theory and strategy for a military victory, and the beginning of the end of American involvement in Vietnam. After two presidents had escalated and expanded the war, the tide had finally turned. Nixon would be forced to wind down the American military effort on the ground in order to try to salvage his policy, reputation, and presidency. The costs of the Vietnam War were too great to sustain.

NOTES

1. Nixon to Kissinger, April 22, 1970, NSC Files/Vietnam Subject Files, Box 88, RNPL.

2. Schmitz, *The Tet Offensive*, 53–76.

3. Abrams to Wheeler, November 24, 1969, "Assessment of Enemy Situation," NSC Files/Vietnam Subject Files: [01] D-A General Abrams II, Nov., Box 66, RNPL.

4. *FRUS, 1969–1976, Vol. 6: Vietnam, January 1969–July 1970*, Document 178.

5. Brown to Kissinger, December 24, 1969, "NSSM 80—Vietnam Portion."

6. Brown to Kissinger, December 24, 1969, "NSSM 80—Vietnam Portion."

7. Vietnam Special Studies Group, "The Situation in the Countryside," January 10, 1970, NSCH Files, Box H001, RNPL; Kissinger to Nixon, undated (January 14, 1970), "The Situation in the Countryside of South Vietnam," NSCH Files, Box H001, RNPL (emphasis in the original).

8. Vietnam Special Studies Group, "The Situation in the Countryside"; Kissinger to Nixon, undated (January 14, 1970), "The Situation in the Countryside of South Vietnam" (emphasis in the original).

9. *FRUS, 1969–1976, Vol. 6: Vietnam, January 1969–July 1970*, Document 167.

10. Abrams to Wheeler, November 24, 1969, "Assessment of Enemy Situation."

11. Lynn to Kissinger, "Vietnam Trip Report," March 2, 1970, NSCH Files, Box H001, RNPL (emphasis in the original).

12. *FRUS, 1969–1976, Vol. 6: Vietnam, January 1969–July 1970*, Document 169.

13. *FRUS, 1969–1976, Vol. 6: Vietnam, January 1969–July 1970*, Document 169.

14. *FRUS, 1969–1976, Vol. 6: Vietnam, January 1969–July 1970*, Document 176.

15. *FRUS, 1969–1976, Vol. 6: Vietnam, January 1969–July 1970*, Document 187.

16. *FRUS, 1969–1976, Vol. 6: Vietnam, January1969–July 1970*, Document 187.

17. *FRUS, 1969–1976, Vol. 6: Vietnam, January 1969–July 1970*, Document 188.

18. *FRUS, 1969–1976, Vol. 6: Vietnam, January 1969–July 1970*, Document 188.

19. *FRUS, 1969–1976, Vol. 6: Vietnam, January 1969–July 1970*, Documents 200 and 218 (emphasis in the original).

20. *FRUS, 1969–1976, Vol. 6: Vietnam, January 1969–July 1970*, Document 205.

21. *FRUS, 1969–1976, Vol. 6: Vietnam, January 1969–July 1970*, Document 208.

22. *FRUS, 1969–1976, Vol. 6: Vietnam, January 1969–July 1970*, Document 217.

23. Kissinger to Nixon, March 27, 1970, "B-52 Operations in Cambodia"; Laird to Nixon, March 24, 1970, "Assessment of MENU Operations," NSC Files/Vietnam Subject Files, Box 105, RNPL.

24. *FRUS, 1969–1976, Vol. 6: Vietnam, January 1969–July 1970*, Document 224.

25. *FRUS, 1969–1976, Vol. 6: Vietnam, January 1969–July 1970*, Document 227.

26. *FRUS, 1969–1976, Vol. 6: Vietnam, January 1969–July 1970*, Document 236.

27. *FRUS, 1969–1976, Vol. 6: Vietnam, January 1969–July 1970*, Document 239.

28. *Public Papers of the Presidents: Richard Nixon, 1970* (Washington, DC: Government Printing Office, 1971), 373–77.

29. Westmoreland to Laird, April 21, 1970, "Courses of Action with Regard to Cambodia"; Pursley to Kissinger, April 22, 1970; National Security Decision Memorandum 56 (hereafter NSDM, followed by number), April 22, 1970, "Actions in Support of the Cambodian Government," NSC Files/Vietnam Subject Files, Box 88.

30. Nixon to Kissinger, April 22, 1970.

31. *FRUS, 1969–1976, Vol. 6: Vietnam, January 1969–July 1970*, Document 253; see also the Office of National Estimates assessment, *FRUS, 1969–1976*, Vol. 6: *January 1969–July 1970*, Document 268.

32. *FRUS, 1969–1976, Vol. 6: Vietnam, January 1969–July 1970*, Document 253.

33. NSDM 56; *FRUS, 1969–1976, Vol. 6: Vietnam, January 1969–July 1970*, Document 248.

34. Haldeman, quoted in Kimball, *The Vietnam War Files*, 26.

35. *FRUS, 1969–1976, Vol. 6: Vietnam, January 1969–July 1970*, Document 254.

36. *FRUS, 1969–1976, Vol. 6: Vietnam, January 1969–July 1970*, Document 256; *FRUS, 1969–1976, Vol. 6: Vietnam, January 1969–July 1970*, Document 258.

37. *FRUS, 1969–1976, Vol. 6: Vietnam, January 1969–July 1970*, Document 259.

38. NSDM 57, April 26, 1970, "Actions to Protect U.S. Forces in South Vietnam," NSC Files/Vietnam Subject Files, Box 88, RNPL. On April 28, Nixon replaced NSDM 57 with NSDM 58, which added the provision that the directive did not affect previously authorized South Vietnamese operations in Cambodia.

39. *FRUS, 1969–1976, Vol. 6: Vietnam, January 1969–July 1970*, Documents 261 and 263; Kissinger to Nixon, April 27, 1970, "Ground Operations in Cambodia," NSC Files/ Haig Chronological Files, Box 965, RNPL.

40. Memorandum of Meeting, April 28, 1970, "Cambodia/South Vietnam," NSC Files/Presidential-HAK Memcons, Box 1024, RNPL.

41. Moorer to Abrams and McCain, May 1, 1970, NSC Files/Vietnam Subject Files, Box 88, RNPL.

42. *FRUS, 1969–1976, Vol. 6: Vietnam, January 1969–July 1970*, Document 267.

43. Kissinger to Nixon, April 28, 1970, and Lord to Kissinger, April 28, 1970, NSC Files/Cambodian Operations (1970), Box 583, RNPL.

44. *Public Papers of the Presidents: Nixon, 1970*, 405–10.

45. *Public Papers of the Presidents: Nixon, 1970*, 405–10.

46. *Public Papers of the Presidents: Nixon, 1970*, 405–10.

47. *Public Papers of the Presidents: Nixon, 1970*, 405–10.

48. *Public Papers of the Presidents: Nixon, 1970*, 405–10.

49. *Public Papers of the Presidents: Nixon, 1970*, 405–10.

50. *Public Papers of the Presidents: Nixon, 1970*, 405–10.

51. *New York Times*, May 3, 1970.

52. *New York Times*, May 2, 1970.

53. *FRUS, 1969–1976, Vol. 6: Vietnam, January 1969–July 1970*, Document 277.

54. *Public Papers of the Presidents: Nixon, 1970*, 411.

55. *FRUS, 1969–1976, Vol. 6: Vietnam, January 1969–July 1970*, Document 277.

56. *FRUS, 1969–1976*, Vol. 1: *Foundations of Foreign Policy, 1969–1972*, Document 66.

57. *Public Papers of the Presidents: Nixon, 1970*, 413; *New York Times*, May 7, 1970.

58. *Public Papers of the Presidents: Nixon, 1970*, 413–23.

59. Nixon, undated (Nixon at the Lincoln Memorial, May 9, 1970), NSC Files, Box 319, RNPL.

60. Frank Church, "War without End: Congress Must Draw the Line," Frank Church Papers, Series 2.2, Box 32, Folder 9, Boise State University, Boise, Idaho (hereafter Church Papers, followed by series/box/folder).

61. Kissinger to Nixon, May 8, 1970, NSC Files, Box 318, RNPL.

62. Kissinger to Nixon, May 4, 1970, "Your May 5 Meetings with Congressional Committees," NSC Files/Cambodian Operations (1970), Box 585, RNPL.

63. LeRoy Ashby and Rod Gramer, *Fighting the Odds: The Life of Senator Frank Church* (Pullman: Washington State University Press, 1994), 315.

64. *Public Papers of the Presidents: Nixon, 1970*, 413–23.

65. "Remarks by Henry A. Kissinger to Senators and Representatives, on the Cambodian Decision," May 12, 1970, NSC Files/Cambodian Operations (1970), Box 585, RNPL; *New York Times*, May 15, 1970.

66. Ashby and Gramer, *Fighting the Odds*, 326–27.

67. Ashby and Gramer, *Fighting the Odds*, 315.

68. *Public Papers of the Presidents: Nixon, 1970*, 476–80.

69. Remarks of Senator Frank Church in the US Senate, June 3, 1970, Church Papers, 2.2/39/10.

70. *Public Papers of the Presidents: Nixon, 1970*, 543–59.

71. *FRUS, 1969–1976, Vol. 6: Vietnam, January 1969–July 1970*, Document 291.

72. Haig to Kissinger, "Lynn Paper, Entitled: Evaluation of Allied Operations in Cambodia," May 30, 1970, NSC Files/Haig Chronological Files, Box 967, RNPL.

73. Kennedy to Buchanan, "Three Week Report on Cambodia," May 25, 1970, NSC Files/Haig Chronological Files, Box 967, RNPL.

74. *FRUS, 1969–1976, Vol. 6: Vietnam, January 1969–July 1970*, Document 299.

75. *FRUS, 1969–1976, Vol. 6: Vietnam, January 1969–July 1970*, Document 299.

76. Joint State/Defense Message to American Embassy Phnom Penh, American Embassy Saigon, MACV, CINPAC, May 21, 1970, NSC Files/Cambodian Operation (1970), Box 588, RNPL.

77. Kissinger to Nixon, undated, "Special NSC Meeting on Cambodia, 3:00 p.m. Friday, May 22, 1970," NSCH Files, Box H028, RNPL.

78. Kissinger to Nixon, undated, "Issues for the May 31 Meeting," NSCH Files, Box H028, RNPL.

79. *Public Papers of the Presidents: Nixon, 1970*, 529–41.

80. *Public Papers of the Presidents: Nixon, 1970*, 543–59.

81. *Public Papers of the Presidents: Nixon, 1970*, 543–59.

82. Memorandum of Conversation, May 31, 1970, NSC Files/Haig Chronological Files, Box 967, RNPL.

83. Memorandum of Conversation, May 31, 1970.

84. Memorandum of Conversation, May 31, 1970.

85. *FRUS, 1969–1976, Vol. 6: Vietnam, January 1969–July 1970*, Document 323 (emphasis in the original).

86. *FRUS, 1969–1976, Vol. 6: Vietnam, January 1969–July 1970*, Document 333.

87. *FRUS, 1969–1976, Vol. 6: Vietnam, January 1969–July 1970*, Document 333.

88. *FRUS, 1969–1976, Vol. 6: Vietnam, January 1969–July 1970*, Document 346.

89. *FRUS, 1969–1976, Vol. 6: Vietnam, January 1969–July 1970*, Document 346.

90. *FRUS, 1969–1976, Vol. 6: Vietnam, January 1969–July 1970*, Document 347.

91. *FRUS, 1969–1976, Vol. 6: Vietnam, January 1969–July 1970*, Document 347.

92. *FRUS, 1969–1976, Vol. 6: Vietnam, January 1969–July 1970*, Document 347.

93. *FRUS, 1969–1976, Vol. 6: Vietnam, January 1969–July 1970*, Document 347.

94. *FRUS, 1969–1976, Vol. 6:Vietnam, January 1969–July 1970*, Document 347.

95. *FRUS, 1969–1976, Vol. 6: Vietnam, January 1969–July 1970*, Document 347.

96. "NSC Meeting: Vietnam Ceasefire and Possible Diplomatic Initiatives," July 21, 1970, NSCH Files/Minutes of Meetings, Box H109, RNPL.

97. "NSC Meeting: Vietnam Ceasefire and Possible Diplomatic Initiatives."

98. "NSC Meeting: Vietnam Ceasefire and Possible Diplomatic Initiatives."

FIVE

The End of the American Century

In February 1941, Henry Luce published his famous essay "The American Century" in support of President Franklin D. Roosevelt's "four freedoms" and efforts to mobilize the United States for entry into World War II. Luce called for Americans to seize the second chance at world leadership that they had fumbled after the Great War with "disastrous consequence for themselves and for all mankind." Peace and prosperity, Luce and other internationalists believed, could be secured only if the United States accepted responsibility for defeating fascism and creating order in the postwar world through the expansion of American values and institutions. It was a war, Luce wrote, "to defend and even to promote, encourage and incite so-called democratic principles throughout the world." Indeed, "as the most powerful and most vital nation in the world," "America and America alone" must determine whether freedom and progress would prevail or the world would face more chaos, economic deprivation, and future wars.[1]

Luce argued that it was essential for the United States to promote the American ideals of freedom, justice, and opportunity for the good of all mankind: "America as the dynamic center of ever-widening spheres of enterprise, America as the training center of the skilled servants of mankind, America as the Good Samaritan, really believing again that it is more blessed to give than to receive, and America as the powerhouse of the ideals of Freedom and Justice—out of these elements surely can be fashioned a vision of the 20th Century to which we can and will devote ourselves." It was in this spirit, he concluded, "all of us are called, each to his own measure of capacity, and each in the widest horizon of his vision, to create the first great American Century."[2]

Such was the confidence with which the United States entered the postwar years. American leaders established the United Nations to promote their political values; the World Bank and the International Monetary Fund, with the US dollar fixed at $35 to an ounce of gold as the currency for international trade, to promote free trade and development; and the North Atlantic Treaty Organization (NATO) in 1949 and the Southeast Asia Treaty Organization (SEATO) in 1954 to sustain Washington's containment policy. The triumph over the Great Depression and victory in World War II over Germany and Japan confirmed for Americans that the United States could overcome any challenge if it had the will and discipline to carry out its policies. Postwar prosperity and power confirmed for Americans the worthiness of their institutions and correctness of their policies and reinforced the idea that their values were universal and desired by all. Washington had all the necessary skills, resources, and military might, if necessary, to triumph in the Cold War.

Only thirty years later, the American Century was over. The US military could achieve only a stalemate in Vietnam and thus a defeat for its policy of limited war to contain communism. Optimism and confidence gave way to division and criticism of the US role in the world, and economic problems replaced postwar prosperity with stagflation. The year from June 1970, when the Nixon administration withdrew American forces from Cambodia and abandoned its quest to defeat North Vietnam (NVN) militarily, to June 1971, with the Supreme Court's rejection of the administration's claims in the *Pentagon Papers* case, marked the end of the postwar era and visions of American omnipotence. In response, Richard Nixon's administration adjusted its policies to conform to these realities. The Vietnam War was no longer problem number one for the president. Rather, insuring his reelection was now the top priority. The administration planned to accomplish this by creating the illusion of peace in Vietnam and shifting the foreign policy focus toward détente with the Soviet Union and improved relations with China. By the middle of 1971, Nixon would reorient American foreign policy away from Vietnam and toward ending the Cold War and establishing what he called a generation of peace.

In the wake of the removal of American forces from Cambodia, Nixon had few good options for moving ahead in Vietnam. He was committed to a continued reduction of American forces, barred from reentering Cambodia by Congress, and unable to fully implement his madman policy due to domestic opposition. Over the next year, the president shifted his definition of what it meant to win in Vietnam from a military victory that allowed him to defeat and impose a settlement on Hanoi to a policy of removing US troops while simultaneously maintaining Nguyen Van Thieu's government in power in Saigon. This would allow the president to run for reelection while claiming to have ended the war and maintained American credibility. A policy emerged that sought to create the appearance of peace in Vietnam built on the winding down of the American combat role and preventing American casualties and détente with the Soviet Union and China. For Vietnam this meant a continued military stalemate. Nixon would extract the United States from the conflict while leaving the South Vietnamese to fight the North Vietnamese in an endless war.

This did not mean that Nixon ceased to employ threats and efforts to use force to influence Hanoi. Yet the president was aware that no new military initiatives would be decisive. In his first eighteen months in office, Nixon had sought to use the madman strategy to achieve victory. Now he would use irrational force or devastating bombing to relieve his frustrations with the war, punish Hanoi for defying him, and keep the North Vietnamese Army (NVA) off balance. This would allow the American troop drawdown to proceed without interruption and buy time for the Army of the Republic of Vietnam (ARVN) to gain strength, all without immediately endangering the Saigon regime.

It was not always clear to Nixon and his national security advisor, Henry Kissinger, from the summer of 1970 to the middle of 1971, what course of action to take in their effort to keep Saigon intact until all US troops were removed and Nixon's reelection was assured. The American leaders continually wavered between alternatives that continued past policies and actions that reflected the president's new policy and goals. Nixon was uncertain at times about the best way to proceed, and that uncertainty was compounded whenever the outlook for his new policy was no better than continued stalemate and ultimate defeat. The dismal set of alternatives Kissinger offered led Nixon to a policy of a drawn-out American retreat designed to mask defeat with success in keeping Thieu in power.

Having failed to achieve victory in Vietnam by 1970, the Nixon administration now reorchestrated the war to serve the political purpose of the president's reelection. Nixon's goal was to maintain the government in Saigon while he withdrew the remainder of American forces from South Vietnam to create the illusion of peace and victory. To that end, Nixon made it clear in July 1970 that he wanted everything possible done to ensure the survival of Lon Nol's regime in Cambodia through aid, covert operations, tactical air strikes, and support from other nations to Phnom Penh. This, he believed, would disrupt NVA forces and keep the fighting away from Saigon. Nixon also told his aides that he "wanted to make a maximum effort in Laos" to tie down North Vietnamese forces and interdict the flow of supplies along the Ho Chi Minh Trail from North to South Vietnam.[3] Again, the purpose was to reduce the direct fighting in South Vietnam to provide Vietnamization an opportunity to succeed. In addition, the president would highlight efforts at negotiations to appease domestic critics. He sought to show how reasonable the American position was and how willing the administration was to end the war, as well as to portray the enemy as intransigent and unreasonable, thereby justifying any new military actions.

By the summer of 1970, Nixon and Kissinger had come to believe that they could convince Hanoi that it would be better to negotiate with Washington now than with Saigon after the Vietnamization of the war was complete. The North Vietnamese would see that it was either peace on Nixon's terms or endless war. As Kissinger prepared to resume his secret talks with North Vietnam in September, he assured President Nixon that he would offer no concessions on the American position that a negotiated agreement had to rest on a mutual withdrawal of US and NVA forces. He understood that "we cannot agree to the replacement in advance of the leaders of the present South Vietnamese Government." Kissinger planned to remind the Hanoi of "our preference for a negotiated settlement, but would underline that the time for this is beginning to run out and at some point we will be committed to our alternative course of Vietnamization." It was therefore up to the North Vietnamese to "choose the way they wish to resolve the conflict. We are nearing the time when the chances for a negotiated settlement will pass, and they will have committed themselves to a test of arms against a strengthened South Vietnam, supported by us in whatever way seems appropriate and necessary."[4]

As Kissinger noted in his postmeeting report to Nixon, he observed signs of positive change in the attitude and approach of Xuan Thuy, and although the North Vietnamese negotiator stated "that Hanoi was prepared to wait a long time for unification of Vietnam," Thuy made some concessions on the political issues he was willing to discuss; he also insisted on another meeting that month and that the secret channel remain open. Still, Thuy made it clear that no agreement could allow the Thieu government to remain in power, a position Nixon noted was "probably the breaking point" in the talks. Kissinger concluded, "It is still difficult to judge whether they are just trying to keep us talking or have real intent of moving on to substantive negotiations."[5] The same could be said about the United States. Nixon and Kissinger were aware that the American negotiating position asked Hanoi to accept defeat in its primary goal of overthrowing the Saigon government and unifying Vietnam under its rule. Thus began another long series of meetings and more public posturing that led to no change.

Prior to Kissinger's next meeting with Thuy, Madame Nguyen Thi Binh, the representative in Paris of the Provisional Revolutionary Government, the political organization of the National Liberation Front (NLF), issued a statement of clarification of that body's negotiating position. The NLF would cease its attacks on American forces in return for a firm commitment to a withdrawal of all U.S. troops by June 30, 1971.[6] Kissinger observed that the proposal "gives the Communists not just a negotiating platform, but a better vehicle for political and propaganda operations against us and against the South Vietnamese Government [GVN]. In fact, it could be designed to serve the Communist cause even more if there were no negotiations than if there were some." The statement "was obviously timed to impact on our elections" and would place "great pressure against the GVN" by appealing to anti-Saigon forces in the South.[7] Kissinger's next meeting with Thuy confirmed for him that the statement was propaganda, not a legitimate negotiation move, and that there was no reason for him to continue to travel to Paris for these meetings unless something new was proposed.[8]

In response to the latest failure in Paris, Nixon delivered a televised address on October 7 to set out what he termed a "major new initiative for peace." Its purpose was to counter the NLF's latest offer, demonstrate Nixon's willingness to negotiate, and gain public support for continuing the war rather than accepting a set deadline for withdrawal. It mirrored Madame Nguyen Thi Binh's proposal, making demands that Nixon knew the North Vietnamese and NLF would reject while making it appear that he was seeking peace in order to gain public support. The president set out five proposals, the most important being a "cease-fire-in-place," without preconditions, as *"part of a general move to end the war in Indochina"* in the hope that it would *"*break the logjam in all the negotiations." The president noted the difficulty of achieving this "in a guerrilla war where there are no frontlines" and warned that it should not be *"the means by which either side builds up its strength."*[9]

The rest of Nixon's proposals were variants of the existing American position. He called for an international Indochina Peace Conference based on the Geneva Accords of 1954. As part of the continued withdrawal of American forces, Nixon stated that he was prepared to "negotiate an agreed timetable for complete withdrawals as part of an overall settlement" in conjunction with "a political solution that reflects the will of the South Vietnamese people" and the "existing relationship of political forces." While the United States was willing to accept the outcome of an agreed-on political process, Nixon insisted that he would not yield to the enemy's demand to "exclude whomever they wish from government," which was "patently unreasonable" and represented the dismantling of the Saigon government. Finally, Nixon sought an *"immediate and unconditional release of all prisoners of war held by both sides,"* a position Hanoi had made clear it would not accept as long as there were American forces in Vietnam. Situating his proposals as part of his larger foreign policy, the president declared that with a cease-fire in Vietnam, "we could have some reason to hope that we had reached the beginning of the end of war in this century. We might be on the threshold of a generation of peace." He concluded by foreshadowing his upcoming effort to move the Vietnam War into the background by focusing on relations with the Soviet Union and China, stating that there was "no goal to which I am more dedicated than to build a new structure of peace in the world."[10]

It was all deception and politics. After the speech, Kissinger called Nixon to congratulate him. The conversation turned to Cambodia. Nixon urged Kissinger to call Anatoly Dobrynin and "say, look don't be foolish, this is a great step forward. Generation of peace, don't you think that is a good line?" The phrase, Kissinger noted, "made all headlines each time you used it. You made a major step forward again." But what was that step, and what was the goal? Nixon confessed, "As you know, I don't think cease-fire is worth a damn, but now that we have done it we are looking down their throats." There was no consistent policy because all of the administration's actions were based on creating an illusion of peace to allow the war to continue. For its part, Hanoi denounced the speech, and the war raged on.[11]

Nixon and Kissinger's awareness that their efforts in Vietnam and Cambodia had not, in any way, won the war and their lack of desire to reach a negotiated settlement at that time became clear throughout the fall of 1970 and the spring of 1971. Less than a week after speaking to the nation, the president announced that he was accelerating the troop removal announced back in April. This meant, he noted, that there would be "205,500 fewer Americans in Vietnam than when I took office."[12] The president did not reveal, however, that economic troubles at home and problems within the American military in Vietnam were placing severe budget restraints on the Pentagon.

The steady withdrawal of American troops meant the war was unwinnable, and soldiers were no longer willing to sacrifice in a cause they believed Washington had abandoned. This led to a breakdown of discipline in the ranks and a crisis for the military in Vietnam. Colonel Robert Heinl Jr.'s article "The Collapse of the Armed Forces," based primarily on an analysis of US troops in 1970, demonstrated the range of problems that beset American forces still in Vietnam. In an explosive opening line, Heinl declared, "The morale, discipline and battleworthiness of the U.S. Armed Forces are . . . lower and worse than at any time in this century and possibly in the history of the United States." Every measure demonstrated that the "army that now remains in Vietnam is in a state approaching collapse, with individual units avoiding or having refused combat, murdering their officers and noncommissioned officers, drug-ridden, and dispirited where not near-mutinous." What was once in Vietnam "the best army the United States ever put into the field" was now "numbly extricating itself from a nightmare war the Armed Forces feel they had foisted on them by bright civilians who are now back on campus writing books about the folly of it all."[13]

The most notable evidence of the breakdown of discipline and the conviction that there was no reason to continue to fight was the fragging of officers by the men. Officially, the Pentagon recorded ninety-six incidents of soldiers killing their officers in 1969, with the number more than doubling in 1970 to 209 incidents. In the Americal Division, fraggings averaged one a week in 1971. The issue of "combat refusal" went beyond just attacks on officers. "Search and evade," which referred to avoiding combat while out in the field, had become prevalent throughout the army. It was "now virtually a principle of war, vividly expressed by the GI phrase, 'CYA (cover your ass) and get home!'"[14]

The military also reflected the social problems that beset American society, including drug use, lack of respect for authority, and racial strife. A congressional investigation found that "10 to 15% of ours troops in Vietnam are now using high-grade heroin, and that drug addiction there is 'of epidemic proportions.'" There were well over one hundred underground newspapers on American military bases, "at least 14 GI dissent organizations," and over a dozen antiwar coffeehouses outside bases that provided literature and forums to discuss desertion and antiwar activities. Though harder to quantify, problems of race were also, Heinl reported, "tearing the services apart." The army was becoming divided, in the words of one noncommissioned officer, "like two street gangs," and racial violence was seen as another indicator of the breakdown of discipline in the ranks.[15]

Major Colin Powell, who served his second tour of duty in Vietnam from July 1968 to July 1969, witnessed many of these problems firsthand and concluded from them that the United States could not win the war. American soldiers by this time remained brave and skilled but "lacked inspiration and a sense of purpose." They clearly understood and reflected the changes on the home front. The public no longer supported the war, President Lyndon Johnson had abdicated rather than run on his record in Vietnam, and the "troops of the ally we had come to aid were deserting at a rate of over 100,000 a year." There was "little of the nobility of purpose" that had seen soldiers through previous wars. Saigon, with leaders such as Nguyen Cao Ky, who openly admired Adolph Hitler, inspired only contempt, whereas American leaders "seemed to believe that by manipulating words," they could "change the truth" about the reality of the war. Racial divisions had appeared on all American bases, and all "were increasingly resentful of the authority that kept them [in Vietnam] for a dangerous and unclear purpose."[16]

At the same time, the North Vietnamese "refused to cooperate" with American military plans. "No matter how hard we struck, NVA troops would melt into their sanctuaries . . . refit, regroup, and come out to fight again." Powell had thought, when in Vietnam in 1962, that it would take half a million men to defeat the NLF and NVA. "Six years later . . . we reached the peak, 543,400, and it was still not enough. Given the terrain, the kind of war the NVA and VC [Viet Cong] were fighting, and the casualties they were willing to take, no defensible level of U.S. involvement would have been enough." As American soldiers kept on dying for a losing cause, Powell could not answer why.[17]

Despite these problems, Kissinger opposed the more rapid drawdown of American forces that Nixon had initiated. "Our biggest bargaining chip between now and the end of Tet (February 1971) is our ability to regulate the timing of the drawdown of our forces," he claimed. "We face the danger of losing this chip," Kissinger believed, by moving too quickly and losing flexibility in negotiations.[18] This only mattered, of course, if the administration was sincerely looking to reach a peace agreement in Paris at this time. But the president was not. His definition of victory had changed. Winning was now defined as the successful withdrawal of American ground forces with the Thieu government still in power and, most importantly, no collapse of Saigon prior to the 1972 presidential election. This meant the balance of forces had to be maintained to preserve a stalemate. Yet, as American troops continued to be withdrawn, enemy strength and advantages naturally grew. This led Nixon to seek opportunities to "hit" Hanoi hard to disrupt its operations and extend the war while he bought time for his other strategies to unfold. He was still looking for bold moves to hurt North Vietnam.

American casualties were decreasing along with the US role in the fighting, but Nixon was prepared for a long war between North and South Vietnam if that was what it took to achieve his understanding of winning. The negotiations were pursued to serve the president's political ends and create the illusion that he was seeking a peaceful resolution of the war, not to end the fighting and bring peace to Vietnam. As Nixon told Kissinger, "Despite all the way we put the cosmetics on . . . our policy is . . . to win the war." That simply meant "letting South Vietnam survive. That's all."[19] Kissinger made clear the divide between the president's public approach and actual policy in the instructions he sent to David Bruce, the new American ambassador to the Paris peace talks, after Nixon's October announcement of his five proposals. The president, Kissinger wrote, "is very emphatic that his new initiative is not designed to be a cover for unilateral American withdrawal. Although our position on withdrawal is phrased somewhat differently in the speech, this is essentially for packaging reasons and is not meant to get us away from the basic principles of his May 14, 1969, speech." Nixon was not "suggesting or accepting a unilateral withdrawal, and he wanted you to know his strong views on this." Moreover, the president would not accept any negotiation that led to the removal of Thieu from office. "On this point also the President's position is very firm," and he believes that Thieu's removal "would be tantamount to the dismantling of the organized noncommunist forces."[20]

In the face of public and congressional opposition, Nixon was not willing to try to keep American forces in Vietnam for much longer, but he did not want to abandon the American commitment to Saigon. What the president saw as his bold military strikes against the NVA/NLF took on a new purpose. Rather than representing an attempt to break the will of Hanoi to continue the war, they were now meant to decrease the pressure on South Vietnam and buy time to continue the program of Vietnamization and the buildup of ARVN forces in order to prop up and maintain the Saigon government as the United States continued to decrease its role in the fighting of the war.

Nixon was also sure that Hanoi was not seeking a negotiated settlement—at least, not one that he was willing to consider. Soviet foreign minister Andrei Gromyko told Nixon that the North Vietnamese would not engage in any further discussions unless Washington was willing to set a timetable for the withdrawal of its forces and establish a coalition government in Saigon. The president told South Vietnamese vice president Nguyen Cao Ky that he knew "Hanoi was playing a game—it had obtained a bombing halt from us in return for entering into talks, but had no intention of reaching a political settlement. While we wanted negotiations, it wanted South Vietnam, and looked on the talks as a screen behind which it could carry on the war without being bombed." Given that, it was necessary "to accept the fact that the value of the Paris talks was mainly in the public relations sense." Nixon assured Ky that the United States "would stand firmly by South Vietnam. Our troop withdrawals would continue (although we would still keep logistical units in South Vietnam), but we would at the same time provide the South Vietnamese with the military and economic assistance which they needed to do the job for themselves."[21]

Nixon's worries about Congress and the funding of the war amplified these concerns. From Saigon, he needed continued improvement of its military and political stability. With elections planned for 1971, it was important that there were no further coups d'état. Every sign of political unrest in Saigon made big headlines in the United States and prompted calls in the media and Congress "to wash our hands of the 'mess in Vietnam.'" It was crucial that South Vietnam not provide "senatorial critics an opportunity to block the Administration's efforts to help Vietnam. The problem was now not so much on the military side but on the economic, since we had to go to the Hill to get appropriations. This was where the real fight lay."[22]

On November 18, Nixon sent a special message to Congress requesting over $1 billion in supplemental appropriations for the war. The president made his case in terms of funding Vietnamization and the Nixon Doctrine and maintaining American credibility and world leadership. Echoing the logic of Luce's "American Century," Nixon argued that "the first six decades of the Twentieth Century taught us that a stable and tranquil world requires American participation in keeping the peace. For us to abdicate that responsibility would be to magnify the world's instability and turmoil for us as well as for our friends." As the Vietnam War demonstrated, it was neither possible nor necessary for the United States to carry out its mission alone. "The overwhelming evidence of the last 25 years—from the Marshall Plan to Vietnamization—is that a systematic program that helps other nations harness their own resources for defense" is the road to collective security and peace.[23] In lobbying members of the Senate, the president noted that his request was "part of the Nixon Doctrine. We wanted to let others do the job themselves; we wanted to get out ourselves. But we must remember the assistance part of the Doctrine. These countries are not going to be building up military machines of their own. We hope that Vietnam and Cambodia will become lesser burdens over time to us. We now see this as the best road in that area."[24] American power would be exerted through support for other nations without entangling American soldiers in the fighting, thereby reducing the costs of wars in the Third World. In essence, Nixon was jettisoning the unpopular strategy of limited war and intervention that had created domestic opposition to American policy in Vietnam, while reaffirming the ideals and axioms of Cold War policy by establishing a new approach to achieving the goals of containment.

After the administration assured Congress that none of the money would be used for US forces or operations in Cambodia in violation of the Cooper-Church Amendment, the funding was approved. The president knew he was facing a constant threat from Congress to take action that would alter his plans or take control of the pace of the American withdrawal out of his hands. Still, the administration did not want free elections in Saigon if the outcome could not be guaranteed. It needed Thieu to win. As Ambassador Ellsworth Bunker noted, no other candidate "would serve U.S. interests as well as Thieu." The main challenge came from General Duong Van Minh. "Minh sees himself as the peace candidate and as such thinks he will be able to arrive at a settlement with North Viet-Nam and the VC," Bunker reported. "Both Minh's eagerness to win the election and to end the war by a negotiated settlement . . . are viewed with profound concern by a large segment of the military, the police and important civilian elements. If Minh were to win," the ambassador continued, "excessive compromises with the Communists or weak and ineffective government would almost certainly set the stage for a military coup. Minh's election, in short, holds out the promise of subsequent serious and dangerous instability." Therefore, a "principal objective of United States policy in Viet-Nam over the next 10 months should be the reelection of President Thieu."[25]

After Minh withdrew from the race because he believed the election was rigged, Nixon was informed that the State Department saw the development as an opportunity to get rid of Thieu. "Turn on him," Nixon asked? "Never, never . . . I hope never." It would be similar to the overthrow of Ngo Dinh Diem, he declared. "Never. Never, never, never." The State Department was "to shut up" concerning the political future of South Vietnam. "They're to say nothing without my approval."[26]

The president wanted, he told Alexander Haig as the general prepared to visit Cambodia and South Vietnam in December 1970, plans to hit Hanoi and keep the North off stride and away from Saigon. With a reduced American fighting force in South Vietnam, and barred from using US forces in Cambodia, Haig, in conjunction with General Creighton W. Abrams, proposed an operation designed to use ARVN troops with US air support to strike "the vital NVA/VC logistic nerve center" in southern Laos. Military commanders were "extremely enthusiastic about this operation, even in view of obvious political difficulties which it will encounter in Washington."[27]

Code-named "Lam Son 719," the plan to interdict the Ho Chi Minh Trail quickly received the president's endorsement. Nixon wanted action, and the operation was designed to demonstrate the effectiveness of Vietnamization. His overall objective, the president stated, was "an enduring Vietnam, namely, one that can stand up in the future; therefore, we must give the NVN a bang." During "the months of February, March and April," Nixon indicated, he would "take the heat and take the risks and then, when the heat is at its highest level we will announce additional withdrawals (below the troop level of 284,000) if warranted." Lam Son 719 was to be an operation that made "a significant strike on choke points" in Laos. It was to be done at the same time as other ongoing battles were fought to show the readiness of ARVN forces to take over the ground war. "We will not justify this on the basis of 'protective reaction,'" Nixon stated, "but, rather, on the basis that while we are cutting down the enemy is building up and, consequently, cannot tolerate this." It was Nixon's belief "that from January 1 to April we can break the back of the enemy" and that the military must *use forces necessary to make operations succeed.*[28] The administration, as Kissinger told Thomas Moorer, had a great deal "riding on this one"[29] as it was part of a larger "game plan." Lam Son 719 was to hit the North Vietnamese hard enough in Laos to demonstrate the ability of Saigon to survive without American forces and in the process prevent any problems with Thieu's reelection in October. "The main thing I'm interested in is just to be sure the South Vietnamese fight well . . . because they're going to be battling in there for years to come," Nixon stated. If that was achieved, then the United States could propose a cease-fire in the fall, a fixed schedule for American withdrawal, and a return of all POWs. Saigon would be told it had a year without heavy fighting to build its strength.[30] The game plan was to end American involvement in time for Nixon's election campaign while preparing Saigon for a continuing war.

After plans for the upcoming attack on Laos were leaked to the press, Nixon and Kissinger briefly reconsidered the operation. Nixon, however, decided that it was vital to go ahead to demonstrate his willingness to take risks and protect his position in the election campaign the next year. Moreover, the president noted that this would be the American army's "last chance for any major positive action since we won't be able to do anything after the dry season ends, and next year we won't have enough troops in place to be able to do anything" in terms of ground operations.[31]

Operation Lam Son 719 was launched on February 7, 1971. Over seventeen thousand ARVN troops, backed by American artillery and air-power, crossed the border into Laos with the goal of disrupting the flow of supplies on the Ho Chi Minh Trail. Positive reports flowed from Saigon concerning the operation, but there were problems from the outset. Hanoi moved a large number of troops into the area to block the ARVN's advance. Both sides sustained heavy losses, including large numbers of downed US helicopters and American crewmen. As South Vietnamese casualties grew, Thieu scaled back the scope of the operation from ninety days to a planned withdrawal in March. Kissinger cabled Bunker on March 1 the he was "profoundly concerned by the way the situation is evolving." Essential to the administration's success in Vietnam was "a minimum basic confidence here that the actions we have taken thus far offer hope of leading to a situation in which the South Vietnamese will be able increasingly to manage their own defenses as U.S. forces continue to be withdrawn at rates comparable to those of the past." The president had supported Lam Son 719 because he was told that, through an attack by ARVN forces, "the Laos trail network would be disrupted with some impact on the enemy's ability to undertake offensive operations during this dry season and the next as well." Now Washington was "beginning to wonder what if anything has been achieved in this regard," given the conflicting reports and the "wide range of modifications to the plan brought on by the host of very real difficulties with which the ARVN had been confronted."[32] Eight days later, Kissinger instructed Bunker that Thieu had to keep up the fighting in Laos through April, as it was "the last chance that ARVN will have to receive any substantial U.S. support on the scale now provided. Thus, this may be our last opportunity to achieve a significant long-range benefit from large offensive operations against the enemy."[33]

Pressure from Washington did not change Thieu's decision. After a symbolic capturing of Tchepone, the originally stated objective, ARVN forces began to withdraw. What had begun with such hope was now a crisis to be managed. The Laos operation had brought the war back in front of the public and reminded people that the administration was no nearer to ending the conflict than when it took office. The media were reporting the operation as a retreat and failure, and images appeared on television of South Vietnamese soldiers hanging onto the skids of American evacuation helicopters. On March 18, Kissinger wrote Bunker that "it would be hard to exaggerate the mystification and confusion caused here by the ARVN's latest scheme of maneuver which envisages a rapid pull-out from Laos."[34] The national security advisor spoke that same day with the president about how to salvage the game plan. They might have to accelerate some aspects to appease public opinion, but they should still go ahead with the plan for a final withdrawal after Thieu's reelection. Nixon stated, "Announce the whole damn thing, and that's that. And the war is dead as an issue" for Nixon's reelection, even though the fighting would be far from over. Without US casualties, the war would again fade from public view. Though it would have no combat role, the United States would still have its airpower and could, Kissinger noted, "do a lot from Thailand and from carriers if the North Vietnamese break the agreement." Nixon responded, "Oh, I see what you mean. Yeah. Okay." [35]

It was to be endless war between North and South Vietnam. In an effort to quiet domestic criticism in the wake of Lam Son 719, Nixon spoke to the nation on April 7. In the days prior to the speech, the president was highly agitated by congressional and press criticism. Referring to "these goddamn Doves," Nixon told Kissinger that he was "determined to just see it through and the hell with them." If the war "fails, it fails." Kissinger assured Nixon that this was "a heroic posture." Nixon responded, "Well, hell, believe it or not, there is no other course for the country. These people—I mean, that's why our domestic side, while I'm interested in their views, why they're irrelevant, they don't know what the hell they are talking about." [36]

The president provided an optimistic and deceptive report to the American public. He claimed that "the South Vietnamese [had] demonstrated that without American advisers they could fight effectively against the very best troops North Vietnam could put in the field" while carrying out a successful operation that disrupted the Ho Chi Minh Trail and damaged Hanoi's capability to conduct the war in South Vietnam. "Consequently, tonight I can report that Vietnamization has succeeded." Moreover, Nixon announced that this success allowed him to increase the withdrawal of Americans from the war. "Between May 1 and December 1 of this year, 100,000 more American troops will be brought home from South Vietnam. This will bring the total number of American troops withdrawn from South Vietnam to 365,000 . . . over two-thirds of the number who were there when I came into office." This meant that "the American involvement in Vietnam is coming to an end. The day the South Vietnamese can take over their own defense is in sight. Our goal is a total American withdrawal from Vietnam. We can and we will reach that goal through our program of Vietnamization." [37]

Nixon indicated that he still hoped he could reach a negotiated settlement, but he was determined not to yield to public pressure for an immediate withdrawal. "If the United States should announce that we will quit regardless of what the enemy does, we would have thrown away our principal bargaining counter to win the release of American prisoners of war." Nor would he accept the overthrow of the government in Saigon. "The issue very simply is this: Shall we leave Vietnam in a way that—by our own actions—consciously turns the country over to the Communists? Or shall we leave in a way that gives the South Vietnamese a reasonable chance to survive as a free people? My plan will end American involvement in a way that would provide that chance. And the other plan would end it precipitately and give victory to the Communists." The war must be ended, Nixon concluded, "in a way that will strengthen trust for America around the world, not undermine it, in a way that will redeem the sacrifices that have been made, not insult them, in a way that will heal this Nation, not tear it apart. I can assure you tonight with confidence that American involvement in this war is coming to an end." [38]

What else could he say but that the operation was a success and that Vietnamization was working? There was no plan to change the strategy or goals. It was now a matter of political survival. Congress was again considering proposals to cut off funding for the war, and Vietnam Veterans against the War (VVAW) was planning demonstrations in Washington for the end of April. From the administration's perspective, either could throw its game plan off course. Nixon was determined to maintain his freedom to use force in Vietnam, control the pace of the American withdrawal, and claim victory when the right time came. Saigon had to be preserved to maintain American credibility, which was necessary, the president believed, to carry out his big-power diplomacy with the Soviet Union and China. The communist powers could not interpret the American withdrawal from Vietnam as a sign of weakness. As Nixon told H. R. "Bob" Haldeman and Kissinger on April 17, he planned to keep bombing North Vietnam and NVA forces, as was currently the case in Laos. "It tells the enemy that in no uncertain terms that, by God, you're going to do—we're going to stay right there, and . . . that we're going to bomb 'em, which we damn well will." That way, once American forces were withdrawn and the prisoners of war were returned, "we'll bomb the hell out of North Vietnam. Get my point? Just bomb the living bejeezus out of it, and everybody would approve of it." [39]

At the same time, Nixon wanted to get the Vietnam War out of the news and shift the focus to the emerging policy of détente. The shocking announcement that the US Ping-Pong team would go to China—the first indication that there might be a thaw in relations with Beijing—helped, as did speculation about a summit with the Soviet Union. Kissinger thought the Ping-Pong story had "driven Vietnam into a secondary rank" and played into "the way we are setting up the Hanoi thing." In the fall "we'll be in a position where we either get a settlement, or announce, together with Thieu, not a complete terminal date, but something in which, for a ceasefire and—and a prisoner exchange, we will give a terminal date." [40] The administration had finally gotten "Vietnam off the front pages and we don't want to get it there again if we can avoid it." [41]

As Nixon told Kissinger on the eve of the VVAW demonstration on April 24, "The war presents a very serious problem. You see, the war has eroded America's confidence up to this point. The people are sick of it, and . . . our game here, of course, must be to deal with it. And we've played it right to the hilt with no support and got—and, as far as the last

Laotian thing, goddamn poor execution on the part of the military. No support from anybody else and a poor excuse military." Yet Nixon worried that all of the administration's effort would come to nothing if Congress forced him to withdraw from Vietnam. "On the other hand, we also have to realize that simply ending the war in the right way may not save the country." The divisions that had developed and the criticisms of America's role in Southeast Asia and the world might lead to the end of US world leadership. "Let's put it this way," Nixon continued. "Let's suppose the war ends; let's suppose that it isn't known until next year; and then the war is over, and then, politically, we go down—the country." There was "no way" they could allow that to happen. That was why, the president declared, "everything has to be played, now, in terms of how we survive." Only peace with honor, which meant the survival of Saigon, could, in Nixon's view, save the nation and America's role in the world.[42]

Nixon stated that he "had no intention of announcing a cave-in" on Vietnam. This was why, Nixon explained, he took such big risks as the Laotian campaign. "The Laotian gamble cost us. It cost us very, very seriously, because we probably did—Well, let me put it this way: had it not been done—I think the comfort we can take from it—had it not been done, there certainly would've been a big summer offensive by the Communists." The downside was that it had revived the antiwar movement after the troop withdrawals had seemingly brought an end to protests. "The war issue was finished last fall. A lot of people thought it was finished, and everybody was relaxed. And that's why we held up rather well in the polls. The action in Laos, itself, dropped us ten points in the polls." This was why it was crucial that peace now be the administration's theme. "I've got to have good news," he told Kissinger, because the "people have got to be reassured." He wanted to be able to make an announcement that summer or fall about troop withdrawals and an end to the American combat role in Vietnam because "people have got to know the war is over. They've got to know that."[43] If all fell into place, "we'll end the goddamn war and blame—and say, 'We ended it, they started it.'" It was necessary to "keep one step ahead" of the opposition in Congress.[44]

The problem with the strategy of reassuring the public that the troop withdrawals demonstrated that the war was over, Nixon believed, was that the antiwar movement and the media were out to prevent him from winning both the war and reelection. The VVAW demonstrations would be news for two weeks of "highly-unconscionable reporting," according to the president. "Well," Kissinger said, "they want to destroy you, and they want us to lose in Vietnam." You have to realize, Nixon said, "that critics of the war are furious that when they thought they had it licked, when they threw Johnson out of office, they thought, 'Well, now, we've won our point on the war.' Now, we've come in, and it looks like we're gonna—they know what it is." The antiwar movement understood that "our policy . . . is to win the war." Vietnamization could not mean defeat. "Our policy is not a withdrawal. Our policy is a withdrawal in a way that will let South Vietnam survive." This was, Kissinger told the president, what drove their opponents to such extremes. They did not want Nixon to win, he said, because "you're [an] anathema" and "you don't panic. You're not Johnson." Nixon agreed, stating, "They know that they never will influence me."[45]

Still, the growing pressure was of concern to the president, particularly the issue of American POWs and the protests by veterans. Hanoi was holding onto American prisoners as leverage to obtain a complete American withdrawal. The wives and families of the POWs had organized and were seeking an end to the war so as to bring them home. Nixon feared that the POW families would endorse the congressional call for a set withdrawal date and join with the veterans in a powerful lobby. "It's our Achilles heel," Nixon told Kissinger. "If those POW wives start running around, coming on to this general election, and veterans, you're in real—we are in troubles [*sic*] like you wouldn't." He needed "a gimmick" to placate them and buy time. "We've got to have something new on POWs. . . . It's got to sound new. That's all. Just . . . put something out, some gobbledygook. You know, take your pick." The only requirement was that it had to be "one we know [Hanoi will] turn down." Kissinger suggested an announcement that the United States was raising the issue in Paris. "That's what we have to do," Nixon agreed. "That's the only thing we have to worry about—realize: I don't give a damn about the Congress, demonstrators, or anything else, but I've got to keep the POW wives from taking off. They could really hurt us. The Congress would pass that so goddamned fast it'd make your head spin, Henry. I know this Congress. On that issue—they would not desert us on the others, but they'd desert us on that issue."[46]

The April–May 1971 demonstrations were some of the largest of the war and certainly reflected the opinion, if not always the tactics, of the majority of Americans. The VVAW had first captured public attention back in January with its "Winter Soldiers" hearings into atrocities committed during the war by American soldiers and the breakdown of discipline within the armed forces. By the time the VVAW began gathering in Washington on April 18, 60 percent of the public thought the war was a mistake and over 70 percent favored a US withdrawal.[47] The weeklong protests culminated with a candlelight march to the Capitol on Thursday, April 22; with more than one thousand veterans throwing their combat medals over a fence onto the Capitol steps on Friday; and with a mass demonstration on Saturday that drew up to five hundred thousand people and with another large rally held in San Francisco on the same day. A small group, calling itself the May Day Tribe, stayed in Washington and conducted a series of random acts of violence that led to a crackdown to drive the protestors out of the city and the arrest of over ten thousand protesters on May 2.

One of the most poignant moments in all of the protests during the Vietnam War occurred when John Kerry addressed the Senate Foreign Relations Committee on behalf of the VVAW. He began his comments by summarizing the findings of the "Winter Soldier Investigation" "at which over 150 honorably discharged, and many very highly decorated, veterans testified to war crimes committed in Southeast Asia." The litany of actions added up to American soldiers having "generally ravaged the countryside of South Vietnam in addition to the normal ravage of war and the normal and very particular ravaging which is done by the applied bombing power of this country." The veterans in Washington and the other veterans they represented were men who had been "given the chance to die for the biggest nothing in history; men who have returned with a sense of anger and a sense of betrayal." They had been caught up in a war that made no sense. There was no threat to the United States, and the claim of fighting for freedom was, to them, "the height of criminal hypocrisy, and it is that kind of hypocrisy which we feel has torn this country apart."[48]

The VVAW had come to protest in the nation's capital because "we feel we have been used in the worst fashion by the administration of this country." The nation had already realized the war was unwinnable, but now people were told they "must watch quietly while American lives are lost so that we can exercise the incredible arrogance of Vietnamizing the Vietnamese." In order to maintain the fiction that America had not failed, "someone has to give up his life so that the United States doesn't have to admit something that the entire world already knows, so that we can't say that we have made a mistake. Someone has to die," Kerry continued, "so that President Nixon won't be, and these are his words, 'the first President to lose a war.'" Kerry asked the nation "to think about that because how do you ask a man to be the last man to die in Vietnam? How do you ask a man to be the last man to die for a mistake?"[49]

In a tight spot, the president returned to the logic of the madman theory as a possible scenario to get what he wanted from Hanoi. Nixon thought that in view of a recent shelling by North Vietnam, "we ought to hit those sites that, normally, we can't bomb now." It was vital to demonstrate to Hanoi "right after these demonstrations, that we're not going to be affected by them." That meant "the only thing to do is to bang 'em." The strikes could be sold to the public as "protective reaction" to threats against American troops. But the main point, Nixon stated, was that "we're going to crack 'em this week."[50] Such actions would also help in Paris, he believed. Kissinger could tell Xuan Thuy that if Hanoi did not accept the American offer on a cease-fire and prisoner exchange, he could not predict what the president would do next. Kissinger would say, "Now, look, this President is extremely tough. You've been wrong every time. If you think you're going to defeat him, if you don't accept this, he will stop at nothing," "imply[ing] that you might do it," that is, "use nuclear weapons." Nixon added, "You can say that. You can say, 'I cannot control him.' Put it that way." Yes, Kissinger responded, "and imply that you might use nuclear weapons." Nixon again scripted it for him. "'He will,' you should say. 'I just want you to know he is not going to cave.'" If Hanoi then publicly revealed the threat, Kissinger said, "I'll deny it." "Oh, sure," Nixon said.[51]

A National Intelligence Estimate (NIE) on South Vietnam at the end of April provided little comfort to the administration. Although it was assumed, for the purpose of the analysis, that the United States would continue to support Saigon militarily and economically beyond 1972, as the American combat role in Vietnam ended, the ARVN would face serious challenges. The prospects for 1971 were positive due to progress in Vietnamization and because the enemy, whose "strength remains substantial," was expected to "rely essentially on the basically conservative tactics observed over the past year. While occasional spurts of larger-scale military activity seem almost certain, particularly in the north, any such activity in South Vietnam would probably be limited in area and duration." However, the outlook for 1972 was filled with problems. Given the reduction of American forces and the upcoming presidential election, Hanoi would certainly increase its military activity. "The aim of this strategy would be to score tactical victories likely to impact adversely on the South Vietnamese and US will to persist in the struggle—specifically, to discredit the Vietnamization program and to encourage sentiment in the US for complete disengagement from the war." Moreover, "there seems little doubt that the communists will continue to maintain an active military and political challenge to the GVN well beyond 1972." A key reason for "Hanoi's ability to stay the course in South Vietnam is the apparent durability of the communist party apparatus there." The NLF cadres "have been able to maintain a viable organization, and this is likely to continue to be the case for the foreseeable future."[52]

Given these realities, "South Vietnamese forces will probably require substantial US support for many years." Saigon's military "lacks the logistical system and technological and managerial skills required to maintain and support a modern fighting force. There are also serious personnel problems, including a shortage of qualified leaders and a propensity for enlisted ranks to desert." With these formidable problems and the uncertain duration of American support, the NIE concluded that the combination of the "doubts concerning the South Vietnamese will to persist, the resiliency of the communist apparatus in South Vietnam, and North Vietnam's demonstrated ability and willingness to pay the price of perseverance are such that the longer term survival of the GVN is by no means yet assured."[53]

Regarding an upcoming round of talks in Paris, Nixon stated in a long conversation with Haig and Haldeman that the United States had to go through with them for appearances, but they were not intended to bring peace. Kissinger had to negotiate for "his little Mickey Mouse game of going over to Paris and seeing those fellows, and so forth and so on. I have no, no illusions about that," Nixon told Haig. "First of all, I asked him—it may be they may not see him. Second, if they do, they're just going to diddle him along, and, and we're not going to do that this time. This is going to be an ultimatum, as far as I'm concerned." Kissinger could have one meeting, but the United States would not get strung along. "He's not going to have two meetings. I mean, he's going to say, 'We're going to have an understanding in this regard,' and then he can give it three days, or four days, or whatever the case is. But, the idea that we will wait and have to have them screw around in those meetings in Paris again, is just not going to happen again," as it had in the fall. "There is really nothing in that record, the previous record . . . to indicate that any progress was made in those talks."[54]

Nor could the United States expect help from the communist superpowers. Kissinger was hopeful that because the administration was making secret overtures to China and holding talks with Russia, Hanoi might be worried. "That's all gobbledygook," Nixon said. "That's a guess. Maybe. Maybe there is; maybe there isn't. But, it's either fish or cut bait now." Haig noted that the administration needed "to have a record. . . . You have to have a record of proposing a fixed withdrawal date, and it being turned down." Nixon concurred. "That record will be made, and then we'll go."[55]

The president wanted to be clear, however, about his goals. The pursuit of détente and improved relations with Beijing did not mean he would abandon Saigon. "The Chinese thing shouldn't—it has nothing to do with it; absolutely nothing to do with it. I mean, if—whatever happens on that will, will just be a dividend. . . . We're going to do the China thing for other reasons." Nixon continued, "You've got the Chinese game, and we've got the Soviet game, and we've got the, the other game, and so forth and so on. Because I know the domestic game at this point. At the present time, we have got to move decisively [unclear] for domestic reasons. Not, not to—we're not—we're not going to change in terms of withdrawal, or anything like that." The Senate was considering the McGovern-Hatfield end-the-war resolution that called for a final withdrawal of all American troops by December 31, 1971, and Nixon was concerned that it might gain passage if he did not appear to be moving toward peace. The talks in Paris were part of keeping up the illusion of progress to prevent Congress from further restricting his power and forcing a final withdrawal. "The Senate votes are the ones I'm concerned about. I've got to have something; something more than simply, 'Well, and—well, we offered the South Vietnamese—or the North Vietnamese, a terminal date, we've got a date.'" It had to be in the form of "the American combat role ends at a certain time, that'll have some impact. Right?" Nixon continued, "We are saying, 'As of a date certain, if you'll give us a cease-fire and release our prisoners, we'll be out.' That's new, and we all know that it's new. And it's very significant. We all know it's very significant. But . . . to the average person in the country, that's just another [unclear] gobbledygook like the one we made before."⁵⁶

Nixon hoped all this could occur prior to his planned meeting with Thieu on June 8. If the talks with the Soviets went well and he could announce a summit, that would have an impact on Congress and make another peace proposal unnecessary. Nixon told Haig that if "the summit thing, if something comes on that, it could have an effect. It could be a big play in early June, if they're ready to announce it." If not, then "we might only have only one ball left, at this time, in the political field, and that's the meeting with Thieu, and the combat troop thing. And that would help. But it would have to come June 8th." If the announcement came any later, "it would be past the votes, and I would hate like hell to go over and have a meeting with him and announce that no more combat troops are going to be there after the Senate had voted a terminal date. . . . I don't want to have actions taken which appear to be in reaction to duress, or to the Senate." Nixon wanted either the summit or the troop announcement, it did not matter which. What did matter, Nixon stated, was having one of them, as they were "the only things that can have any effect on the Congressional situation. See, that will really hit 'em, it will hit with a great shock. The other things—SALT [the Strategic Arms Limitation Treaty]—will help some sophisticated people."⁵⁷

Nixon returned to the Paris negotiations at the end of the meeting. "You understand," he stated, "with Henry bouncing back and forth with Paris and those goddamn trips," the North Vietnamese would "like to string it along, because they know very well that we don't do anything" when talks are being held. Yet Nixon wanted to bomb the North again. "We're going to hit 'em," he told Haig. "I mean, they can't turn down an offer like that, and they can't make some of the jackass statements they make without paying some consequences, and that's the only thing we've got left. We're just about ready to hit 'em again, so I—so they—see, that's another reason for you, when you're talking to Henry, must be pressing Thieu. I mean, we—look, we can't diddle any more. That's the whole point." The only thing "that really matters is the talk that's going on in the Senate at the present time."⁵⁸

Nixon was determined to end the war on his terms and schedule. If Congress cut off the funding and said the United States had to be out in December, "what do you do then? Then what's happened to Vietnam?" The administration had "fought a long battle, and we can win it. But, right now, we've got to shoot our bullets and shoot them in good enough time." After the meeting with Thieu, the president said, he could announce that South Vietnam "will assume the full combat responsibility at a certain time, that's pretty goddamn good news, isn't it?" As Haldeman noted, everyone knew the United States was propping up the Thieu government. Nixon responded that was right, so Washington had to "just do it and do it well." Paris was a dead end, Nixon stated. Hanoi was not "going to talk," Nixon declared. "Why the hell should they?" The North Vietnamese know "we're going to get out anyway. You see my point?" They were well aware of the domestic restraints the president faced.[59]

In their effort to stay ahead of the political opposition, Nixon and Kissinger softened the American negotiating position. The American "package," as Kissinger presented it on May 31, included a willingness to set a specific date for the removal of all American forces, a cease-fire-in-place with international supervision, no infiltration of outside forces, and the release of the POWs. It no longer included mutual withdrawal of forces but still insisted on keeping the Thieu government in power. While Kissinger thought an agreement on this basis would put Saigon "in a good position," the proposal would demonstrate that the administration had "improved our negotiating record," should Hanoi remain intransigent and thus "strengthen our position both here at home and around the world."[60]

Nixon refused to accept the remaining issue, the removal of the current government in Saigon, as a condition for an agreement. He intended to stand behind Thieu, who Washington was sure would win the October election, or Ky or Minh if one of them happened to win. Suppose Thieu did lose, Nixon stated. It would not make much difference, given that the leaders in Saigon "live at our sufferance, anyway. They'd have to come along."[61] The main point, Nixon told Kissinger and Haig, was that Washington was not going to "overthrow" the government in Saigon. "We're not going to turn the country over—17 million people—over to the Communists against their will. Put that down and get those sons-of-bitches to say it that way." He was emphatic, telling Haig to make sure they added "with the bloodbath that would be sure to follow" to their statements that he would not allow a change of government in Saigon.[62]

It infuriated Nixon and Kissinger that their opposition in the Senate continued to push them on withdrawal. Recalling for Kissinger a recent conversation with John Sherman Cooper, Nixon said that he had told the senator that all he had done since coming to the White House was pull out troops. Yet Cooper, Frank Church, and the other doves remained his opponents even though they knew "damn well where we are" in reducing the American role in the war and what the situation would be the following year. In addition, Nixon fumed to his national security advisor that they were not getting any help from the military in Vietnam with making things look good either. In keeping with their constant finger-pointing to explain the failure of their policy, Kissinger told the president that "the real problem is that [Military Assistance Command, Vietnam] is just not on top of its job." Either Melvin Laird was not pushing them hard enough, or "because Abrams has just quit, they're not making their extra-special effort . . . that makes the difference between success and failure" on the battlefield.[63]

Nixon concurred with Kissinger's point. The American commanders were "just sitting out there like the French used to sit," he said. The president stated that he wanted a new general, someone like Lieutenant General William DePuy, assistant chief of staff of the army, to go to Saigon. "He's a cocky little bastard," Nixon stated, and they could "let him go out there and . . . shape them up." They could bring Abrams home the next time they announced a troop withdrawal and make the change. The announcement could be, "'We're finished there.' Hand De-Puy with what we have left. That there's been no deal, and tell him don't worry, he'll—he'll be looking for our opportunity to smack 'em." It remained doubtful, however, if a greater military effort would work. Kissinger put the odds at no better than one in three that North Vietnam would agree to the American terms. Nixon acknowledged he was right, and said, "I'm not being hopeful."[64] It was an oblique admission that their earlier policy of military victory had failed. Now they had to make sure it did not hurt them in the reelection campaign. Still, Nixon again emphasized the need to keep the Vietnam War out of the news while he turned to détente and big-power diplomacy to position himself as the peace candidate in 1972.

Yet it proved difficult to avoid news of the war. On June 13, 1971, the *New York Times* began publishing excerpts from the *Pentagon Papers*, a classified study of the Vietnam War from the Harry S. Truman administration until May 1968, containing over three thousand pages of analysis and four thousand pages of documents. Commissioned in 1967 by then secretary of defense Robert McNamara, the *Pentagon Papers* revealed the credibility gap between what four administrations had told the American public about Vietnam and their actual policies, actions, and knowledge of the war. Nixon had the Department of Justice obtain a temporary restraining order on the publication of the study on the ground that disclosure of classified material compromised national security. In a 6–3 decision, the Supreme Court ruled that the administration had failed to make its case and allowed the publication of the *Pentagon Papers* to resume.

In the midst of the initial debates over the leaked documents, McGovern-Hatfield was defeated in the Senate on June 16 by a vote of 55–42. A month later, the administration revealed that Kissinger had made a secret trip to Beijing and that the president had accepted Mao Zedong's invitation to visit China the next year. Nixon and Kissinger hoped that this news might prompt Hanoi to accept the latest American offer. After meeting with Le Duc Tho in late July, Kissinger told Nixon that "the shock of your impending Peking visit" left him unsure about how to precede on the only issue left, "the replacement by us of Thieu." Neither side, however, was yet willing to give in on this point. Hanoi insisted on a coalition government without Thieu in return for an end to the fighting, and Washington refused to yield.[65]

Kissinger thought Hanoi faced a dilemma that caused "real anguish" for the North Vietnamese. "They have fought for many years to gain control over South Vietnam or at least a friendly government," Kissinger told Nixon, "and they cannot clearly see how they will achieve that aim if they stop fighting. On the other hand, they do not see how they can achieve it if they continue." It was a position Hanoi found hard to confront because "their cadres and their public opinion, who have fought so hard and lost so much, may find it very hard to swallow a settlement under which Thieu remains." Yet Le Duc Tho made it clear the war would continue. He told Kissinger "that 'no Vietnamese' would accept an agreement without knowing the political future of South Vietnam." Kissinger also reported that Tho, "referring indirectly to the Peking trip," had said "there was no 'magical way' of settling the Vietnam problem, and that only the participants could end the war. He emphasized their independence and the support they were getting from 'socialist countries.'"[66]

Despite the lack of evidence, Nixon and Kissinger continued to develop scenarios in which Hanoi would fold to American pressure. Discussing on August 17 another upcoming trip to Paris by Kissinger, Nixon dismissed the negotiations as Kissinger's "just going over there and yakking around, you know, and they go over the same ground, and maybe, maybe—well, we'll settle one little, miserable point." Kissinger agreed, stating that he did not expect a settlement. Still, there was an advantage because, after it failed, "they [would] get hit with [the] Russian" news. That, Kissinger stated, was "going to be a real jolt to them." He was referring to the forthcoming announcement that Nixon would travel to Moscow in May 1972 for a summit meeting with Soviet leaders. Kissinger noted that Hanoi would stall so that it did not appear to be reaching an agreement under pressure, but the North Vietnamese would have to yield. "They can see—in other words, they will see inevitability," Nixon said. Kissinger concurred. Hanoi would see "their two big allies are dealing with us before the war in Vietnam has ended. Both of them have invited you to their capitals while the war is still going on. Both of them, no matter what they tell them, have a vested interest to make sure that they don't screw it all up because they obviously have their own fish to fry." This meant that even if the communist superpowers did not apply "direct pressure, the mere fact that they are seeing you," would influence Hanoi and the North Vietnamese still know "we've got them off the front pages—no matter what happens—until the middle of November."[67]

In other words, Kissinger stated, the Vietnam War was no longer the story. Under Lyndon Johnson, it was the only foreign policy issue; "therefore, the slightest twitch was a headline." Now, it was hard for

Hanoi to make news as "we've made Vietnam a small country in Asia." If the North tried to disrupt the trip to Beijing in February or Moscow in May, Kissinger speculated, the American public would turn against Hanoi. The national security advisor went so far as to predict a peace settlement in November. Nixon, however, was not as sure. "The American public isn't going to like anymore so-called 'escalation'" that would come from an American response to an enemy offensive. "That's the problem we've got."[68]

The president was right. Public opinion would not accept another stepped-up American military effort. Nixon's only option was to continue to aid Saigon, remove the remaining US forces, and plan for endless fighting in Vietnam. Combined with the state of the military in Vietnam, congressional restraints, and public opinion, another factor restraining the president's actions was the state of the economy. The Vietnam War had brought an end to the post–World War II economic boom and prosperity. By 1971, unemployment in the United States was above 6 percent and increasing, and inflation was rising as well, approaching 5.9 percent that summer. Moreover, the United States was, for the first time in the twentieth century, experiencing a trade deficit with the rest of the world. Current economic theory could not account for the combination of high unemployment and high inflation, leading to a new concept, stagflation, to explain an inflationary cycle during a recession.

In response, Nixon began experimenting with drastic government intervention into the economy. In March, he signed an executive order imposing wage and price controls on the construction industry to try to stop the dramatic rise in the costs of commercial building. On August 15, Nixon shocked the nation when he announced his new steps to address the economic crisis. The United States would abandon the Bretton Woods arrangement and stop converting dollars into gold at a fixed rate. In addition, he was imposing wage and price controls on the whole economy for ninety days in an effort to stop a further growth in inflation, as well as a 10 percent tax surcharge on imports to redress the trade imbalance by making imports more expensive. The American economy could no longer afford all of the global commitments the nation had made after World War II.

The failure in Vietnam had exposed the hubris behind the concept of the American Century and the limits to American power. As the problems that faced the nation mounted—stalemate in Vietnam, internal divisions, economic crisis—Richard Nixon was forced to abandon his quest for a decisive military victory. In its place, he sought to salvage American credibility and his political future thorough a complicated calculus of reducing American casualties while continuing the war. On November 12, 1971, the president announced the end of US participation in offensive ground operations and the withdrawal of another forty-five thousand troops. His short-term political strategy of creating the illusion of peace was working, but the war was hardly over. It was defeat in disguise.

NOTES

1. Henry Luce, "The American Century," *Life*, February 17, 1941. The four freedoms were freedom of speech and of religion and freedom from want and from fear.

2. Luce, "The American Century."

3. *FRUS, 1969–1976, Vol. 7: Vietnam, July 1970–January 1972*, Documents 1 and 4; see also Senior Review Group Meeting, September 15, 1970, "Short-Term Cambodia Strategy (NSSM 99)," NSCH Files/Minutes of Meetings, Box H111, RNPL.

4. *FRUS, 1969–1976, Vol. 7: Vietnam, July 1970–January 1972*, Document 31.

5. *FRUS, 1969–1976, Vol. 7: Vietnam, July 1970–January 1972*, Document 35.

6. *FRUS, 1969–1976, Vol. 7: Vietnam, July 1970–January 1972*, Document 41.

7. *FRUS, 1969–1976, Vol. 7: Vietnam, July 1970–January 1972*, Document 43.

8. *FRUS, 1969–1976, Vol. 7: Vietnam, July 1970–January 1972*, Document 45.

9. *Public Papers of the Presidents: Nixon, 1970*, 825–28 (emphasis in the original).

10. *Public Papers of the Presidents: Nixon, 1970*, 825–28 (emphasis in the original).

11. *FRUS, 1969–1976, Vol. 7: Vietnam, July 1970–January 1972*, Document 46.

12. *Public Papers of the Presidents: Nixon, 1970*, 836.

13. Col. Robert D. Heinl Jr., "The Collapse of the Armed Forces," *Armed Forces Journal* (June 1971), 30–37.

14. Heinl, "The Collapse of the Armed Forces."

15. Heinl, "The Collapse of the Armed Forces."

16. Colin Powell, *My American Journey* (New York: Random House, 1995).

17. Powell, *My American Journey*.

18. *FRUS, 1969–1976, Vol. 7: Vietnam, July 1970–January 1972*, Document 29.

19. *FRUS, 1969–1976, Vol. 7: Vietnam, July 1970–January 1972*, Document 190.

20. *FRUS, 1969–1976, Vol. 7: Vietnam, July 1970–January 1972*, Document 47.

21. *FRUS, 1969–1976, Vol. 7: Vietnam, July 1970–January 1972*, Documents 58 and 76.

22. *FRUS, 1969–1976, Vol. 7: Vietnam, July 1970–January 1972*, Document 76.

23. *Public Papers of the Presidents: Nixon, 1970*, 1074–79.

24. *FRUS, 1969–1976, Vol. 7: Vietnam, July 1970–January 1972*, Document 70.

25. *FRUS, 1969–1976, Vol. 7: Vietnam, July 1970–January 1972*, Document 100.

26. *FRUS, 1969–1976, Vol. 7: Vietnam, July 1970–January 1972*, Document 248.

27. Haig to Kissinger, December 15, 1970, NSC Files/Haig Special Files, Box 1012, RNPL; see also Haig, "Trip Report," NSC Files/Special Files, Box 1011, RNPL.

28. *FRUS, 1969–1976, Vol. 7: Vietnam, July 1970–January 1972*, Document 96 (emphasis in the original).

29. *FRUS, 1969–1976, Vol. 7: Vietnam, July 1970–January 1972*, Document 127.

30. *FRUS, 1969–1976, Vol. 7: Vietnam, July 1970–January 1972*, Document 131.

31. *FRUS, 1969–1976, Vol. 7: Vietnam, July 1970–January 1972*, Document 117.

32. *FRUS, 1969–1976, Vol. 7: Vietnam, July 1970–January 1972*, Document 142.

33. *FRUS, 1969–1976, Vol. 7: Vietnam, July 1970–January 1972*, Document 147.

34. *FRUS, 1969–1976, Vol. 7: Vietnam, July 1970–January 1972*, Document 156.

35. *FRUS, 1969–1976, Vol. 7: Vietnam, July 1970–January 1972*, Document 157; see also *FRUS, 1969–1976, Vol. 7: Vietnam, July 1970–January 1972*, Document 178.

36. *FRUS, 1969–1976, Vol. 7: Vietnam, July 1970–January 1972*, Document 174.

37. *Public Papers of the Presidents: Richard Nixon, 1971* (Washington, DC: Government Printing Office, 1972), 522–27.

38. *Public Papers of the Presidents: Nixon, 1971*, 522–27.

39. *FRUS, 1969–1976, Vol. 7: Vietnam, July 1970–January 1972*, Document 185.

40. *FRUS, 1969–1976, Vol. 7: Vietnam, July 1970–January 1972*, Document 185.

41. *FRUS, 1969–1976, Vol. 7: Vietnam, July 1970–January 1972*, Document 186.

42. *FRUS, 1969–1976, Vol. 7: Vietnam, July 1970–January 1972,* Document 188.
43. *FRUS, 1969–1976, Vol. 7: Vietnam, July 1970–January 1972,* Document 188.
44. *FRUS, 1969–1976, Vol. 7: Vietnam, July 1970–January 1972,* Document 200.
45. *FRUS, 1969–1976, Vol. 7: Vietnam, July 1970–January 1972,* Document 190.
46. *FRUS, 1969–1976, Vol. 7: Vietnam, July 1970–January 1972,* Document 191.
47. Small, *Johnson, Nixon, and the Doves,* 214–15.
48. US Senate, Committee on Foreign Relations, *Legislative Proposals Relating to the War in Southeast Asia: Hearings,* 180–210.
49. US Senate, Committee on Foreign Relations, *Legislative Proposals Relating to the War in Southeast Asia: Hearings,* 180–210.
50. *FRUS, 1969–1976, Vol. 7: Vietnam, July 1970–January 1972,* Document 191.
51. *FRUS, 1969–1976, Vol. 7: Vietnam, July 1970–January 1972,* Document 190.
52. *FRUS, 1969–1976, Vol. 7: Vietnam, July 1970–January 1972,* Document 195.
53. *FRUS, 1969–1976, Vol. 7: Vietnam, July 1970–January 1972,* Document 195.
54. *FRUS, 1969–1976, Vol. 7: Vietnam, July 1970–January 1972,* Document 197.
55. *FRUS, 1969–1976, Vol. 7: Vietnam, July 1970–January 1972,* Document 197.
56. *FRUS, 1969–1976, Vol. 7: Vietnam, July 1970–January 1972,* Document 197.
57. *FRUS, 1969–1976, Vol. 7: Vietnam, July 1970–January 1972,* Document 197.
58. *FRUS, 1969–1976, Vol. 7: Vietnam, July 1970–January 1972,* Document 197.
59. *FRUS, 1969–1976, Vol. 7: Vietnam, July 1970–January 1972,* Document 197.
60. *FRUS, 1969–1976, Vol. 7: Vietnam, July 1970–January 1972,* Document 206.
61. *FRUS, 1969–1976, Vol. 7: Vietnam, July 1970–January 1972,* Document 218.
62. *FRUS, 1969–1976, Vol. 7: Vietnam, July 1970–January 1972,* Document 227.
63. *FRUS, 1969–1976, Vol. 7: Vietnam, July 1970–January 1972,* Document 218.
64. *FRUS, 1969–1976, Vol. 7: Vietnam, July 1970–January 1972,* Document 218.
65. *FRUS, 1969–1976, Vol. 7: Vietnam, July 1970–January 1972,* Document 237.
66. *FRUS, 1969–1976, Vol. 7: Vietnam, July 1970–January 1972,* Document 237.
67. *FRUS, 1969–1976, Vol. 7: Vietnam, July 1970–January 1972,* Document 246.
68. *FRUS, 1969–1976, Vol. 7: Vietnam, July 1970–January 1972,* Document 246.

SIX

Denouement

As Richard Nixon finished his third year in office, the war in Vietnam remained a stalemate with neither side able to gain the upper hand. Negotiations in Paris had broken down again as Hanoi was unwilling to reach an agreement that left President Nguyen Van Thieu in power, and Washington would not yield on mutual withdrawal and a political process that left the current government in power in Saigon. Yet the dynamics of the war had changed. Nixon's efforts to buy time for his pursuit of victory through troop withdrawals and Vietnamization had forced the president to lower American troop levels to a point that, by the fall of 1971, US forces could no longer engage in offensive operations and were now in Vietnam solely in a defensive capacity and to serve as leverage in negotiations.

Hanoi remained determined to topple the Thieu regime and to unify Vietnam under its rule. Its military and negotiating strategies continued to work toward that end throughout 1972. As Le Duc Tho told Henry Kissinger, "You are faced with many difficulties in Indochina. You want to get out of these difficulties. The last few years you have been trying to go here and there to seek a way out. . . . I think you make the problem more complicated for yourself, because you don't get the results you expect. There is no magical way to settle the problem of Vietnam outside of serious negotiations here in Paris on the basis of our proposals and your proposals." In other words, the United States had attempted to defeat Hanoi and failed. There was no means, the North Vietnamese negotiator believed, for the United States to achieve a military victory, and acknowledgment of this reality was necessary for peace. "If the war continues," Tho stated, "we are firmly confident in our success, in our victory."[1]

Still, Nixon remained committed to Saigon, and negotiations broke down after Thieu's reelection in October 1971. The October elections were blatantly corrupt, and Thieu's continued hold on power did not create any greater legitimacy or support for his regime. The United States had cast its support of the elections in Saigon in terms of an expression of the free will of the South Vietnamese people and their right to determine their political future, which the Nixon administration wanted to see guaranteed by any peace agreement. In response, Xuan Thuy told Kissinger that the more the United States explained its position, "the more the actual situation belies your assertions. I really did not expect that after the election for the Lower House in South Vietnam and after the activities of Ambassador [Ellsworth] Bunker towards the candidates in South Vietnam, that Mr. Special Advisor Kissinger would still affirm that the United States wants fair elections in South Vietnam, that you want to abstain from influencing the results, and that you want the South Vietnamese people to freely express their views." Rather, it appeared to Hanoi "that the United States, one way or another, wants to maintain the Nguyen Van Thieu Administration in power in order to implement neocolonialism in South Vietnam." Le Duc Tho noted that Hanoi had "repeatedly reiterated that if the United States Government maintains the Nguyen Van Thieu Administration, then we can come to no settlement at all."[2]

Prior to the vote, a lengthy National Security Council discussion of Vietnam on September 20 set out clearly the central unresolved problem Washington faced in Vietnam. Speaking about Saigon, Chairman of the Joint Chiefs of Staff Admiral Thomas Moorer stated that he believed the United States had provided the Army of the Republic of Vietnam (ARVN) with the opportunity to win the war. "From the military point of view, the South Vietnamese should be able to pull their own weight and provide their own security. This is not so much a matter of hardware and equipment, but of political structure and national will." Nixon stated that he agreed. "They have the equipment, weapons, and airforce which the other side doesn't have." Yet no significant progress had been made, and the enemy remained relentless. Still, Nixon remained determined to see Saigon survive. "Our choice may be difficult, but the only one there who can run the country is Thieu. Whether there will be a referendum or elections, and the people vote for or not for, Thieu is the only one there. [Nguyen Cao] Ky can't do it, and [Duong Van] Minh is unbelievable. There's a real war on, finding a new leader is very difficult, and we're going to back Thieu. . . . We must take that hard line."[3]

The United States, Nixon continued, had to put the best face on the situation and make it appear that it was succeeding, as American credibility was at stake. After all, "we've gone through a lot—the demonstrations in 1969, the Cambodia demonstrations, and those last May, but we're still around. We have been able to survive." It was essential that this continue. If the United States pulled out now and Saigon fell, the

American people "would heave a sigh of relief. We could have lived with that for a year and a half. Then the consequences would come—an unmitigated disaster in terms of our foreign policy in the future." American credibility would be ruined, given the doubts many nations already had about the United States. "Because of neo-isolationism, our moves towards the Chinese and the Soviets, and the Nixon Doctrine itself, there are surely some doubts that the U.S. can be relied upon. After the U.S. let Diem down, that is after the murder of Diem, for us to say that Thieu is out because he didn't do what we wanted—I can see the whole thing unravel starting from Southeast Asia, Indonesia, and Thailand, and all the way to Japan. What we really confront is what has been a long and terrible trial for U.S. foreign policy: will it fail or succeed?"[4] Thus, even though the American phase of the war was winding down, it was imperative that Washington continue to prop up Saigon, even in the face of so much opposition.

This complex problem had to be juggled carefully, the president noted. Moscow and Beijing could misinterpret détente and the shift to containment through negotiation rather that confrontation, in conjunction with Vietnamization, as weakness. Nixon therefore saw his actions in Vietnam as crucial to dispelling this perception. No matter the type of settlement reached, Nixon remained determined to back South Vietnam militarily. On the one hand, Nixon noted, "the China initiative is very important, even though we only agreed to discuss differences. We do have differences with China, but within 15 years it will be a significant power, and the question is will we discuss these differences or fight about them? So we're starting now." Similarly, it was vital to talk with the Soviets and stabilize the Cold War conflict. "We give a little, and they give a little, and no position has changed. To be able to play these games, it is doubly important that the U.S. not fail in Vietnam"; otherwise, the rest of the world would say, "'My God, can we depend on the U.S.?' So, realistically, we have to see it through, and the way is to stand by Thieu and support him." He would announce in November the end of American ground operations in Vietnam as a sign of progress, but the United States had to face the fact that its success depended on keeping Thieu in power. "We must stick through this way," Nixon concluded.[5] Thus, any agreement reached in Paris would be for the purpose of the president's reelection and not as the basis of a final end to the war. The president had no intention of allowing Saigon to fall.

A conversation between Nixon and Kissinger in late November 1971 made this clear. In a preview of what would occur after the election the following year, Nixon told Kissinger what he was preparing to do. "The day after that election—win, lose, or draw—we will bomb the bejeezus out of them. Because then, to hell with history." Kissinger encouraged the president, stating, "History will think well of you, then." This would be, the president said, a no-holds-barred air campaign. "I'd take out the railroads; I'd take out the air force; I'd take out the—you know, just, just knock the shit out of 'em for three months." Hanoi, the president continued, did not realize it, but they would have to contend with him one way or another next November—"they have to deal with, here, a man, who if he wins the election will kick the shit out of them, and if he loses the election will do it even more. Now, there's where we are." Nixon continued, "Some would say, 'Well, if you lost the election, the editorials will scream: He doesn't have a mandate,' and so forth. Bullshit! I couldn't care less. I could care, then, about seeing that America didn't lose the war. And getting back our prisoners, which is even more important at that time. See? I'm telling you: we've got cards then, and we'd be ready." Although the main targets would be military, Nixon noted, "incidentally, I wouldn't worry about a little slop over, and knock off a few villages and hamlets, and the rest." He concluded by telling Kissinger he needed to let the North Vietnamese know in private the president's determination to preserve the Saigon government and the ends he would go to after the election. "I really would. I'd finish off the goddamn place. . . . Bomb Haiphong. You know, the whole thing. I would put a crippling blow on it. Go on for 60 days of bombing. Just knock the shit out of them." Kissinger replied, "Absolutely. Absolutely!"[6] Through airpower, Nixon believed, he could ensure the survival of Saigon.

President Nixon would run for reelection in 1972 as a peace candidate, as the man who had ended the Vietnam War and lessened the tensions of the Cold War. To this end, on January 25, 1972, Nixon revealed to the nation that Henry Kissinger had been engaged in secret negotiations with North Vietnam since August 1969, had met with representatives of Hanoi on twelve occasions, and had made peace offers that were not yet part of the public record. Specifically, the president noted that the United States was willing, within six months of a peace agreement and cease-fire in Southeast Asia, to withdraw all of its forces from South Vietnam, exchange all prisoners of war, and support a new presidential election in Saigon.

The next month, on February 21, 1972, Richard Nixon began his historic visit to China where he met with the communist leaders of a nation the United States had refused to recognize since the Chinese Revolution in 1949. Three months later, the president would be exchanging toasts with Soviet leaders inside the Kremlin to celebrate the signing of the Strategic Arms Limitation Treaty. Upon his return, Nixon went directly to the Capitol, where he spoke to a joint session of Congress. He declared that "for decades, America has been locked in hostile confrontation with the two great Communist powers, the Soviet Union and the People's Republic of China. We were engaged with the one at many points and almost totally isolated from the other, but our relationships with both had reached a deadly impasse." Now that had all changed: "In the brief space of 4 months, these journeys to Peking and to Moscow have begun to free us from perpetual confrontation. We have moved toward better understanding, mutual respect, point-by-point settlement of differences with both the major Communist powers."[7]

Progress had been made, Nixon stated, in reducing the threat of war and shifting American Cold War policy from confrontation to negotiation. Meeting the people in the communist world, Nixon claimed, "made me more determined than ever that America must do all in its power to help that hope for peace come true for all people in the world." The summits of 1972 "are part of a great national journey for peace." Harking back to Henry Luce, the president asserted that "an unparalleled opportunity has been placed in America's hands. Never has there been a time when hope was more justified or when complacency was more dangerous. We have made a good beginning. And because we have begun, history now lays upon us a special obligation to see it through. We can seize this moment or we can lose it; we can make good this opportunity to build a new structure of peace in the world or we can let it slip away." Nixon declared that he was determined to seize the moment to bring a generation of peace. "Then the historians of some future age will write of the year 1972, not that this was the year America went up to the summit and then down to the depths of the valley again, but that this was the year when America helped to lead the world up out of the lowlands of constant war, and onto the high plateau of lasting peace."[8]

The Vietnam War received just a brief mention that belied the reality of the moment. As the president spoke, the fighting in Vietnam was at a level not seen since the 1968 Tet Offensive. On March 30, 1972, North Vietnamese forces began the so-called Easter or Spring Offensive. With negotiations deadlocked and US forces no longer engaged in ground combat, North Vietnam launched a conventional attack on South Vietnam with divisions crossing the demilitarized zone into the northernmost provinces, followed by attacks in the central highlands and northwest of Saigon in early April. The North Vietnamese scored early victories, capturing Quang Tri City and An Loc and coming close to taking Kontum City and splitting South Vietnam into two. A defeat of South Vietnam would disprove Nixon's claims that his policy of Vietnamization had succeeded in bringing peace and jeopardize the president's reelection bid. Nixon responded first with American airpower in support of ARVN forces in South Vietnam, then with Operation Linebacker, a sustained bombing campaign in North Vietnam to destroy military installations and disrupt supply lines and to punish Hanoi. He also ordered the mining of Haiphong Harbor to interrupt the flow of equipment into North Vietnam.

The American bombing ultimately proved effective in halting the offensive, but the North Vietnamese and National Liberation Front (NLF) did gain control of new territory along South Vietnam's borders and in the Mekong Delta. The blunting of Hanoi's attack did not alter the fact that the war remained a stalemate. The Spring Offensive also exposed Vietnamization as a failure in enabling Saigon to stand alone against Hanoi. There were few signs that, without the massive American air campaign, the largest yet in the war, the South could thwart the North's attack. The Easter Offensive also increased congressional pressure for a final end to American participation in the war and gave the North Vietnamese a stronger position once negotiations resumed in Paris. Finally, it demonstrated that the war would ultimately be settled by the Vietnamese and not the United States. The halting of the offensive only provided a false impression that Washington was in control of Saigon's fate.

Negotiations in Paris resumed in July. The Nixon administration was ready to settle the American role in the war. When Kissinger again met with North Vietnamese negotiators, the United States dropped the demand for a mutual withdrawal. Political pressure, economic problems, and a shift of emphasis to détente and talk of building a generation of peace made the president eager to claim he ended the war. Hanoi, seeing the opportunity to secure a final removal of all US forces from Vietnam, dropped its demand for the removal of Thieu from office prior to a cease-fire and a release of American prisoners of war. Having seen the initial success of the Spring Offensive prior to the American bombing, North Vietnamese leaders were willing to continue the war against Saigon without a regime change. On October 22, an agreement was reached that called for a cease-fire with all Vietnamese forces in place, followed by final withdrawal of all American military forces from Indochina, return of POWs, recognition of the NLF's political organization, the Provisional Revolutionary Government, as the legal authority in the territory it controlled, and establishment of a vague National Council of National Reconciliation to determine the political future of Vietnam.

From Washington's point of view, this was the best deal it could achieve in its effort to claim it had achieved peace with honor in successfully containing North Vietnam and preserving an independent South Vietnam. Nixon was also convinced, in the wake of the Spring Offensive, that American airpower would be decisive in sustaining South Vietnam. From Saigon's vantage, however, the agreement represented defeat in disguise. Thieu well realized that the presence of North Vietnamese Army (NVA) forces in South Vietnam and legal recognition of the NLF spelled his regime's demise. Therefore the South Vietnamese president rejected the settlement, making it clear that he would break with the Nixon administration and publicly criticize the proposed peace deal. Nixon, with his reelection virtually assured, decided to stick with Saigon for the moment while still reaping the political benefits of an agreement. Kissinger informed the North Vietnamese that the United States could not sign the treaty because some details had to be worked out. Yet, on October 26, Kissinger announced in a press conference that "peace was at hand," although the administration still had to work out some of the technical points and ambiguities in the arrangement. On the campaign trail in West Virginia, Nixon acknowledged that a breakthrough had been made, though the details were still being discussed. Thieu had effectively blocked the treaty's signing.

Nixon won a landslide victory on November 7 based on his self-presentation as a president who was bringing a generation of peace after three decades of war and Cold War tensions. Peace in Vietnam, however, remained an illusion. Negotiations resumed in late November but broke off on December 13. Nixon was in a bind. Although he had carried forty-nine states in the election, the Democrats controlled the legislature and, when Congress convened in January, would clearly move to cut off funding for the war and force Nixon to withdraw the remainder of American forces. The president was racing the clock if he wanted to shape the final agreement and claim he had brought peace to Vietnam. Nixon responded to the breakdown of negotiations in two ways—by bombing North Vietnam and pressuring Thieu to yield on the peace agreement. On December 18, Nixon launched Linebacker II, an around-the-clock air attack concentrated on Hanoi and Haiphong that lasted for eleven days, accompanied by the second mining of Haiphong Harbor. Over seventeen hundred sorties were flown, more than seven hundred by American B-52 bombers, dropping approximately twenty thousand tons. Nixon and Kissinger claimed the intent was to force Hanoi back to the negotiations, ready to make necessary concessions for a final agreement. This gave Nixon the opportunity to demonstrate that he planned to continue to fight in Vietnam well after any agreement was reached.

Saigon, however, was just as much a target. Nixon's action was designed to demonstrate to Thieu that he could count on Nixon to defy his critics and unleash American power in a manner similar to how it was employed during the Spring Offensive to protect South Vietnam after a treaty was signed. On December 17, the president wrote Thieu that he was making his final effort to get him to join with the United States in reaching a peace agreement and "to convey my irrevocable intention to proceed, preferably with your cooperation but, if necessary, alone." The military action he would initiate the next day, Nixon stated, was "meant to convey to the enemy my determination to bring the conflict to a rapid end—as well as to show what I am prepared to do in case of violation of the agreement." It was time for the United States and South Vietnam to present a united front in the negotiations. A refusal by Saigon to join Washington "would be an invitation to disaster—to the loss of all that we together have fought for over the past decade. It would be inexcusable above all because we will have lost a just and honorable alternative." If Thieu continued to balk, however, Nixon made it clear that he "would seek a settlement with the enemy which serves U.S. interests alone."[9]

Critics dubbed the December air attacks the Christmas bombings, and Democratic congressional leaders promised to take immediate action to prevent a continuation of the American military role in Vietnam. Nixon, after winning a landslide victory in November, saw his approval ratings plummet into the mid-30 percent range, a level they never recovered from with the revelations about Watergate. Thus, for Nixon to achieve his goal of a peace settlement that kept Thieu in power and allowed for future American military strikes, he needed to force Saigon to comply with the treaty negotiated by the United States.

In a second letter to Thieu delivered on January 5, 1972, Nixon wrote that there was little more he could add to previous communications, "including my December 17 letter, which clearly stated my opinions and intentions. With respect to the question of North Vietnamese troops, we [will] again present your views to the Communists as we have done vigorously at every other opportunity in the negotiations. The result is certain to be once more the rejection of our position. We have explained to you repeatedly why we believe the problem of North Vietnamese troops is manageable under the agreement, and I see no reason to repeat all the arguments." Nixon continued by stating again that "the gravest consequences would then ensue if your government chose to reject the agreement and split from the United States. As I said in my December 17 letter, 'I am convinced that your refusal to join us would be an invitation to disaster—to the loss of all that we together have fought for over the past decade. It would be inexcusable above all because we will have lost a just and honorable alternative.'" Nixon continued by stating that "I can only repeat what I have so often said: the best guarantee for the survival of South Vietnam is the unity of our two countries which would be gravely jeopardized if you persist in your present course. The actions of our Congress since its return have clearly borne out the many warnings we have made." Ambassador Bunker, with Kissinger's approval, inserted the following statement immediately before the last sentence: "Should you decide, as I trust you will, to go with us you have my assurance of continued assistance in the post-settlement period and that we will respond with full force should the settlement be violated by North Viet-Nam. So once more I conclude with an appeal to you to close ranks with us."[10]

When the final agreement was reached, Nixon wrote Thieu again in an effort to ensure that Saigon did not sabotage the treaty. The president noted that he understood Thieu's concern with the continued presence of NVA forces in the South and that he agreed with the South Vietnamese president that "the question of national survival is your most solemn obligation." To that end, Nixon insisted, "the most essential element for the security of South Vietnam, in addition to the courageous efforts of your own people, is the maintenance of unity between the United States and the Republic of Vietnam and with it our continued economic and military assistance. All the actions I have undertaken in recent months have been guided by this consideration of preserving for your country the support which is essential for our mutual objectives." Thieu had to recognize, Nixon stated, that "the only alternative to the pursuit of the course I have followed is the cutting off by the U.S. Congress of all future support to the Republic of Vietnam." Therefore, "any further delay would be totally counterproductive and have disastrous consequences for us all." Failure to act would result in "an inevitable and immediate termination of U.S. economic and military assistance." The president repeated once more that he was prepared to "react strongly in the event the Agreement is violated. . . . It is my firm intention to continue full economic and military aid."[11]

Thieu finally yielded, and on January 23, 1973, Nixon announced that "we today have concluded an agreement to end the war and bring peace with honor in Vietnam and in Southeast Asia." A cease-fire would begin on January 27. Within sixty days, all American forces would be withdrawn from South Vietnam and all POWs released. A Council of National Reconciliation was to be established to determine the political future of South Vietnam, while "the United States will continue to recognize the Government of the Republic of Vietnam as the sole legitimate government of South Vietnam." The president claimed that he had achieved all he set out to gain in the negotiations and stated that the nation should be "proud that America did not settle for a peace that would have betrayed our allies, that would have abandoned our prisoners of war, or that would have ended the war for us but would have continued the war for the 50 million people of Indochina."[12]

It was yet one more deception. The Paris agreement did not mean peace for Vietnam. Rather, it guaranteed continued war in South Vietnam. North Vietnamese forces remained in the South, and no one expected the political arrangements in the Paris treaty to provide a peaceful settlement. This was why Thieu had resisted the final agreement, why Hanoi was willing to yield on its insistence that there would be no agreement as long as Thieu remained in office, and why the Nixon administration secretly promised continued assistance and military retaliation when the fighting resumed.

Nixon, however, had miscalculated. Although he planned to continue to support and supply Saigon and to employ airpower to protect the ARVN from the NVA, he was unable to do so because of political changes at home. The Christmas bombings had weakened the president's position after the election. The beginning of the trial of the Watergate burglars, along with the Senate hearings on the scandal, brought forth new revelations of the administration's misconduct during the election, further eroding Nixon's political strength. By April 30, his top advisors, H. R. Haldeman, John Ehrlichman, and White House Counsel John Dean, were fired or forced to resign as the political crisis moved closer to the Oval Office. The Case-Church Amendment, narrowly defeated in August 1972, passed Congress in June 1973. It prohibited any further US military action in Vietnam, Cambodia, or Laos without congressional approval in advance. The next month, Congress passed the War Powers Resolution, which required the president to notify Congress within forty-eight hours of any military action and to receive authorization within sixty days to continue the operation. While Nixon claimed these restrictions were unconstitutional, he was in no position to challenge Congress, and they rendered him unable to provide any air support once the fighting resumed in Vietnam. The revelations about misconduct and the cover-up of the Watergate break-in led to Nixon's resignation on August 8, 1974.

Sporadic fighting occurred throughout 1973 as both sides sought to strengthen their forces and positions. North Vietnam, recognizing Nixon's inability to respond, improved the Ho Chi Minh Trail so that it could be used to move trucks, tanks, and artillery. This allowed Hanoi to support its nearly doubled force of approximately 200,000 NVA, along with 90,000 NLF troops, against 710,000 ARVN soldiers backed by over 400,000 armed civilian guards by the end of the year. In April 1974, North Vietnam began sustained attacks against Saigon's troops to improve its position and prepare for a major offensive to be launched on March 1, 1975. NVA forces quickly gained territory in the central highlands, and simultaneous attacks were initiated in the north of South Vietnam in Quang Tri Province and to the west of Saigon. Thieu decided to sacrifice the northernmost provinces for a defensive enclave further south, leading to a rapid disintegration of Saigon's fortunes. By April 18, enemy troops were preparing to enter Saigon, and the capital fell to NVA/NLF forces on April 30. The Vietnam War was finally over.

NOTES

1. *FRUS, 1969–1976*, Vol. 7: *July 1970–January 1972*, Document 236.

2. *FRUS, 1969–1976*, Vol. 7: *July 1970–January 1972*, Document 254.

3. *FRUS, 1969–1976*, Vol. 7: *July 1970–January 1972*, Document 259.

4. *FRUS, 1969–1976*, Vol. 7: *July 1970–January 1972*, Document 259.

5. *FRUS, 1969–1976*, Vol. 7: *July 1970–January 1972*, Document 259.

6. *FRUS, 1969–1976*, Vol. 7: *July 1970–January 1972*, Document 278.

7. *Public Papers of the Presidents: Richard Nixon, 1972* (Washington, DC: Government Printing Office, 1973), 660–66.

8. *Public Papers of the Presidents: Nixon, 1972*, 660–66.

9. *FRUS, 1969–1976, Vol. 9: Vietnam, October 1972–January 1973*, Document 189.

10. *FRUS, 1969–1976, Vol. 9: Vietnam, October 1972–January 1973*, Document 248.

11. *FRUS, 1969–1976, Vol. 9: Vietnam, October 1972–January 1973*, Document 278.

12. *Public Papers of the Presidents: Richard Nixon, 1973* (Washington, DC: Government Printing Office, 1974), 18–20.

Conclusions

The Nixon years, with the exception of the Paris Peace Agreement, have received much less study than any part of the Vietnam War from 1945 to 1975. Remarkably, given Nixon's efforts to win the war, there is no study that examines the crucial first years of his policy toward Vietnam. There are a number of reasons for this. For a long time there were fewer documents available on the Nixon presidency and foreign policy, a situation compounded by legal issues related to Watergate and the president's resignation that further delayed the release of much material beyond the slow process of declassification. In addition, the overshadowing focus of scholars of the Nixon years has been on Watergate and détente. Finally, in comparison to the desire to understand the origins of the Vietnam War, what has mainly been seen as the inevitable winding down of a failed enterprise has made the Vietnam War during the Nixon years, with the exception of the Paris Peace, of less interest to historians.

These structural and interpretive reasons were compounded by the difficulty of finding an interpretive narrative for the kaleidoscope of events of the time period and the deliberate deceptions of the Nixon White House concerning its policy. Moreover, Nixon's and Kissinger's views have shaped much of the scholarship and understanding of their policy. Over the years, from their early days in office through the writing of their memoirs and other works, Nixon and Kissinger have offered a consistent position on their Vietnam policy, albeit one that varies in the credit they allot to each other. The president and his national security advisor argue that they came to office bequeathed an ill-run, mismanaged, and unpopular war that, nonetheless, was vital to American interests and had to be properly managed so they could successfully address other crucial foreign policy issues, most notably Cold War relations with the Soviet Union and China. They have asserted that their approach to Vietnam, Vietnamization of the war and a gradual withdrawal, was necessary to secure an end to the war that would allow for Nixon's opening toward China and his effort to reshape the Cold War through the policy of détente.

Given that Nixon and Kissinger understood the Vietnam War in traditional Cold War terms where the United States faced an enemy that was intractable and unreasonable in its negotiations (convinced seemingly that the United States would soon quit), they believed that American credibility and moral standing in the world were on the line. This made it essential that Washington defend Saigon to prevent a communist take-over and the subsequent bloodbath Nixon claimed would result if South Vietnam fell to communism. Eschewing the "easy and popular" decision to leave Vietnam, Nixon claimed that his administration saw the war through to a successful conclusion by a combination of military pressure, triangle diplomacy with the communist superpowers, and diplomatic skill despite the opposition of Congress, the press, and the antiwar movement. In other words, Nixon and Kissinger contend that the Vietnam War was skillfully managed in such a manner that the president was able to achieve a peace with honor and carry out his policy of détente.

Jeffrey Kimball has written the only monograph on Nixon's entire Vietnam policy, *Nixon's Vietnam War*. He casts Nixon's policy as an effort at gradual de-Americanization of the war and a negotiated settlement that would allow the United States to disengage from Vietnam with few negative consequences to American interests. Kimball emphasized improvisation and contingency in Nixon's policy. Vietnamization was, according to Kimball, a central part of Nixon's policy, but it was never an overarching strategy. Rather, it was part of an ever shifting use of different tactics—military pressure, linkage, and negotiation—by Nixon to extract the United States from Vietnam with American credibility intact.

Kimball's examination of Nixon's policies is also focused on the psychological dimension of the president's policymaking, and in the process places a great deal of emphasis on the president's relationship with Henry Kissinger and their efforts to shape their own legacies. "Nixon's peculiar psychology and the odd relationship he had with Henry Kissinger," Kimball writes, "profoundly influenced the strategy he used in seeking to achieve his globalist goals in Vietnam." Moreover, while Kimball makes the madman theory a crucial component of his analysis, he believes it was one of many options the president had to choose from, including Vietnamization, negotiations, and pacification to end the war, and he believes Nixon abandoned it as early as the fall 1969. From that point on, as Kimball has emphasized further in his indispensable subsequent work, *The Vietnam War Files*, the Nixon administration turned to negotiations, and more specifically, the strategy of a decent interval, to extract the nation, and President Nixon's reputation, from the quagmire of the Vietnam War.[1]

A significant declassification of documents (along with the moving of the Nixon papers to the Nixon Presidential Library) is allowing for a deeper and richer understanding of Nixon's presidency and his Vietnam policy and calls for historians to revise the misunderstandings and get beyond the deceptions. Very few, if any, of Nixon's and Kissinger's claims correspond to the documentary evidence. By following the narrative set out by Nixon and Kissinger, and examining the Nixon years as a whole to explain the ending the war, scholars have overlooked Nixon's quest for military victory and hence the failure of his policy in Vietnam.

To adequately understand Nixon's decisions, it is necessary to examine his policy from 1969 to 1973 in two parts, and not as a whole as most scholars have done. The years 1969–1970 were spent in pursuit of victory, and it was only the failures of Nixon's efforts, combined with mounting political and economic problems, that led to a shift in 1971 that sought an acceptable exit strategy focused on détente. Thus, for the first two years of his presidency, Nixon pursued escalation and victory in the Vietnam War, not extraction. The effort to preserve American credibility through a military triumph is the crucial aspect of Nixon's policy that most of the current works overlook in the focus on Vietnamization as a policy only designed to gradually extract the United States from the war, and leads to an incorrect understanding of Nixon and his policies in Vietnam. That is, after four years of escalation and stalemate under Johnson, Nixon still sought victory through military means to impose a settlement that would maintain an anticommunist government in Saigon. He did so despite the fact that senior-level analysis throughout the executive branch led to the conclusion that the war could not be won.

While the Tet Offensive was a crucial turning point in the war, Nixon sought to defy its lessons and the changes it had brought domestically. Instead of taking what he termed the popular position and initiating a plan to end the war, the president turned to deception and covert policies to escalate and expand the war while creating the appearance that he sought peace. Driven by his desire to maintain American credibility, convinced of his own ability to accomplish what Johnson could not, and determined not to be the first American president to lose a war, Nixon implemented a complex set of policies in Vietnam that he believed would defeat North Vietnam and force Hanoi to capitulate to his terms in Paris.

In pursuing escalation, Nixon faced a difficult problem: public demand for an end to the war and congressional pressure to sustain the negotiations in Paris undermined his pursuit of a military victory. Nixon's policies were designed to get around these obstacles. He believed that through expansion of the war to Cambodia, escalation of the bombing through his madman policy, Vietnamization and the Nixon Doctrine, and successful manipulation of public opinion, he could still militarily force the enemy to submit to America's terms: the survival of the anticommunist government in Saigon. Yet, the strains on the military (the need for more men, the breakdown of discipline, fatigue, and stalemate), compounded by the economic problems at home and domestic political opposition, made it clear that Nixon's continued pursuit of victory was doomed to failure no matter what Congress did, just as Nixon was told in early 1969.

Thus, praise for Richard Nixon's foreign policy acumen is greatly overstated. Specifically, there was no grand design for détente that guided all of his decisions as the president and his supporters have claimed. Rather, his priority upon taking office was victory in Vietnam.

The conceptualization of Vietnam as something Nixon had to manage and make sure did not interfere with his real foreign policy goals of détente with the Soviet Union and China has events backwards. Similarly, the lying, deception, and attacking his "enemies" abroad and at home were the norm for the Nixon White House and connected to his efforts in Vietnam as the president had to employ covert actions and deceit to carry out his escalation and expansion of the war. The falsification of records to hide the secret bombing of Cambodia and the illegal wiretaps placed on staff and reporters phones to try and find out who leaked information about the operation were the first steps on the road to Watergate.

Nixon's decision to continue the war in Vietnam in 1969 had devastating consequences for Vietnam and the United States. The seven years of additional fighting incurred millions of casualties, further destruction of the land and infrastructure of Vietnam, and expansion of the fighting into Cambodia and Laos. For the United States, it also meant deeper political and social divisions, a worsening economy, and the political crisis of Watergate culminating in the resignation of President Nixon. In the process, it brought an end to the postwar consensus on containment, shattered the notion of an American Century, and saw prosperity yield to stagflation and an abandonment of the Bretton Woods system. The credibility gap became a chasm as distrust of the government grew and all institutions in American society were questioned.

Nixon's continued pursuit of military victory and the ultimate collapse of Saigon demonstrated that military action was not the key determinant in the struggle. The United States could maintain a stalemate and artificially prop up the Saigon government, but there are limits to power in determining the political behavior of other nations and the influence of the United States to shape events. The deception that arose from success in achieving a stalemate and having local collaborators hid the fundamental problem the United States faced in the war: the lack of any political legitimacy of the Saigon government. It doomed the American enterprise in Vietnam. All the U.S. troops, bombs, training of ARVN, nation building efforts, and resources could not overcome that powerful reality.

NOTE

1. Kimball, *Nixon's Vietnam War*, xii; *The Vietnam War Files*.

Bibliographic Essay

The papers at the Richard Nixon Presidential Library, Yorba Linda, California, are the essential starting point for understanding President Nixon's policy toward Vietnam. The most important records are the National Security Council (NSC) Files, including the Vietnam Subject File, Vietnam Country File, Cambodian Operations File, Alexander M. Haig Chronological Files, Alexander M. Haig Special Files, and Presidential/ HAK Memcons; the National Security Council Institutional Files (NSCH), including Meeting Files, Minutes of Meetings, National Security Study Memorandums (NSSMs), and National Security Decision Memorandums (NSDMs); the Kissinger Office Files, including HAK Administrative and Staff Files, HAK Trip Files, Country Files–Far East–South Vietnam, and Country Files–Far East–Vietnam Negotiations; and the Henry A. Kissinger Telephone Conversation Transcripts. Other important collections include the oral histories conducted with various members of the Nixon administration, available at the Nixon Library; the Papers of Henry A. Kissinger, Manuscript Division, Library of Congress, Washington, DC; and H. R. Haldeman, *The Haldeman Diaries: Inside the Nixon White House: Multimedia Edition* (Santa Monica, CA: Sony Electronic Publishing Co., 1994).

Significant published primary document collections include Department of State, *Foreign Relations of the United States (FRUS)*, Vol. 1: *Foundations of Foreign Policy, 1969–1972*; Vol. 6: *Vietnam, January 1969–July 1970*; Vol. 7: *Vietnam, July 1970–January 1972*; Vol. 8: *Vietnam, January–October 1972*; Vol. 9: *Vietnam, October 1972–January 1973*; Vol. 10: *Vietnam, January 1973–July 1975* (Washington, DC: Government Printing Office, 2003, 2006, 2010); and *Public Papers of the Presidents: Richard Nixon, 1969–1973* (Washington, DC: Government Printing Office, 1970–1975).

Useful memoirs by leading participants include Clark Clifford with Richard Holbrooke, *Counsel to the President: A Memoir* (New York: Random House, 1991); William Colby, *Lost Victory: A Firsthand Account of America's Sixteen-Year Involvement in Vietnam* (Chicago: Contemporary Books, 1989); Daniel Ellsberg, *Secrets: A Memoir of Vietnam and the Pentagon Papers* (New York: Viking, 2002); Henry A. Kissinger, *White House Years* (Boston: Little, Brown and Company, 1979), *Years of Upheaval* (Boston: Little, Brown and Company, 1982), and *Ending the Vietnam War: A History of America's Involvement in and Extrication from the Vietnam War* (New York: Simon and Schuster, 2003); Richard Nixon, *RN: The Memoirs of Richard Nixon* (New York: Grosset and Dunlop, 1978), *No More Vietnams* (New York: Arbor House, 1985), and *In the Arena: A Memoir of Victory, Defeat, and Renewal* (New York: Simon and Schuster, 1990); and H. R. Haldeman with Joseph DiMona, *The Ends of Power* (New York: Times Books, 1978).

On Nixon's policy toward Vietnam, Jeffrey Kimball, *Nixon's Vietnam War* (Lawrence: University Press of Kansas, 1998), is the place to start. See also his *The Vietnam War Files: Uncovering the Secret History of Nixon-Era Strategy* (Lawrence: University Press of Kansas, 2004). Lewis Sorley, *A Better War: The Unexamined Victories and Tragedy of America's Last Years in Vietnam* (New York: Harcourt Brace, 1999), provides a favorable interpretation that supports Nixon's claim to have achieved an honorable peace that was lost due to congressional action. Andrew Johns, *Vietnam's Second Front: Domestic Politics, the Republican Party, and the War* (Lexington: University Press of Kentucky, 2010), places Nixon's views in the context of those of other Republican leaders. David F. Schmitz, *The Tet Offensive: Politics, War, and Public Opinion* (Lanham, MD: Rowman & Littlefield, 2005), provides the context for the war and Nixon's decisions.

Essential studies of Nixon's foreign policy include Stephen E. Ambrose, *Nixon: The Triumph of a Politician, 1962–1972* (New York: Simon and Schuster, 1989); William Bundy, *A Tangled Web: The Making of Foreign Policy in the Nixon Presidency* (New York: Hill and Wang, 1998); Robert Dallek, *Nixon and Kissinger: Partners in Power* (New York: HarperCollins, 2007); Joan Hoff, *Nixon Reconsidered* (New York: Basic Books, 1994); Frederik Logevall and Andrew Preston, eds., *Nixon in the World: American Foreign Relations, 1969–1977* (New York: Oxford University Press, 2008); Richard Reeves, *President Nixon: Alone in the White House* (New York: Simon and Schuster, 2001); Jonathan Schell, *The Time of Illusion: An Historical and Reflective Account of the Nixon Era* (New York: Knopf, 1976); Franz Schurmann, *The Foreign Politics of Richard Nixon: The Grand Design* (Berkeley: Institute of International Studies, 1987); Melvin Small, *The Presidency of Richard Nixon* (Lawrence: University Press of Kansas, 1999); Melvin Small, ed., *A Companion to Richard M. Nixon* (Malden, MA: Wiley-Blackwell, 2011); Anthony Summers, *The Arrogance of Power: The Secret World of Richard Nixon* (New York: Viking, 2000); and Tad Szulc, *The Illusion of Peace: Foreign Policy in the Nixon Years* (New York: Viking, 1978).

For policy toward Cambodia, see Kenton Clymer, *The United States and Cambodia, 1969–2000: A Troubled Relationship* (New York: Routledge-Curzon, 2004); and William Shawcross, *Sideshow: Kissinger, Nixon and the Destruction of Cambodia*, rev. ed. (New York: Simon and Schuster, 1987). On détente, see Raymond Garthoff, *Détente and Confrontation: American-Soviet Relations from Nixon to Reagan*, 2nd ed. (Washington, DC: Brookings Institution, 1994); and Keith L. Nelson, *The Making of Détente: Soviet-American Relations in the Shadow of Vietnam* (Baltimore: Johns Hopkins University Press, 1995). Regarding Nixon's policy toward China, Evelyn

Goh, *Constructing the U.S. Rapprochement with China, 1961–1974: From "Red Menace" to "Tacit Ally"* (New York: Cambridge University Press, 2004), is the place to start.

For studies on the Vietnamese perspective on the war, start with Lien-Hang T. Nguyen, *Hanoi's War: An International History of the War for Peace in Vietnam* (Chapel Hill: University of North Carolina Press, 2012); and Robert Bingham, *Guerilla Diplomacy: The NLF's Foreign Relations and the Vietnam War* (Ithaca, NY: Cornell University Press, 1998). See also Cheng Guan Ang, *The Vietnam War from the Other Side* (New York: Routledge-Curzon, 2002); and David Elliot, *The Vietnamese War: Revolution and Social Change in the Mekong Delta, 1930–1975* (Armonk, NY: M. E. Sharpe, 2003).

Studies on Henry Kissinger include Mario Del Pero, *The Eccentric Realist: Henry Kissinger and the Shaping of American Foreign Policy* (Ithaca, NY: Cornell University Press, 2010); Jussi Hanhimäki, *The Flawed Architect: Henry Kissinger and American Foreign Policy* (New York: Oxford University Press, 2004); Seymour Hersh, *The Price of Power: Kissinger in the Nixon White House* (New York: Summit Books, 1983); Walter Issacson, *Kissinger: A Biography* (New York: Simon and Schuster, 1992); Bruce Mazlish, *Kissinger: The European Mind in American Policy* (New York: Basic Books, 1976); Roger Morris, *Uncertain Greatness: Henry Kissinger and American Foreign Policy* (New York: Harper and Row, 1977); Robert Schulzinger, *Henry Kissinger: Doctor of Diplomacy* (New York: Columbia University Press, 1989); and Jeremy Suri, *Henry Kissinger and the American Century* (Cambridge, MA: Harvard University Press, 2007).

For broader studies of the Vietnam War that include chapters on Nixon's policy, see Larry H. Addington, *America's War in Vietnam: A Short Narrative History* (Bloomington: Indiana University Press, 2000); David Anderson, ed., *The Columbia History of the Vietnam War* (New York: Columbia University Press, 2010); Frances Fitzgerald, *Fire in the Lake: The Vietnamese and the Americans in Vietnam* (Boston: Little, Brown and Company, 1972); James William Gibson, *The Perfect War: The War We Couldn't Lose and How We Did* (New York: Vintage, 1986); George Herring, *America's Longest War: The United States and Vietnam, 1950–1975*, 3rd ed. (New York: Knopf, 1996); Stanley Karnow, *Vietnam: A History* (New York: Penguin, 1991); A. J. Langguth, *Our Vietnam: The War, 1954–1975* (New York: Simon and Schuster, 2000); Robert Mann, *A Grand Delusion: America's Descent into Vietnam* (New York: Basic Books, 2001); George Donelson Moss, *Vietnam: An American Ordeal*, 3rd ed. (Upper Saddle River, NJ: Prentice Hall, 1998); Robert D. Schulzinger, *A Time for War: The United States and Vietnam, 1941–1975* (New York: Oxford University Press, 1997); Neil Sheehan, *A Bright Shining Lie: John Paul Vann and America in Vietnam* (New York: Random House, 1988); and Marilyn B. Young, *The Vietnam Wars, 1945–1990* (New York: HarperCollins, 1991).

The impact of bombing in Vietnam is assessed in Mark Clodfelter, *The Limits of Air Power: The American Bombing of North Vietnam* (New York:

Free Press, 1989); and Robert Anthony Pape, *Bombing to Win: Air Power and Coercion in War* (Ithaca, NY: Cornell University Press, 1996). On the 1972 Spring Offensive, see Stephen P. Randolph, *Powerful and Brutal Weapons: Nixon, Kissinger, and the Easter Offensive* (Cambridge, MA: Harvard University Press, 2007). See Anthony S. Campagna, *The Economic Consequences of the Vietnam War* (New York: Praeger, 1991), and Allen J. Matusow, *Nixon's Economy: Booms, Busts, Dollars, and Votes* (Lawrence: University Press of Kansas, 1988), on the economic impact of the Vietnam War on the United States. The issue of POWs is addressed in Michael Allen, *Until the Last Man Comes Home: POWs, MIAs, and the Unending Vietnam War* (Chapel Hill: University of North Carolina Press, 2009). Crucial analysis of the American military during the Nixon years is found in Jeffrey Clarke, *Advice and Support: The Final Years, 1965–1973* (Washington, DC: Center of Military History, US Army, 1988); Col. Robert D. Heinl Jr., "The Collapse of the Armed Forces," *Armed Forces Journal* (June 1971): 30–37; Kyle Longley, *Grunts: The American Combat Soldier in Vietnam* (Armonk, NY: M. E. Sharpe, 2008); and Ronald Spector, *After Tet: The Bloodiest Year in Vietnam* (New York: Free Press, 1994).

The antiwar movement and public opinion are examined in Terry Anderson, *The Movement and the Sixties: Protest in America from Greensboro to Wounded Knee* (New York: Oxford University Press, 1995); Charles DeBenedetti with Charles Chatfield, *An American Ordeal: The Antiwar Movement of the Vietnam Era* (Syracuse, NY: Syracuse University Press, 1990); George H. Gallup, ed., *The Gallup Poll: Public Opinion, 1935–1971*, Vol. 3: *1959–1971* (New York: Random House, 1972); *Gallup Opinion Index*, Nos. 33 and 35 (Princeton, NJ: Gallup International, 1968); Godfrey Hodgson, *America in Our Time: From World War II to Nixon—What Happened and Why* (New York: Vintage, 1976); David W. Levy, *The Debate over Vietnam* (Baltimore: Johns Hopkins University Press, 1991); Melvin Small, *Johnson, Nixon, and the Doves* (New Brunswick, NJ: Rutgers University Press, 1989); *Antiwarriors: The Vietnam War and the Battle for America's Hearts and Minds* (Wilmington, DE: Scholarly Resources, 2002); Robert R. Tomes, *Apocalypse Then: American Intellectuals and the Vietnam War, 1954–1975* (New York: New York University Press, 1998); Tom Wells, *The War Within: America's Battle over Vietnam* (Berkeley: University of California Press, 1994).

There is a growing literature on the Paris Peace Treaty. The most important studies are Pierre Asselin, *A Bitter Peace: Washington, Hanoi, and the Making of the Paris Agreement* (Chapel Hill: University of North Carolina Press, 2002); Larry Berman, *No Peace, No Honor: Nixon, Kissinger, and Betrayal in Vietnam* (New York: Free Press, 2001), and "A Final Word on the Decent Interval Strategy," *Passport: The Newsletter of the Society for Historians of American Foreign Relations* 34 (December 2003): 32–33; Lloyd Gardner and Ted Gittinger, *The Search for Peace in Vietnam* (College Station: Texas A&M University Press, 2004); Jussi Hanhimäki, "Selling the

'Decent Interval': Kissinger, Triangular Diplomacy, and the End of the Vietnam War, 1971–73," *Diplomacy and Statecraft* 14 (March 2003): 159–194; George Herring, ed., *The Secret Diplomacy of the Vietnam War: The Negotiating Volumes of the Pentagon Papers* (Austin: University of Texas Press, 1983); Arnold Isaac, *Without Honor: Defeat in Vietnam and Cambodia* (Baltimore: Johns Hopkins University Press, 1983); Jeffrey Kimball, "The Case of the 'Decent Interval': Do We Now Have a Smoking Gun?" *Passport: The Newsletter of the Society for Historians of American Foreign Relations* 32 (December 2001): 35–39, and "Decent Interval or Not? The Paris Agreement and the End of the Vietnam War," *Passport: The Newsletter of the Society for Historians of American Foreign Relations* 34 (December 2003): 26–31; Luu Van Loi and Nguyen Anh Vu, *Le Duc Tho–Kissinger Negotiations in Paris* (Hanoi: Goio Publishers, 1996); Gareth Porter, *A Peace Denied: The United States, Vietnam, and the Paris Agreement* (Bloomington: Indiana University Press, 1975); and Frank Snepp, *Decent Interval: An Insider's Account of Saigon's Indecent End* (New York: Random House, 1977).

Index

About the Author

David F. Schmitz is the Robert Allen Skotheim Chair of History. He is the author of *Brent Scowcroft: Internationalism and Post-Vietnam War American Foreign Policy* (2011); *The Triumph of Internationalism: Franklin D. Roosevelt and a World in Crisis, 1933-1941* (2007); *The United States and Right-Wing Dictatorships, 1965-1989* (2006); *The Tet Offensive: Politics, War, and Public Opinion* (2005); *Henry L. Stimson: The First Wise Man* (2001); *Thank God They're on Our Side: The United States and Right-Wing Dictatorships, 1921-1965* (1999); *The United States and Fascist Italy, 1922-1940* (1988); *Architects of the American Century: Individuals and Institutions in Twentieth-Century U.S. Foreign Policymaking* (edited with T. Christopher Jespersen, 2000); and *Appeasement in Europe: A Reassessment of U.S. Policies* (edited with Richard D. Challener, 1990).

A specialist in twentieth-century U.S. history and American foreign policy, he teaches courses on U.S. foreign policy, America in Vietnam, twentieth-century U.S. history, and the history of rock 'n' roll. Professor Schmitz has received the Robert A. Fluno Award for Distinguished Teaching in Social Science, the G. Thomas Edwards Award for excellence in Teaching and Scholarship, Paul Garrett Fellowship, and Burlington Northern Foundation Faculty Achievement Award from Whitman College; the Arnold L. and Lois Graves Award in the Humanities from Pomona College; and grants from the National Endowment for the Humanities, Franklin D. Roosevelt Four Freedoms Foundation, and the Herbert Hoover Presidential Library Association.